POETRY IN ENGLISH
AN INTRODUCTION

POETRY IN ENGLISH
AN INTRODUCTION

Charles Barber

St. Martin's Press   New York

All rights reserved. For information, write:
St. Martin's Press, Inc., 175 Fifth Avenue, New York, NY 10010
Printed in Hong Kong
First published in the United States of America in 1983

ISBN 0-312-61888-3

Library of Congress Cataloging in Publication Data

Barber, Charles Laurence
   Poetry in English.

   Bibliography: p.
   Includes index.
   1. English poetry—History and criticism.
I. Title
PR502.B27   1983   821'.009   82-23099
ISBN 0-312-61888-3

Contents

Foreword

There are so many ways of approaching poetry, of enjoying
it, of assimilating it. Poetry performs so many functions: it
leads us into the infinity of human imagination, as when
Milton tries to justify the ways of God to man; it can, in Pope,
express 'what oft was thought but neer so well expressed':
it can, with Vaughan, reveal Eternity 'like a Great Ring of
pure and endless light', or, with Eliot, show us the waste land
of spiritual sterility; it can convey the ecstasy of love in
Donne's passionate intensity, or record the Whitsun Weddings
in Larkin's cautious camera-work; it can capture Yeats's
tragedy of Cuchulain, of father killing his son in ignorance,
or compel us, say, to the correct compassion James Kirkup
creates in his account of a heart operation.

Poetry corresponds to and interprets human experience in
all its variety: and to the poetry of England has been added
poetry written in English in many other countries: Ireland,
Scotland and Wales, to begin with, and then, of course, the
United States, and the countries which are or have been within
the Commonwealth, as well as countries such as the Phillipines
where lively poetry has been written in recent years.

Poets who write in English draw upon a vast wealth of
achievement in the past; they are part of a long, noble
tradition. Some of them write in full consciousness of what
has gone before them, developing, adapting, echoing; others
react against their predecessors — as Wordsworth and Coleridge
sought to move away from what had become, in their time,
an outworn poetic diction. As Ezra Pound put it, there needs
to be an impulse 'to make it new' — in whatever way the
poet chooses.

In this *Introduction*, Dr Barber conveys not only the variety of techniques but the wealth of subject matter to be found in poetry written in English; he has selected examples of different kinds of poetry, simple and sophisticated; his comments illuminate the strengths and subtleties to be enjoyed in reading poems, discovering their variety and realising how skilfully poets can express our thoughts and emotions, putting them into patterns of words and images, using metre and often rhyme to make them memorable. For poetry encapsulates human experience in a unique way, economically and precisely, stimulating and satisfactorily. It is there in profusion for our enrichment, and Dr Barber is an excellent guide.

Stirling, 1982   *A. N. Jeffares*

Preface

This book is an introduction to English poetry, intended for the general reader who wishes to extend the range of his reading and find new things to enjoy. It should be useful for students in their final two or three years at school, especially those who are beginning the serious study of poetry, for example for examination purposes. It should also be useful to first-year students of English literature in universities and colleges. Particular attention has been paid to the needs of overseas students, by glossing difficult words in the poems quoted, and by offering historical and cultural background-information where it helps understanding. Some of this material will not be necessary for home students, but I hope that it will not reduce their enjoyment of the book.

Particular prominence is given to English poets who are commonly studied in the upper forms of schools and in first-year university courses, but some attention is given to all the major English poets since 1500, and to many minor ones. Not much is said about English poetry before 1500, except for Chaucer, who is obviously indispensable. Burns and Yeats are both discussed, but it has not been possible in a book of this size to give a full account of the splendid traditions of Scots and Anglo-Irish poetry.

Short poems which are analysed in any detail are reproduced in full in the text. This is clearly impossible with longer poems, and it is highly desirable that, when such poems are discussed at all closely, you should have your own copy of the poem open beside you.

I am only too strongly aware of the old proverb about leading a horse to the water. I am convinced, however, that a book of this kind can help people to react to poetry and to enjoy it better, by removing prejudices and misunderstandings, and by introducing them to new kinds of poetic experience; to do this is one of the main aims of the present work.

CHARLES BARBER

Acknowledgements

I am grateful to Professor A. N. Jeffares, who suggested that I should write this book, and who has been unfailingly helpful while I have been doing so. I am also indebted, for advice on points of detail in their particular specialist fields, to three friends at the University of Leeds: Ann Massa, Arthur Ravenscroft and Alistair Stead. For information about the Yoruba *oriki*, I am indebted to Dr Karin J. Barber of the University of Ifè.

The author and publishers also wish to thank the following who have kindly given permission for the use of copyright material:

Faber & Faber Ltd and Harcourt Brace Jovanovich, Inc., for 'Whispers of Immortality' and other short extracts from *Collected Poems 1909–1962* by T. S. Eliot; The Marvell Press (England), for an extract from the poem 'Lines on a Young Lady's Photograph Album' by Philip Larkin from *The Less Deceived*; A P Watt Ltd on behalf of Michael and Anne Yeats, and Macmillan Publishing Co. Inc., for the poems 'Sailing to Byzantium', 'The Coming of Wisdom with Time' and 'He Tells of the Perfect Beauty' from *Collected Poems* by William Butler Yeats. Copyright renewed in the U.S. by Bertha Georgie Yeats.

1 *The Nature of Poetry*

What is Poetry?

We are all familiar with poems of various lengths and kinds.
But what are we to include in our definition of poetry? The
nursery rhymes we learnt as children? The rhymes we use to
memorise the number of days in each month? The commer-
cial verses in Christmas cards? The advertising jingles on
television? The words of the latest pop-song? Where shall we
draw the line?

An example

Let us begin by looking at an example of a poem. We would
probably all agree that the following short work by William
Wordsworth (1770–1850) is a poem:

> She dwelt among the untrodden ways
>   Beside the springs of Dove,
> A Maid whom there were none to praise
>   And very few to love:
>
> A violet by a mossy stone   5
>   Half hidden from the eye!
> — Fair as a star, when only one
>   Is shining in the sky.
>
> She lived unknown, and few could know
>   When Lucy ceased to be;   10
> But she is in her grave, and, oh,
>   The difference to me!

The poem tells us of a girl who lived in a remote country area: the Dove is a river in the Peak District of Derbyshire, a hilly region which in Wordsworth's time had little contact with the outside world. In the second stanza, the poet suggests the beauty and delicacy of the girl by calling her a *violet,* a flower which is sweetly scented and richly coloured, but unobtrusive: there is nothing gaudy or assertive about a violet. The girl, we understand, was sweet and quiet. Living in a remote area, she was half-hidden from people's knowledge, as the violet is by a mossy stone. The moss suggests the dampness of the hedge-bottom and woodland which are typical habitats of the violet, but it also emphasises the natural setting in which the girl lived: she was in a remote region, but was surrounded by natural growth. Her remoteness, loneliness, and beauty are then suggested by a different comparison: she was like a star shining in the sky without competitors. The only time when just one star is visible in this way is when darkness is beginning to fall (or alternatively in the early morning, before it is quite light); the comparison therefore evokes a twilight atmosphere, foreshadowing the rest of the poem. In the final stanza, the poet reveals that the girl is dead, and suggests the grief that this has caused him. The expression *ceased to be* (10) is impersonal and prosaic: the death was merely a statistic in the records, and hardly anybody knew about it. But precisely at this point the poet reveals his personal knowledge of the girl, by using her name for the first time ('*Lucy* ceased to be'); and he immediately goes on to imagine her death in a way which is more concrete and more moving ('she is in her grave'). The poet makes no attempt to describe his feelings about the death: it is sufficient for him to reveal his emotional commitment to Lucy in the final line of the poem, and leave the description of her in the rest of the poem to make its own effect.

Poetry and verse

One obvious feature of that poem is that it is in *verse.* Unlike prose, it is divided into *lines* of a predetermined length, and these divisions are independent of those demanded by grammar or meaning, as can be seen in lines 7 and 8, where the line-division comes between a grammatical subject (*one*) and its verb (*is shining*). Moreover, the lines have a regular kind of rhythm: in general, unstressed and stressed syllables alternate. A clear example is line 2, where the stressed syllables are -*side, springs,* and *Dove.* There are indeed departures from this stressed-unstressed pattern, as in line 7 (in which *Fair* is obviously stressed and *as* unstressed); but the pattern is so strong in the poem that we feel such departures from it simply as variations on a theme.

Moreover, the poem is divided into stanzas of four lines each. In every stanza, the first and third lines have four main stresses, while the second and fourth have only three. In addition, every line ends with a rhyme: in each stanza, the first line rhymes with the third, and the second with the fourth.

All these features — division into lines, regular rhythm, stanzaic structure, rhyme — are common in English poetry. They are not all essential, however: much English verse is unrhymed and unstanzaic (for example, Milton's *Paradise Lost,* Wordsworth's *Prelude*). Indeed, the only essential distinguishing feature between English verse and English prose is probably the fact that verse is divided into lines, a division which is independent of the normal phrase-, clause-, sentence- and paragraph-divisions which are also found in prose. It is true that verse, in addition, normally has a more regular rhythm than prose; the degree of regularity, however, can vary greatly in different poems; moreover, some prose is highly rhythmical; so that it is difficult to lay down regular rhythm as an absolute criterion for distinguishing verse from prose. But division into lines does seem to provide such a criterion.

Being composed in verse is an essential characteristic of English poetry: if a work is written in prose, we do not call it a poem. It is true that people sometimes refer to a particular work as a 'prose-poem'; the expression might be used, for example, of Virginia Woolf's novel *The Waves* (1931), or John Ruskin's description, in *The Stones of Venice* (1851), of St Mark's Square. Here, however, we should understand the word *poem* to be used metaphorically: what is meant is that the prose-work in question has many of the characteristics commonly found in poetry (such as density of verbal texture, richness of metaphor, marked rhythms, imaginativeness). Such 'prose-poems', however, are to be categorised as prose-works of a particular kind, not as poetry: all English poetry is in verse.

Imaginative literature

But is the converse true? Is all English writing in verse to be classified as poetry? It is not reasonable to say so. We usually restrict the term *poetry* to the kind of discourse which we call *literature,* or more fully *imaginative literature.* Poetry is literature written in verse.

We all know in a general way what kinds of things we mean by literature — plays, novels, short stories, and things of that sort. And we can distinguish literature from other kinds of discourse, such as are found (for example) in a scientific text-book, a philosophical treatise, a manual of technical instructions, a history-book, a theatre-programme, a work of religious or political propaganda, or a tourist-guide. On the other hand, it is not easy to define literature, for it can do many different things. It can celebrate, console, praise, satirise, entertain. It can arouse strong emotions in us, and liberate us from them. Above all, perhaps, we go to literature for illumination: it does not set out to convey information (as a chemistry text-book does), or to teach us skills (as many handbooks do), or to promote the aims of a political or religious organisation (as propaganda does), or to persuade us to buy something (as advertising does); what it does for us above all is to illuminate human life, and to educate our feelings about it. It has to be conceded, on the other hand, that not all literature succeeds in doing this; and moreover it could be argued that other kinds of discourse can also illuminate (for example works of philosophy and of science). Let us therefore add another criterion, and say that literature is in some sense *fiction,* and invites the reader to use his imagination.

Literature is fictional in that it does not claim that its statements are factual or literally true. This is obvious enough with the novel and with drama, in which the author offers us imaginary characters and events; this is the case even when he handles true events, such as historical material, since what he gives us is an imaginative reconstruction of the events, not a historical documentation of them. But poetry too is fiction: when a poet offers us events, moods, attitudes, emotions, or whatever, he does not invite us to believe that they are a transcription of something that has happened; rather, he invites us to experience them. This applies even if the poet is talking about himself and his experiences, as Wordsworth appears to be doing in the Lucy poem. Perhaps there really was a girl called Lucy in Dovedale who was loved by the poet and who died; or perhaps the whole thing is just an imaginative invention of the poet. Whichever is the case, the poem remains exactly the same to the reader: whether or not Lucy really existed is quite irrelevant. When a poet says *I*, we have to take this to refer to a fictional narrator, not to the historical person who wrote the poem.

Poetry, then, is imaginative literature written in verse. It is possible for other kinds of discourse to be written in verse, but we do not then call them poetry. It would be possible to put a chemistry text-book, or even a railway timetable, into verse, but the result would not be poetry (unless the versifier did a great deal more than just put the information into metrical form). Similarly, because their aims and functions are different from those of literature, we do not recognise as poetry the advertising jingles used on television, or even mnemonic rhymes, like the one which begins:

> Thirty days hath September,
> April, June, and November.

On the other hand, pop-song lyrics and many nursery-rhymes clearly fall within our definition of poetry. Inevitably, there are borderline cases. A mnemonic rhyme or a skipping-rhyme may have an imaginative power in its use of language that makes us respond to it as poetry. A work that sets out to be religious or political propaganda may transcend its aims and become literature. And the borderline between fact and fiction can be a very uncertain one, as may be seen in much autobiography, and in the memoirs of politicians.

Bad poetry is poetry

Our definition of poetry has nothing to do with value-judgements. We regard poetry as being a particular kind of discourse (literature) written in verse; we may, therefore, recognise as poetry works which we disapprove of, or which we find dull or trivial. The case is exactly parallel with that of the drama or the novel. We give the name 'novels' to works which meet certain criteria (for example, that they are fictional prose narratives of a certain minimum length, handling characters and events recognisably resembling those of the real world); whether particular novels are good, bad, or indifferent is quite a separate question.

It is necessary to say this, because some people dismiss poems which they find unimportant by saying that they are 'not poetry'. This is an unfortunate usage, because it confuses the criteria for a genre with value-judgements on members of the genre. If you find particular poems (those, say, of Patience Strong or of Stephen Duck) quite intolerable, then you should say that they are bad poems (and explain why you think so), not that they are 'not poetry'. In any case, opinions about the value of particular poems vary from reader to reader, and from age to age.

Metre

English poetry is divided into lines, and these lines have some kind of rhythmic pattern. In Wordsworth's Lucy poem the lines have four main stresses and three main stresses alternately, and within each line there is an alternation of unstressed and stressed syllables; some lines depart from the regular unstressed–stressed sequence, but it is sufficiently common in the poem to be felt as an underlying rhythmic pattern throughout. Such an underlying rhythmic pattern is called *metre*; and metrical patterns of some kind appear to be basic to all poetry.

Some of the effects of metre are not fully understood. Perhaps the repeated rhythmic beat sharpens the hearer's perceptions, making him more receptive; it may even suspend resistance to what is being said in the poem. Other effects of metre are clearer: it can throw emphasis on particular words; it can set up expectations, and then produce effects by either satisfying or defeating them; it can contribute to the sense of emotional control in a poem, our feeling that the poet is ordering experience, not being carried away by it.

Metrical systems

The metrical systems that are possible depend on the characteristics of the language in question. In Modern English (the English language since about 1500) it is not possible to use a metrical system like that of the Latin poets of the first century BC. In classical Latin poetry, the metres consisted of patterns of long and short syllables; these length-patterns did not coincide with the arrangement of the stresses in the line, for it was possible for the main stress in a word to be carried by either a long or a short syllable; and part of the poet's art was the counterpointing of the length-pattern against the stress-pattern. There have been many attempts to imitate classical Latin metres in English poetry (notably in the sixteenth century), but, for reasons which will become clear later, the system just will not work in English.

Within the limitations of a given language, however, more than one type of metrical system is possible, and the system dominant at a given time may be an accident of cultural history. In the course of English history there has been more than one type of metrical system. In Old English (the English language before about 1100), the poets used an alliterative system. Each line was divided into two half-lines, and in each half-line two of the syllables constituted 'lifts'; there were rules, concerned with syllable-length and stress, as to what syllables could be lifts. Some of the lifts alliterated with one another, that is, they began with the same speech-sound: the first lift of the second half-line always alliterated with one of the lifts in the first half-line, and sometimes with both. A limited number of stress-patterns were permissible in a half-line; but, provided one of these patterns was used, there was no restriction on the total number of syllables: in the Old English epic poem *Beowulf* a half-line can have as few as four syllables and as many as eight.

Metres of the alliterative type were still in use in the later fourteenth century, as in the famous anonymous poem *Piers Plowman*, though the metrical rules were now less strict than in Old English poetry. But while *Piers Plowman* was being written in the South-West Midlands, Geoffrey Chaucer (*c.* 1343–1400) was writing in London, and using quite a different style of versification: for Chaucer uses rhyme, and a kind of metre familiar in most later English poetry. His versification was almost certainly influenced by French and Italian poetry.

Since Chaucer's time, there have been various theories about English metre, but two types of view have predominated, and the versification of most English poetry in the modern period can be made to fit one or both of these views (whether or not the poet in question subscribed to the theory himself, or indeed had any metrical theories at all). For brevity we can call these two systems 'the stress-feet system' and 'the syllable-counting system'.

The 'stress-feet' metrical system

This system is influenced by classical Latin theories, but with stress playing the part which in Latin was played by syllable-length. In classical Latin poetry, each line of verse had to consist of a number of small units called *feet* (Latin *pedes*), usually of two or three syllables. For example, an iamb was a foot consisting of a short syllable followed by a long, while a trochee had a long syllable followed by a short, an anapaest two short followed by a long, a spondee two long, a pyrrhic two short, a dactyl a long followed by two short, and so on. For each type of metre, the number of feet in the line was prescribed, and there were rules about the types of feet that could be used and the positions in the line that they could occupy.

When, in the late Middle Ages and Renaissance, this system was adapted for the description of English poetry, stressed and unstressed syllables took the place of the Latin long and short syllables. So an English iamb is an unstressed syllable followed by a stressed one (as in the word *above*), a trochee has a stressed syllable followed by an unstressed one (as in the word *happy*), and so on.

When we analyse English metres by the stress-feet system, we say that the lines in a given metre have a certain fixed number of feet: there are two-foot lines, three-foot lines, four-foot lines, five-foot lines, and six-foot lines. In imitation (but imperfect imitation) of classical usage, these are often called dimeters, trimeters, tetrameters, pentameters, and hexameters respectively. We then specify the type of foot used — iamb, trochee, anapaest, or whatever — which is the same throughout the line. So we can say that Wordsworth's Lucy poem has four-foot iambic lines and three-foot iambic lines alternately (or we can call them iambic tetrameters and iambic trimeters).

You will remember, however, that in the Lucy poem not all the lines are exactly iambic: that is, they do not invariably follow the pattern of unstressed syllable followed by stressed syllable. The theory deals with this by saying that the poet can replace one or more feet in any line by feet of a different kind, and can take other liberties, such as inserting an additional unstressed syllable at the beginning or end of a line. In line 7 of the Lucy poem, a trochee is substituted for the expected iamb in the first foot of the line.

As an example of scansion (metrical analysis) by the stress-feet method, let us take a short passage of William Shakespeare (1564–1616) written in about 1593 in blank verse (unrhymed iambic five-foot lines). The division of each line into feet is shown by vertical lines, while stressed syllables are marked with an oblique stroke over the top and unstressed syllables with a cross. The stresses shown are plausible ones, but of course there are other possible ways of reading the lines.

He can|not live, | I hope, | and must | not die

Till George | be pack'd | with post-|horse up | to heaven.

I'll in, | to urge | his hat|red more | to Clarence

With lies | well steel'd | with weigh|ty ar|guments,

And if | I fail | not in | my deep | intent,

Clarence | hath not | anoth|er day | to live.

(*Richard III*, I.1.145–50)

In the scansion it is assumed that *heaven* (2) was spoken as one syllable, and that *arguments* (4) had a stress on its third syllable as well as its first, as was perfectly possible in sixteenth-century pronunciation. It will be seen that the rhythms of the passage are very regular: there are few departures from the iambic pattern, which communicates itself unmistakably to the hearer. There are indeed a few departures, such as the use of a trochaic foot and a pyrrhic foot at the beginning of line 6, and the addition of an unstressed syllable at the end of line 3; but twenty-four of the thirty feet, in my reading, are iambs.

In the course of Shakespeare's career, the rhythms of his blank verse became increasingly free, and in his late plays the underlying iambic pattern is much less obvious. This is illustrated by the following passage, which was written in about 1610:

I had thought | (Sir) to | have held | my peace, | until

You had drawn | oaths from | him not | to stay; | you (Sir)

Charge him | too cold|ly. Tell | him, you | are sure

All in | Bohem|ia's well: | this sat|isfaction,

The by-|gone-day | proclaim'd, | say this | to him . . .   5

(*The Winter's Tale*, I.2.28–32)

Of the twenty-five feet, only twelve are iambs in my reading of the passage. Notice too the greater tendency, compared with the earlier passage, for the grammar and the meaning to overrun the end of the line (as in lines 1–2), and for heavy stops to occur inside the line (as in line 3). Nevertheless, the hearer still feels the passage as iambic verse.

Most English verse of the post-medieval period is written in iambic metres, but other metres are occasionally used. 'Nurse's Song' by William Blake (1757–1827) is in an anapaestic metre:

When the voi|ces of chil|dren are heard | on the green

And laugh|ing is heard | on the hill,

My heart | is at rest | within | my breast

And ev|erything else | is still.

The stanza consists of alternate four-foot and three-foot anapaestic lines. Anapaests give a lilting quality to the movement, and can easily sound sing-song and childish. In 'Nurse's Song' they are obviously used to give a childlike quality to the verse, but Blake is careful not to overdo it, and slips in several iambic feet among the anapaests.

Trochaic metres, too, are sometimes used, as in *The Song of Hiawatha* (1855) by the American poet, Henry Wadsworth Longfellow (1807–82):

> From his | lodge went | Hia|watha,
> Dressed for | travel, | armed for | hunting;
> Dressed in | deerskin | shirt and | leggings,
> Richly | wrought with | quills and | wampum.

The metre is four-foot trochaic.

Syllable-counting

Some English poets have based their versification, not on feet, but on the number of syllables in the line. In the sixteenth century, one popular metre was 'fourteeners' — lines of exactly fourteen syllables, rhyming in couplets. Another was 'Poulter's Measure', which consisted of lines of twelve syllables and fourteen syllables alternately, again rhyming in couplets, as in the following lines by Henry Howard, Earl of Surrey (1517–47):

If care do cause men cry, why do not I complain?
If each man do bewail his woe, why show I not my pain?
Since that amongst them all I dare well say is none
So far from weal, so full of woe, or hath more cause to moan.

The lumbering movement of those lines, and the painfully pedestrian effect, are rather typical of poetry written in this measure.

Another time when syllable-counting was practised was the period from the later seventeenth century to the later eighteenth, the age of Dryden, Pope, and Johnson. In this age, it was common to refer to poetry as 'numbers', and they did indeed believe that verse should have a fixed number of syllables per line. The commonest metre used was the ten-syllable line, usually in rhymed couplets, as in the following playful lines by Alexander Pope (1688–1744) about Hampton Court Palace:

> Close by those Meads for ever crown'd with Flow'rs,
> Where Thames with Pride surveys his rising Tow'rs,
> There stands a structure of Majestick Frame,
> Which from the neighb'ring Hampton takes its name.
> Here Britain's Statesmen oft the fall foredoom   5
> Of Foreign Tyrants, and of Nymphs at home;
> Here thou, Great Anna! whom three realms obey,
> Dost sometimes Counsel take — and sometimes Tea.
> (The Rape of the Lock, III. 1–8)

Where there is any possible doubt about the number of syllables in a word, Pope indicates his intentions by his spelling: so *Flow'rs* (1) has one syllable, not two, and *neighb'ring* (4) has two syllables, not three. Pope observes syllable-number very strictly, and if ever you find a line of his verse that appears to have the wrong number you can be pretty sure that there is a mistake in your text.

Pope and his contemporaries knew that many earlier poets, including ones for whom they had great admiration (like Shakespeare), did not conform to their rule of syllable-number. This they considered a sad deficiency in these earlier poets, who had been unfortunate to be born in a less refined age than their own, before the true secret of English versification had been discovered. Then, in the seventeenth century, Mr Waller and Mr Dryden had 'refined our numbers', and the really polished age of English poetry had begun. The concept of 'refining our numbers' includes several different things: the use of smooth and regular rhythms, the avoidance of successive vowel-sounds, the employment of a certain kind of poetic vocabulary, and also the syllable-counting principle.

A metrical system based on syllable-number, by itself, leaves many questions unanswered, since it tells us nothing about the rhythms used in the lines. In practice, the poetry of Pope and his contemporaries can be scanned on the stress-feet system: the passage from *The Rape of the Lock* can be analysed as five-foot iambic verse, like the Shakespeare passages already examined. It is perhaps best, therefore, to regard strict syllable-counting as an additional restriction which can be added to the stress-feet system, rather than as a wholly independent system.

Free verse

The stress-feet system can be used to analyse the metres of most post-medieval English poems, but not all. Only with difficulty, for example, can it be applied to 'free verse', verse with completely unpredictable line-lengths, the pioneer of which was the American poet Walt Whitman (1819–92). The following example of free verse is by D. H. Lawrence (1885–1930), and is the opening of a poem called 'Snake':

> A snake came to my water-trough,
> On a hot, hot day, and I in pyjamas for the heat,
> To drink there.
>
> In the deep, strange-scented shade of the great dark
>   carob-tree
> I came down the steps with my pitcher   5
> And must wait, must stand and wait, for there he
>   was at the trough before me.
>
> He reached down from a fissure in the earth-wall in
>   the gloom
> And trailed his yellow-brown slackness soft-bellied
>   down, over the edge of the stone trough
> And rested his throat upon the stone bottom,
> And where the water had dripped from the tap, in a   10
>   small clearness,
> He sipped with his straight mouth,
> Softly drank through his straight gums, into his slack
>   long body,
> Silently.

The lines vary in length from three syllables (13) to twenty (8); and the poem is not in stanzas, but in sections or paragraphs of varying length. Lawrence, clearly, is trying to make the movement of the verse mirror the sense: line 6 has a beautiful pausing movement, produced by the repetition ('must wait, must stand and wait'); and line 8, which is very long and yet which constitutes only one intonation-group, enacts marvellously the movement of the snake down from the fissure into the trough. This is undeniably verse: it is in lines, and is markedly rhythmical. But there seems little point in trying to scan it. We could, admittedly, say that the first line was an iambic tetrameter, the second an iambic pentameter, the third an iambic trimeter, and so on. But since the point of a metrical analysis is to show an underlying pattern, this procedure would be futile. We cannot even say with certainty that the movement of the poem is predominantly iambic. In the face of such a poem, we have to admit that the stress-feet system, though a useful tool of analysis, has no universal validity.

Rhythm

The metre of a poem is an abstraction, an underlying theoretical pattern. We must distinguish it from the *rhythm* of the poem. This is the actual movement of the words as spoken, which often departs from the metrical pattern. It would indeed be possible for the rhythm of a poem to be identical with its metre throughout, but such a poem would be monotonous, because too predictable. So in practice the rhythms of a poem always depart from the theoretical metre, and the hearer is aware of the contrast between the two: there is a kind of counterpointing effect between the movement of real English speech and the fixed underlying pattern.

The rhythm of English speech

One of the major features of the rhythm of spoken English, and the kind of effect it can have in verse, is illustrated by the following line, which is the opening of a sonnet by Sir Thomas Wyatt (1503–42):

The lŏng lóve thát ĭn mў thŏught dŏth hárbŏur.

The stress-marks show the natural way of reading the line. If it is read in this way, it is striking that the first three words, *The long love*, move more slowly than the rest of the line, suiting the movement to the sense. What makes them move more slowly? It has nothing to do with the intrinsic length of vowels or consonants in English: in present-day speech, for example, both *long* and *love* have short vowels. The words move slowly because there are two successive stressed sylla- bles; and the basic principle of the rhythm of spoken English is that the speaker tries to have equal spaces between *stresses*.

Consider the following two sentences of present-day English, spoken with the stresses as shown:

(i)   I've ă néw hórn ŏn mў cár nów.

(ii) I've gŏt ă néw dĭstríbŭtŏr ŏn mў mínĭvăn tŏdáy.

In (i) there are eight syllables, and in (ii) there are fifteen, almost twice as many; and yet, if they are spoken with the stresses as marked, the two sentences take almost exactly the same length of time to speak. This is because they both have four stressed syllables; and it is the stressed syllables that the speaker tries to space out evenly. Where there are many successive unstressed syllables, the speaker goes very fast, because he has to squash them all into a single time-unit; and where there are successive stressed syllables he goes slowly. So the sequence *-strĭbŭtŏr ŏn mў mín-* in (ii) occupies the same length of time as *néw hórn* in (i): both of them occupy one time-unit, the space between two stresses. The rhythm of English, in other words, is stress-timed; and to the best of our knowledge it has been so for many centuries. Not all lan- guages have this characteristic: in some (such as French) the speaker tries to space *all* syllables equally, so that a sentence with fifteen syllables takes nearly twice as long to speak as one with eight syllables.

To return to the Wyatt line, it is now clear why the first

three words move slowly. Both *long* and *love* are stressed (the normal pattern for the adjective—noun construction), and both are monosyllables. They are followed by three unstressed syllables, and the time-interval between *long* and *love* is the same as that between *love* and *thought*. Indeed, the first three syllables of the line occupy the same length of time as the remaining seven, two time-units in each case. In general, successive stressed syllables slow down the movement of English, while successive unstressed syllables make it go fast.

It is not to be thought that Wyatt had any theories about stress-timing. Poets do not need to have theories about language in order to use it effectively; and many other poets have shown in their work that in practice they know how to utilise the rhythmic characteristics of the language. In *An Essay on Criticism* (1711), Pope refers to poetry in which

> expletives their feeble aid do join,
> And ten low words oft creep in one dull line.

The 'creeping' effect of that last line is achieved by the sequence of ten monosyllables, eight of which are stressed (all except *And* and *in*). 'To his Coy Mistress', by Andrew Marvell (1621—78), ends with the couplet

> Thús, though wĕ cánnŏt máke oŭr sún
> Stánd stíll, yĕt wĕ wíll máke hĭm rún.

Notice the slowing-down effect of the three consecutive stressed monosyllables (*sun/Stand still*): the sun is not actually made to stop, but it does move in a very slow and majestic way. In the final line, half the time is occupied by the first two syllables, *Stand still,* so that the remainder of the line goes very fast — it really does run.

The technique can be used in the reverse direction: if consecutive stresses slow the movement down, conversely the insertion of a pause may induce the reader to use consecutive stresses. Consider the opening of 'The Good Morrow', by John Donne (1573—1631):

> I wonder by my troth what thou and I
> Did, till we lov'd? were we not wean'd till then?
> But suck'd on country pleasures, childishly?

The break at the end of the first line, coming as it does between subject and verb, almost compels the reader to stress the word *Did,* and indeed to make it the most prominent word in the sentence. It is this strong stress on *Did* (and the accompanying intonation-pattern) which gives the sentence its colloquial ring.

This last example assumes that the reader inserts a pause at the end of a line of poetry. Nowadays, many actors and poetry-readers pretend that verse is not written in lines: they speak poetry without giving any indication of the where-abouts of the line-endings. This is absurd: if the poet had wanted his work to be read in this way, why did he not write it as prose? The line is a basic structural feature of poetry, and the hearer should be conscious of it. This does not mean that we should read poetry as if there were a full-stop at the end of each line: if the sense runs on into the next line, the intonation of the speaker's voice must keep it open. But it does mean that at the end of each line there must be at the very least a momentary hesitation, so that the line-structure is apparent to the hearer. The effects that poets achieve often depend on the pause at the line-ending, and we shall see more examples later.

Reading aloud

Rhythm is a central feature of poetry, and so it is necessary that a poem should be *heard.* Since the introduction of print-ing and the achievement of almost universal literacy, we have all become text-centred and print-centred, and tend to think of language as something written. In the past, however, poets have written to be heard — spoken, recited, sung. To appre-ciate them fully, we too need to speak them, recite them, sing them. For the experienced reader of poetry this may indeed be unnecessary: his aural imagination may be suffic-iently developed for him to 'hear' the poetry in his head, even when he reads silently. The inexperienced reader, however, needs to hear poetry read aloud, and to read it aloud himself whenever possible. For readers whose native tongue is not English, it is essential to hear readings by native speakers as often as possible, because non-native speakers inevitably carry over features from their own language into their reading of English, and may easily misread the rhythms of poetry; particular difficulty is likely to be encountered by speakers of tone-languages, such as Burmese, Chinese, Igbo, Thai, and Yoruba.

A Comparison: Wyatt and Surrey

In discussing rhythm, we looked at the opening line of a sonnet by Wyatt. This sonnet was translated from the Italian of Petrarch (Francesco Petrarca) (1304–74). It happens that a younger contemporary of Wyatt's, the Earl of Surrey, translated the same Petrarch sonnet. The two translations are interestingly different in their rhythms, and it is instructive to compare them. They also differ in other ways, and a more general comparison of the two poems will point forward to other topics to be discussed later.

The theme of the sonnets is fairly conventional: the poet loves a lady; he allows his desire for her to become too apparent, whereupon she is angry and rebuffs him; he retreats into silence; what remains for him but to die for love? Wyatt's version runs as follows:

> The long love that in my thought doth harbour
> And in mine heart doth keep his residence
> Into my face presseth with bold pretence
> And therein campeth, spreading his banner.
> She that me learneth [teaches] to love and suffer   5
> And will that my trust and lust's negligence
> Be reined by reason, shame, and reverence,
> With his hardiness [boldness] taketh displeasure.
> Wherewithal unto the heart's forest he fleeth,
> Leaving his enterprise with pain and cry,   10
> And there him hideth and not appeareth.
> What may I do when my master feareth,

But in the field with him to live and die?
For good is the life ending faithfully.

And here is Surrey's version:

Love that doth reign and live within my thought,
And built his seat within my captive breast,
Clad in the arms wherein with me he fought
Oft in my face he doth his banner rest.
But she that taught me love and suffer pain,   5
My doubtful hope and eke [also] my hot desire
With shamefast [modest] look to shadow [conceal]
   and refrain,
Her smiling grace converteth straight [immediately]
   to ire.
And coward love then to the heart apace
Taketh his flight, where he doth lurk and plain
   [lament]   10
His purpose lost, and dare not show his face.
For my lord's guilt thus faultless bide [endure]
   I pain.
Yet from my lord shall not my foot remove:
Sweet is the death that taketh end by love.

Rhythms in the two sonnets

Both poems are written in five-foot iambic metre, but the
rhythmical differences between them are striking. Surrey's
sonnet has a very regular rhythm, with few departures from
the iambic pattern. The only common departure is the
inversion of the first foot in the line (the use of a trochee
instead of an iamb), which happens in lines 1, 3, 4, 10, 13,
and 14. This particular variation does not cause two successive stressed syllables to occur within the line, and there are
very few variations of the kind that do cause this to happen:
in my reading of the poem, the only examples of juxtaposed
stresses within the line are *love then* (9) and *my lord's guilt*
(12). The regularity of the rhythm means that most lines
have exactly five stressed syllables; indeed, it is possible to
read the poem giving five stresses to *all* the lines. This fact,

together with the rarity of successive stressed syllables, gives an even distribution of emphasis within the lines: inside each line, no particular word or phrase is highlighted by the rhythm, and there are five areas of about equal prominence.

In Wyatt's poem there are greater departures from the iambic pattern, and more lines with fewer than five stresses: in my reading, there are only four stresses in lines 1, 4, 5, 11, and 12, and only three stresses in line 8. The departures may in fact be fewer than appears to the modern reader: Wyatt probably intended an additional stress on the final syllables of *residence* (2), *negligence* (6), *reverence* (7), and *faithfully* (14), as was perfectly possible in sixteenth-century pronunciation. Moreover, it is possible that in line 6 Wyatt intended *lust's* (in the original manuscript spelt *lustes*) to be pronounced as two syllables. But even so, it is clear that Wyatt's rhythms are much freer than Surrey's. This freedom enables him to vary the pace at which different phrases move, and to highlight particular parts of a line. We have already seen how, in line 1, the juxtaposition of stressed syllables makes *long love* move more slowly than the rest of the line; a similar slowing-down is seen in line 9, with *heart's forest.* The less even distribution of emphasis, as compared with Surrey, is partly due to the smaller number of stresses: in line 8 there are only three stressed syllables, and so only three words are given any prominence (*hardiness, taketh, displeasure*). But other factors contribute to the effect, as in line 3:

Into my face presseth with bold pretence.

Here the word *presseth* has great prominence. In part, this is achieved by syntax: the line contains three grammatical units, the verb standing alone in the centre of the line with a preposition-phrase on each side of it; this isolates *presseth*, and makes it stand out. The effect is much reinforced, however, by the two successive stressed syllables (*face press-*): the reader is obliged to pause before *presseth*, which is thus isolated for attention. Intonation (the varying musical pitch of the voice during speech) also plays a part: the grammatical structure is such that a new tone-group begins at *press-*, which is spoken at a higher musical pitch than any other

word in the line. The effect of all these things is to highlight
presseth as the key-word of the line. Similarly, *campeth* and
spreading stand out in line 4, but less strongly, since there are
no successive stressed syllables.

Rhymes in the two sonnets

Surrey's rhymes are all exact, and are straightforward masculine ones. Even the final rhyme of the poem, *remove/love*,
was exact, since there was a common variant of *love* with a
long vowel, making it rhyme with such words as *move* and
prove. Wyatt, on the other hand, has the rhymes *harbour/
banner/suffer/displeasure*. These are not full rhymes at all,
but simply words with identical final unstressed syllables.
This use of partial rhymes makes Wyatt's poem sound more
tentative than Surrey's, less certain and confident. On the
other hand, the final rhyme of the sonnet was an exact one:
as we have seen, Wyatt probably intended the final syllable of
faithfully to be stressed, and in such a case the *-y* was
commonly pronounced to rhyme with *die*.

Diction in the two sonnets

Surrey's Love is more aristocratic than Wyatt's: he reigns (1),
and has built a *seat* ('capital city, throne') (2). Wyatt's Love,
by contrast, *harbours* in his thought (1): this means that he
lodges or encamps there (without the associations of lurking
or concealment that the word now has). At the end of the
poem, similarly, Surrey's Love is his *lord*, while Wyatt's is
his *master*. In lines 3–4, Wyatt uses verbs of physical action
(*presseth, campeth, spreading*), which give vigour to the
writing; Surrey's lines are limper: he has the verb *fought*,
but then in rhyme-position the extremely inert verb *rest*.
In line 6, Surrey has the rather conventional phrase *hot desire*;
Wyatt's expression, *lust's negligence*, is not only more striking, but also implies self-criticism. Moreover, the lady wishes
his desires to be controlled (*reined*), whereas Surrey's lady
wishes him to conceal (*shadow*) his desire beneath a modest
appearance: Wyatt is concerned with morality, Surrey with
appearances (though in justice we must add that Surrey also

says *refrain*). In Wyatt's time, *reined* would have had a more physical effect than it has for us, since it was still a living metaphor: men as a matter of course rode on horseback, and knew what it was like to feel the pull on the reins and the effort required; whereas for us the word has become a dead metaphor, just a synonym for 'hold back, control'.

At line 9 we reach the 'turn' of the sonnet, when Love runs away. Surrey handles this well, with his eloquent *lurks and plains*; but Wyatt's writing is superb:

> Wherewithal unto the heart's forest he fleeth,
> Leaving his enterprise with pain and cry.

The second of these lines, with its vivid and evocative *pain and cry*, has a remarkable intensity; but perhaps the word that marks the difference between the two poets is *forest* in the line before — a word that does not occur in the Italian original, but is Wyatt's own addition. Here we have to use our historical imagination, and conjure up for ourselves what a forest meant to Englishmen in the early sixteenth century — when human habitations were thinly scattered in an often wild landscape, and there were still wolves in the British Isles. A forest was a place of darkness, obscurity, danger (wild animals, brigands), a place where one could lose one's way and die; but it could also be a hiding-place, a refuge. Such, Wyatt is saying, is the human heart, with its darknesses, its dangers, its half-understood desires, which threaten (like wild animals or brigands) to savage the forces of reason and civilisation. This movement of the poem into the inner life, the obscurity and instability of man's heart, is typical of Wyatt.

In the final three lines, Surrey disclaims moral responsibility for what has happened: he is *faultless* (12), and it is his lord who is the guilty one. This lord, of course, is Love, who is simply a mythological projection of the poet's own desires: so Surrey's shifting of the guilt to Love is a casuistical evasion of responsibility (which is not found in the Petrarch original). The final lines of the two poems are characteristically different: the key-words in Surrey's line are *sweet, death,* and *love;* while those in Wyatt's are *good, life,* and *faith.* Surrey's line is somewhat self-indulgent, imagining the sweetness of dying for love. Wyatt's line is also nominally about death (*ending*), but its emphasis is in fact upon living (*life*), and moreover living under the dictates of morality (*good, faithfully*).

Surrey's poem is nearer to the Italian original than Wyatt's, both in substance and in spirit, and is a smooth and elegant piece of writing. Wyatt, however, has taken the material and turned it into something of his own: with its use of English speech-rhythms, its self-criticism, its firmly moral stance, and its evocation of the darkness of the human heart, Wyatt's sonnet is a new and independent work of art, and quite a remarkable one.

Rhyme

The earliest English poetry, Anglo-Saxon alliterative verse, made no use of rhyme; and the alliterative tradition continued to the end of the Middle Ages. From the twelfth century onwards, however, we find English poetry of a different kind, using rhyme, and with metres based on syllable-counting or on stresses. This development was perhaps due to the influence of medieval Latin hymns, and, later, of French and Italian poetry. Since the fourteenth century, rhyme has been a common feature of English poetry.

To form a full rhyme, two words must have identical vowels in stressed syllables; if anything follows these vowels it must also be identical; but what precedes the stressed vowels must be different. Identity and difference refer to pronunciation, not spelling. Examples of full rhymes are *flee/agree, hand/stand, mother/brother, trippingly/skippingly, great/mate*. But *great* does not rhyme with *grate*, because what precedes the vowel is identical. A rhyme may extend over more than one word: *make it* rhymes with *take it*, and *Bacchus* with *lack us*.

The commonest rhymes in English poetry are so-called masculine ones, rhymes in which there are no unstressed syllables following the stressed ones (*flee/agree, hand/stand*); but quite often we also find feminine ones, in which one unstressed syllable follows the stressed one (*ringing/singing, leather/together*). It is not common to find rhymes in which two or more unstressed syllables follow the stressed one (*sincerity/prosperity*); such rhymes easily sound comic, and indeed are sometimes used for humorous effect.

Functions of rhyme

When two words rhyme in a poem, they are brought into relationship: we are made to feel some kind of connection between them. Blake's 'London' (1794) opens thus:

> I wander thro' each charter'd street,
> Near where the charter'd Thames does flow,
> And mark in every face I meet
> Marks of weakness, marks of woe.

The rhymes bring *street* and *meet* into association, reinforcing the sense of numerous chance outdoor encounters. The link between *flow* and *woe* suggests that it is not only the river that flows: there is a flowing movement of the sad-faced people through the streets. Moreover, the mere fact of being rhyme-words gives greater prominence to these four words.

Rhymes also increase our consciousness of the line-ending, and so reinforce the metrical pattern. A rhyme at the end of a sentence gives a sense of finality and completeness. In Shakespeare's plays, a scene in unrhymed verse often ends with a rhymed couplet, which acts as a scene-ending signal for the audience; even in some prose dramas, such as the comedies of Wycherley and Congreve in the Restoration period, it is common for a scene to be ended with a rhymed couplet.

If there is a regular pattern of rhymes in a poem, this may give us a sense of order being imposed on experience: metre and formal rhyme-schemes are a means of exercising control over the feelings, subjecting emotion to the discipline of form.

Partial rhymes

A poet is under no obligation to use full rhymes, and poems

often contain inexact rhymes; this is one way of introducing variety into a poem, and has the effect of loosening the tie between the rhyming words, and reducing the rigidity of the rhyme-scheme. Some historical knowledge is necessary, however, before we declare that a rhyme is exact or inexact: as we have seen, in the Wyatt and Surrey sonnets the rhymes *remove/love* and *die/faithfully* were exact ones when the poems were written. In Shakespeare's poetry, the vast majority of the rhymes were exact ones; examples of such rhymes, which are no longer exact, are *age/pilgrimage, alone/gone, are/prepare, break/speak, brood/blood, come/tomb, die/memory, ear/bear, have/grave, one/alone, pass/was,* and *war/bar;* these are all taken from the *Sonnets.*

Because of changes in pronunciation, there are numerous such rhymes which were once exact but which are now not rhymes at all. Because of the influence of earlier poets, however, many of these rhymes have continued to be used. There is an example of such a traditional or literary rhyme in Wordsworth's 'Lucy' poem, when in the second stanza he rhymes *stone* with *one*. In Shakespeare's time this had been a perfect rhyme, but in Wordsworth's it was not. In the eighteenth and nineteenth centuries such inexact but traditional rhymes are common.

Assonance and half-rhyme

Sometimes, however, poets who use inexact rhymes are not following tradition but on the contrary doing something new. In the present century, for example, some poets have made extensive use of assonance and of half-rhyme, as an alternative to rhyme. Assonance is an identity of vowels without identity of the following consonants, as in *groan/home.* Half-rhyme is identity of following consonants (and sometimes of preceding consonants too), with difference of vowels: *force/face, those/ways.* (Some writers use the word *assonance* to include also what I call *half-rhyme,* but it is useful to distinguish the two types.) Assonance and half-rhyme are often found in 'popular' kinds of poetry, such as broadside ballads and nursery-rhymes:

One for the master, and one for the *dame,*
And one for the little boy who lives down the *lane.*
(‘Baa, baa, black sheep’)

In these works such usages are perhaps a mark of naivety or lack of poetic skill; but some poets have used assonance and half-rhyme as a sophisticated technique. The powerful and moving poem ‘Strange Meeting’ by Wilfred Owen (1893– 1918) is written in five-foot lines in couplets, but uses half- rhyme instead of full rhyme. It begins as follows:

It seemed that out of battle I escaped
Down some profound dull tunnel, long since scooped
Through granites which titanic wars had groined.
Yet also there encumbered sleepers groaned,
Too fast in thought or death to be bestirred.   5
Then as I probed them, one sprang up, and stared
With piteous recognition in fixed eyes,
Lifting distressful hands as if to bless.
And by his smile, I knew that sullen hall,
By his dead smile I knew we stood in Hell.   10

The effect is remarkable, the half-rhymes bringing together words and ideas which we do not normally associate. At the same time, the neatness and certainty which rhymed couplets tend to produce are quite absent: Owen’s combination of couplet with half-rhyme produces a curious mixture of con- viction and diffidence — the couplet-form giving the effect of conviction, while the half-rhymes make its expression diffi- dent. Owen grew up in the Edwardian Age, and the couplets perhaps reflect a sense of the orderliness and confidence of that late-imperial period; but now, towards the end of the First World War, amidst the carnage of the Western Front, Owen modulates the couplets into the nuances and half-lights of half-rhyme: the certainties and pieties of that pre-war world have dissolved. But Owen has convictions and passion- ate feelings about the war, and the half-rhymes help him to express them without falling into the rhetoric of the past.

Other poets who have made considerable use of assonance or half-rhyme include Gerard Manley Hopkins (1844–89), Robert Graves (1895–), and W. H. Auden (1907–73).

Rhyme-schemes: heroic couplets

There are poems, such as Milton's 'Lycidas', in which there are rhymes, but no set pattern of rhymes. Most often, however, a poet chooses a rhyme-scheme for a poem and sticks to it. One popular form is rhymed couplets, in which successive lines rhyme in pairs. Rhymed couplets are often used with five-foot iambic lines, and this combination is called Heroic Couplets. Heroic couplets can be used for narrative poetry: much of Chaucer's *Canterbury Tales* is written in this metre, and Chaucer handles the couplets so as to give a free-flowing style in which the sense often overruns the couplet-boundary. A different treatment of the heroic couplet is seen in Pope:

> Damn with faint praise, assent with civil leer,
> And without sneering, teach the rest to sneer;
> Willing to wound, and yet afraid to strike,
> Just hint a fault, and hesitate dislike;
> Alike reserv'd to blame, or to commend,   5
> A tim'rous foe, and a suspicious friend.
>
> (*Epistle to Dr Arbuthnot*)

In that extract from Pope's famous satirical portrait of Addison, the couplets are end-stopped: a natural grammatical pause occurs at the end of each couplet, so that the poem moves forward one couplet at a time. Used in this way, the rhymed couplet gives neatness and point, an epigrammatic quality. In the passage, this effect is enhanced by the use of antithesis: each line falls into two contrasting halves, and the contrast is often accentuated by alliteration (*hint/hesitate*, *foe/friend*). The effect is rapier-like: each couplet makes a thrust, and the rhymes make each thrust sound deadly.

The heroic couplet was especially popular in the period from Dryden to Johnson; it was not used only for satire, but also for pastoral, elegy, narrative, and many other forms. The age admired neatness, polish, and decorum, and its couplets are often end-stopped, though not always as regularly as in that Pope passage.

Stanzas

Stanzaic verse is also common in English poetry, especially for shorter poems. A stanza is a group of lines with a predetermined metre and sequence of rhymes, the same for each stanza of the poem. A popular stanza is the one used in Wordsworth's 'Lucy' poem: a rhyme-scheme a b a b, with the lines alternately four-foot and three-foot iambic. Some poems have longer and more complicated stanzas: Spenser's *Faerie Queene* (1596) uses a stanza rhyming a b a b b c b c c, the lines being five-foot iambic except for the last in the stanza, which is six-foot.

Stanzas provide units for the progression of a poem, part of the structure within which the poet orders his material. They also set up expectations in the reader, just as metre does; and the poet may sometimes surprise us by defeating our expectation, for example by running the sense on from the end of one stanza into the next (as Donne does in 'Hymn to God my God, in my sickness'), or by introducing subtle variations in a complicated rhyme-scheme (as Keats does in 'To Autumn').

A stanzaic pattern, like a metre, is a constriction on a poet, a formal discipline to which he voluntarily submits himself. It is a means by which the poet controls the expression of his feelings, prevents his writing from being just a cry. In a poem which is highly charged emotionally, the reader is often conscious of this function of stanzaic form: the pattern is keeping the feeling under control. For example, in the beautiful love-lyric 'Go lovely rose', by Edmund Waller (1608–87), the strict stanzaic form imposes emotional control, while in *The Deserted Village* (1770) by Oliver Goldsmith (1730–74) the intense nostalgic feeling is contained within the heroic couplet. Less obvious rhyme-patterns can have a similar effect, as in 'A far cry from Africa' by the West Indian poet Derek Walcott (1930–). This is about the struggle between the Mau Mau liberation movement and the British in Kenya. Because of his upbringing, Walcott feels conflicting loyalties (to black nationalism, to English history and culture), and a helplessness in the face of the suffering of individuals on both sides. He is 'poisoned with the blood of both', and how can he choose, he asks, 'Between this Africa and the English tongue I love'? The poem has an intricate rhyme-scheme, which helps to give a sense of control over powerful conflicting emotions.

Set forms

A similar sense of discipline is given by the use of certain set forms that have arisen in European poetry: these are not stanzaic, but have a recognised metrical and rhyming pattern to which the poet conforms.

One such form is the sonnet, which arose in Italy in the Middle Ages and was introduced into England early in the sixteenth century. The sonnet has exactly fourteen lines, a group of eight (the octave) followed by a group of six (the sestet); at the 'turn' of the sonnet, between the octave and the sestet, there is some change of direction or theme or mood. Italian sonnets had lines of eleven syllables. The octave rhymed a b b a a b b a. There was more variety in the sestet, which could have either two or three rhymes, with such patterns as c d c d c d and c d e c d e. When the sonnet came to England, the metre adopted was five-foot iambic. Some poets have used the strict Italian type of rhyme-scheme: all of Milton's sonnets, for example, conform to it. English, however, is less rich in rhymes than Italian, and most English sonneteers have therefore used a rather freer rhyme-scheme, invented by Surrey: a b a b c d c d e f e f g g. This is the rhyme-scheme used in Shakespeare's sonnets. With this pattern, the turn sometimes comes after the twelfth line instead of after the eighth.

The Italian sonneteers usually wrote whole sequences of sonnets. Many of them were concerned with love, and a sequence might be addressed to one particular mistress, or concern the poet's fluctuations of fortune in his relationship with her. Sonnet sequences were copied by English poets of the late sixteenth century: the pioneer was Sir Philip Sidney (1554—86), with his *Astrophel and Stella,* and he was followed by Daniel, Drayton, Spenser, Shakespeare, and many others. Most Elizabethan sonnets are about love, but the form lends itself to many different themes: Donne's outstanding sonnets are religious, while Milton's are often political. After Milton, the sonnet fell out of favour, but was revived by Wordsworth (who favoured the strict Italian form), and was popular throughout the nineteenth century; distinguished practitioners include Keats and Hopkins.

There were other set forms in French and Italian poetry, often with refrains or repeated lines as well as strict rhyme-schemes, but none of them ever caught on in English as the sonnet did. There are, however, scattered examples of them: Wyatt's 'Ye old mule' is a rondeau; Hopkins's 'The child is father to the man' is a triolet; Auden's 'Hearing of harvests rotting in the valley' is a sestina; and William Empson (1906—) has published two moving examples of the villanelle, 'It is the pain, it is the pain endures' and 'Missing dates'. English, however, does not seem to lend itself very well to these strict forms, and the only ones to have had much currency are those used in recent times for comic purposes — the limerick and the clerihew.

Blank Verse

The earliest English poetry was unrhymed, and even in later times there was a tradition of unrhymed poetry. Classical Greek and Latin poetry had not used rhyme, and this carried weight with classically educated English poets. John Milton (1608–74), in a brief foreword to *Paradise Lost* (1667), defends his use of unrhymed verse by invoking classical precedent:

> The measure is English heroic verse without rhyme, as that of Homer in Greek, and of Virgil in Latin; rhyme being no necessary adjunct or true ornament of poem or good verse, in longer works especially, but the invention of a barbarous age, to set off wretched matter and lame metre.

Milton himself, however, had used rhyme in many shorter poems, and was to use it again in some of the choruses of *Samson Agonistes* (1671).

By far the commonest kind of unrhymed verse in post-medieval English is blank verse: unrhymed five-foot iambics. The inventor of this metre was Surrey, and it first occurs in a translation from the Latin, his rendering of two books of Virgil's *Aeneid,* published in 1557. The metre was taken up by writers for the theatre, and by Shakespeare's time was the standard one in English drama. At first, dramatic blank verse was relatively stiff and inflexible, with regular iambic rhythms and with most lines end-stopped: such is the blank verse of Thomas Kyd's *Spanish Tragedy* (1592), and of the early plays of Christopher Marlowe (1564–93). It was above all Shakespeare who developed blank verse, making it into a marvellously varied and expressive instrument.

In the seventeenth century, Milton developed his own variety of blank verse for use in epic. The metre continued to be popular even in the eighteenth century, despite the predilection of that age for the heroic couplet. The Romantics, too, made extensive use of blank verse, especially in longer poems such as Wordsworth's *Prelude,* and it was one of the standard metres all through the nineteenth century.

Poetic Diction

There is a tendency in most ages for certain words, phrases, and grammatical constructions to be considered inherently suitable for poetry: a specific 'poetic diction' develops, which sets off the language of poetry from that of prose or of speech. To contemporaries, this language often seems so self-evidently the way in which poetry should be written that to them it appears perfectly natural and transparent, whereas to a later age it may appear highly artificial. This is one reason why every age needs new translations of foreign works. When Pope translated Homer into eighteenth-century heroic couplets, he had an enormous success with the reading-public. His readers were not struck, apparently, by any incongruity between Pope's style and the manner and matter of the original: he was just writing poetry in the way everybody knew it should be written. For us, however, the incongruity is plain, and we feel Pope's translation to be an obviously eighteenth-century work.

As an age tends to have its poetic diction, so individual poets too may have theirs. Indeed, a powerful poet may influence a whole age's idea of the kind of language suitable for poetry. Or at the least he may have followers who are so influenced, even if there are opposing schools of thought. One such influential poet was Edmund Spenser (*c.* 1552—99).

Spenser's diction

Poets influenced by Spenser, especially in the seventeenth century, tend to draw on his minor poems rather than on *The Faerie Queene.* Especially influential was *The Shepherd's Calendar* (1579), the diction of which is more eccentric and more extreme than that of *The Faerie Queene.* Spenser is well-known for his use of archaisms, but the poetic language that he invented contained other elements as well. There are, in addition to archaisms, words from regional dialects, learned literary words, ordinary everyday words, pseudo-rusticisms, and brand-new inventions of Spenser's own. In *The Faerie Queen* the rustic element is largely absent, and the more typical blend is of the literary and the archaic.

Both poems influenced many minor seventeenth-century writers, especially writers of pastoral, who often lift whole phrases from Spenser, and even copy his mistakes (as when he misunderstands the meaning of some archaic expression). His influence waned in the later seventeenth century, but even in the middle of the eighteenth century there was a substantial Spenserian poem, James Thomson's *The Castle of Indolence* (1748). In the Romantic period, with its love of the medieval past, there was a renewed interest in Spenser, and his language once again became influential, for example in the poetry of Keats.

Milton's diction

More general and pervasive was the influence of Milton, especially on the eighteenth century. His minor poems affected eighteenth-century poetic diction more than the grand style of *Paradise Lost,* so let us look at one of his sonnets, published in 1645. It is addressed to the nightingale, whose

song is propitious to lovers, and calls on the bird to sing
before the owl prophesies the poet's doom; in past years the
nightingale has sung too late for the poet's relief, but without
reason, since the poet serves both the Muse and Love.

> O Nightingale, that on yon bloomy Spray
> Warbl'st at eve, when all the Woods are still,
> Thou with fresh hope the Lover's heart dost fill,
> While the jolly Hours lead on propitious May,
> Thy liquid notes that close the eye of Day,   5
> First heard before the shallow Cuckoo's bill,
> Portend success in love; O if Jove's will
> Have link'd that amorous power to thy soft lay,
> Now timely sing, ere the rude Bird of Hate
> Foretell my hopeless doom in some Grove nigh: 10
> As thou from year to year hast sung too late
> For my relief; yet hadst no reason why,
> Whether the Muse, or Love call thee his mate,
> Both them I serve, and of their train am I.

Unlike Spenser's poetry, this sonnet contains no archaisms. It
does, however, use words which had fallen out of everyday
speech and had become purely poetic or literary, such as
warble 'sing' (2), *eve* 'evening' (2), *lay* 'song', 'poem' (8), and
grove 'small wood' (10). There are other words in which this
process had begun, but which were perhaps still heard in
normal speech: *yon* 'that', 'the one over there' (1), *spray*
'twig', 'shoot' (1), *ere* 'before' (9), and *nigh* 'nearby' (10); in
eighteenth- and nineteenth-century writing these were purely
poetic or literary words, whereas in the sixteenth century
they had been ordinary everyday usage. The same is true of
a couple of grammatical features. Milton addresses the nightingale as *thou* instead of *you*; this is in accordance with
traditional usage, in which *thou* was used (among other
things) to address anything non-human — a god, an inanimate
object, an abstraction, an animal, a ghost. In Milton's time,
however, *thou* was dying out as a normal part of educated
speech, and by the following century had become (except in
some regional dialects) a purely literary form. The same is
true of the insertion of non-emphatic *do* into affirmative

statements, as in *Thou . . . dost fill* (3) (instead of *Thou . . . fillest*); this too was dying out as an everyday usage during the seventeenth century.

Moreover, there are words in the poem which are purely literary, and which have never been anything else. One such is *bloomy* 'full of blossoms, flowery', which has never been a colloquial word; a fondness for adjectives ending in -*y* is a feature of the poetic diction of the period from Milton to Thomas Gray (1716–71) — *breezy, dewy, glassy, heathy, mazy, pearly, shady, watery, wavy,* and so on. Another is *liquid,* when used specifically of sounds in the sense 'pure and clear'.

The sonnet also uses periphrasis, and word-meanings influenced by Latin. Periphrasis is the use of a descriptive phrase in place of a word, as when Pope, in his 'Pastorals', writes *the feather'd choirs* (meaning 'birds'). An example in the Milton sonnet is *the rude Bird of Hate* (9) meaning 'the owl' (a creature whose cry was thought to be ominous of death), or possibly 'the cuckoo'. An example of a word given a different meaning under classical influence is seen in line 4, where *Hours* does not have its usual English meaning, but is used (like Latin *Horae*) to mean 'the female divinities who preside over the changes in the seasons'; Milton is the first recorded user of the word in this sense.

There is a tendency in the sonnet to give every noun an appropriate adjective: *bloomy spray, jolly Hours, propitious May, liquid notes, shallow cuckoo, soft lay, hopeless doom.* These adjectives are usually general rather than particular, as indeed are the nouns themselves. We know that the nightingale sat on a bloomy spray, but we have no idea what kind of tree it was, what the blossoms looked or smelt like, what size, shape, or colour the leaves or branches were. This preference for the general rather than the particular is typical of English poetry in the period from Milton to Gray; indeed, it was a tenet of the neo-classical literary theory that dominated poetry in that period. A character in Samuel Johnson's *Rasselas* (1759) says:

> The business of the poet . . . is to examine, not the individual, but the species; to remark general properties

and large appearances: he does not number the streaks of the tulip, or describe the different shades in the verdure of the forest.

It was the poets of the Romantic and Victorian periods who believed that poetry should capture the specific, particular, and idiosyncratic, rather than the general and typical. With Milton's *bloomy spray* contrast Tennyson's

> More black than ashbuds in the front of March
> ('The Gardener's Daughter')

or Keats's

> The coming musk-rose, full of dewy wine,
> The murmurous haunt of flies on summer eves.
> ('Ode to a Nightingale')

Notice that the distinction between general and particular is quite different from that between abstract and concrete: Milton's *bloomy spray* is concrete, but not particular.

Eighteenth-century diction

The influence of this Miltonic style on the poetic language of the eighteenth century can be illustrated by the following extract from a very early work by Pope, his 'Pastorals' (1709):

> Hear how the birds, on ev'ry bloomy spray,
> With joyous music wake the dawning day!
> Why sit we mute, when early linnets sing,
> When warbling Philomel salutes the Spring!
> Why sit we sad, when Phosphor shines so clear,   5
> And lavish Nature paints the purple year?

We could almost believe that Pope wrote that with the Milton sonnet open in front of him. Admittedly in Pope it is morning (Phosphor is the morning star), whereas Milton's sonnet is an evening one; but Pope has the nightingale (*Philomel*), and echoes Milton's phraseology (*bloomy spray, warbling*).

As in Milton, each noun tends to have an appropriate but rather general adjective (*joyous music, early linnets, warbling Philomel, lavish Nature*). In *the purple year* (6) we see another example of Latin influence on meaning: here *purple* means 'brilliant, beautiful, gay', under the influence of Latin *purpureus,* which in poetry could have similar meanings. In the word *Nature* (6) we see the eighteenth-century love of personification: poems of the period are often littered with figures like Envy, Fear, Hope, and Joy. A famous example is Thomas Gray's line

Youth on the prow, and Pleasure at the helm

('The Bard').

The eighteenth-century poets, as could be expected, developed their vocabulary in many ways differently from Milton, even though he was a strong influence. In addition to the adjectives in -*y* already mentioned, their poetic words include *adore, adorn, ambrosial, azure, breast, Ceres* 'corn', *charm, congenial, decent, enamelled, eve* 'evening', *fabric* 'edifice', 'building', *fancy, flood* 'river', 'sea', *fury, gale* 'breeze', *generous, genial* 'festive', 'conducive to growth', 'cheering', *glade, glebe* 'earth', 'soil', 'cultivated land', *grove, hearth, lawn* 'glade', 'grassland', *lay* 'poem', 'song', *liquid, mead* 'meadow', *melt, morn* 'morning', *Muse, nymph* 'girl', 'woman', *odour, oft, pasture, rill, sable* 'black', *silver, sire* 'father', *soft, swain* 'shepherd, man', *tresses, turf, urn, vain, verdant, vernal, warble, zephyr.* The favourite words vary from poet to poet, but there is a solid core of poetic language which they can all draw on.

From the middle of the century there is a movement towards a more 'Gothic' type of poetry, and a cult of melancholy, leading to some shift in the favourite poetic words (again much influenced by Milton, especially 'Il Penseroso' and 'Lycidas'). The newer favourites include *cell, cloister, ghastly, hermit, ivy, melancholy, mossy, myrtle, pale, pallid, pilgrim, rude, ruin, shroud, tomb, tower,* and *yew.*

Nineteenth-century diction

What is often called the poetic diction of the eighteenth

century was, more strictly speaking, characteristic of the period from about 1660 to 1790, from the poetry of John Dryden (1631–1700) to that of Samuel Johnson (1709–84). In the late eighteenth century, the reaction against this poetic language had already begun, with Blake's *Songs of Innocence* and *Songs of Experience* (1789–94), and the publication of *Lyrical Ballads* (1798) by Wordsworth and Coleridge. These poets were consciously hostile to the poetry of the previous age, and in a preface to the second edition of *Lyrical Ballads,* in 1800, Wordsworth attacked 'what is usually called poetic diction'; he argued that the language of a large part of every good poem must (except for metre) in no respect differ from that of prose; and he claimed that his own poems in the volume were written in 'a selection of the real language of men in a state of vivid sensation'.

Nevertheless, a great deal of nineteenth-century poetry (including much of Wordsworth's own) does use a special poetic diction. It is less uniform than that of the eighteenth century, and so less easy to define, but all the same it clearly distinguishes much poetry from prose, and still more from everyday speech. Many poets looked back for inspiration to English poetry before the time of Dryden, and especially to the age of Shakespeare, and they often adopted words and grammatical forms from that earlier age. Spenser became influential again, while Milton continued to be a potent force. The use of a distinctively poetic language is not confined to minor poetry, but is found in much of the best writing of the age. Consider, for example, the final stanza of Keats's 'Ode on a Grecian Urn' (1820):

> O Attic shape! Fair attitude! with brede
> Of marble men and maidens overwrought,
> With forest branches and the trodden weed;
> Thou, silent form, dost tease us out of thought
> As doth eternity: Cold Pastoral!   5
> When old age shall this generation waste,
>   Thou shalt remain, in midst of other woe
> Than ours, a friend to man, to whom thou say'st,
> 'Beauty is truth, truth beauty,' — that is all
>   Ye know on earth, and all ye need to know.   10

This contains many things which were never heard in the everyday language in Keats's time. Archaic grammatical features include the use of the singular pronoun *thou*, and its associated verb-forms (*dost, shalt, say'st*); the use of *ye* as a variant of *you* (10); the use of *doth* (5) instead of *does*; and the insertion of unstressed *do* in affirmative statements (*Thou . . . dost tease*) (4). Poetic forms in the vocabulary include *brede* 'braid', 'things plaited or intertwined' (1); *maidens* 'girls', 'young unmarried women' (2); *overwrought* 'worked all over', 'having its surface figured or decorated' (2); and *weed* 'small plants', 'grass' (3).

The colloquial tradition

So in all ages, it seems, there is a special poetic diction, marking off poetry from everyday language. Equally, however, there always seems to be an opposing force, a drive for the colloquial and 'non-poetic' in poetry.

In some kinds of writing, indeed, the use of a less highly wrought style was positively encouraged by literary theory. The neo-classical theory of poetry, which was powerful from the Renaissance until the end of the eighteenth century, contained the doctrine of the three styles: the high style, which was grandiloquent and made extensive use of figurative language; the middle style, which was less exalted; and the low style, which made little use of figures, and was the nearest to ordinary usage. The style chosen ought to depend, the theory held, on the subject-matter and the kind of poetry being written: the high style was to be used in epic and tragedy, the middle style in comedies and love-poetry, and the low style in pastoral poetry and satire. The low style provided a precedent for a colloquial kind of style, and a poet might well extend it into other kinds of poetry.

Indeed, it seems no exaggeration to say that there is a continuous colloquial tradition in English poetry, existing alongside the more literary tradition, and sometimes in conflict with it. The two strands may occur in the work of a single poet, and even meet inside a single poem. Post-medieval poets in whom the colloquial strand has been prominent include Sir Thomas Wyatt, John Donne, and George Gordon,

Lord Byron (1788–1824). In Wyatt it is found in the 'Satires', but also in some of his finest love-poetry:

> They flee from me that sometime did me seek
> With naked foot stalking in my chamber.
> I have seen them gentle, tame, and meek
> That now are wild, and do not remember
> That sometime they put themself in danger
> To take bread at my hand; and now they range
> Busily seeking with a continual change.

This is completely lacking in conventional poetic language, and its rhythms are strongly suggestive of real speech. The word-order is completely natural: in the whole stanza, the only concession to the demands of metre and rhyme is the placing of *me* before *seek* in the first line.

Donne is a writer of many moods and many styles, and can be wildly hyperbolical and fantastic. Beneath most of his work, however, we feel the steady pressure of the idiom and movement of speech. We have already seen how he achieves a colloquial effect at the beginning of 'The Good Morrow'; and many of his love-poems open with phrases which are both colloquial and strikingly dramatic:

> Busy old fool, unruly sun,
> Why dost thou thus,
> Through windows, and through curtains call on us?
> > ('The Sun Rising')

> For Godsake hold your tongue, and let me love
> > ('The Canonization')

> Love, any devil else but you,
> Would for a given soul give something too
> > ('Love's Exchange')

> Dear love, for nothing less than thee
> Would I have broke this happy dream
> > ('The Dream')

I long to talk with some old lover's ghost
                                    ('Love's Deity')

Whoever comes to shroud me, do not harm
    Nor question much
That subtile wreath of hair, which crowns my arm
                                    ('The Funeral').

Donne did not write for the theatre, but it was not for nothing that he lived in the greatest age of the English drama.

In Byron, the colloquial strain is seen especially in the great satirical works, *The Vision of Judgment* (1822) and *Don Juan* (1819—24), as in the opening stanza of the former poem:

> Saint Peter sat by the celestial gate:
>   His keys were rusty, and the lock was dull,
> So little trouble had been given of late;
>   Not that the place by any means was full,
> But since the Gallic era 'eighty-eight'   5
>   The devils had ta'en a longer, stronger pull,
> And 'a pull altogether', as they say
> At sea — which drew most souls another way.

(In *the Gallic era 'eighty-eight'*, Byron is referring to the period of the French Revolution and the European wars which followed.) The scene is set at the gate of Heaven, of which St Peter is gatekeeper, and the informal (even flippant) manner of the writing is in deliberate contrast with the supposed solemnity of the setting. This is only one of several styles used in the poem, but the colloquial element makes a substantial contribution to its overall effect.

Other poets in whom the colloquial strain appears are Shakespeare, Hopkins, the Irish poet W. B. Yeats (1865—1939), the American poet Robert Frost (1874—1963), and T. S. Eliot (1888—1965). Colloquialism is also a powerful force in much recent poetry from New Commonwealth countries, where writers have felt the need to develop an authentic local voice; poets in whom the strain is strong include Edward Brathwaite (1930–) in the West Indies, Wole Soyinka (1935–) in Nigeria, and Okot p'Bitek (1931) in East Africa. On the other hand, there are some poets from whose work it is almost entirely absent, notably Spenser and Milton and poets much influenced by them, such as Alfred, Lord Tennyson (1809–92). It might be thought that Pope too belonged to this group, but in fact his mature work contains some strikingly colloquial passages, such as the opening of the *Epistle to Dr Arbuthnot* (1734):

> Shut, shut the door, good John! fatigu'd I said,
> Tie up the knocker, say I'm sick, I'm dead,
> The Dog-star rages! nay 'tis past a doubt,
> All Bedlam, or Parnassus, is let out:
> Fire in each eye, and papers in each hand,
> They rave, recite, and madden round the land.

The artificiality of 'poetic diction' is likely to be most obvious to people at times of cultural and social upheaval, when there is a change in sensibility and literary expectations. At such times, poets will try to establish new ways of writing, and so there are periodic 'poetic revolutions'. The Elizabethan style is succeeded by the Metaphysical, the Metaphysical by the Augustan, the Augustan by the Romantic, the Romantic by the neo-metaphysical style of the early T. S. Eliot. The initiators of such poetic revolutions often theorise or propagandise about them, as Wordsworth does in the preface to *Lyrical Ballads,* and they are likely to argue that the old style is artificial, and their own style natural: Wordsworth claims to write poetry in 'the real language of men'. But the Augustans similarly had thought that Metaphysical poetry was forced and artificial, whereas their own poetry was the product of Nature and Reason. The arguments produced at such times of change seldom illuminate the nature of poetry: Wordsworth's theories about the language of poetry, as Coleridge showed in his *Biographia Literaria* (1817), just will not hold water. But such arguments do help us to understand what poets are reacting against, what they are trying to do, and how they are trying to do it.

Metaphor

In the 'Lucy' poem, Wordsworth calls the girl a violet. This is an example of metaphor, defined by the *Oxford English Dictionary* as 'The figure of speech in which a name or descriptive term is transferred to some object different from, or analogous to, that to which it is properly applicable'. Other examples of metaphor already quoted are Wyatt's use of the word *forest* to describe his heart, and Keats's *dewy wine* to denote liquid (dew or rain-water) in the musk-rose. The *OED* definition seems to imply that metaphors are always nouns, but in fact we usually include similar transfers with other parts of speech: when Wyatt says that his lust should be reined by reason, he is using the verb *to rein* metaphorically: its literal meaning is 'to pull on the reins of a horse'; Wyatt uses it in the transferred sense 'to control one's desires'.

Metaphor is one of the powerful tools that poets use, but it is by no means confined to poetry: it also occurs in prose, and in speech. Indeed, the language is full of dead metaphors: the first person to talk about the *foot* of a hill or the *mouth* of a river, or to say that he *saw* ('understood') what somebody meant, was using a metaphor; but the usage later became so common that it ceased to be a metaphor at all, and was simply one of the accepted meanings of the word in question. Poets, however, often try to create new metaphors.

A metaphor is always a two-sided thing: there is the original literal meaning of the word, and there is the new transferred meaning. So, in the Wordsworth poem the word *violet* is shifted from its literal meaning 'a kind of flower' to its metaphorical one 'a sweet girl'. It is convenient to have a terminology to refer to these two sides of a metaphor, and one has been invented by the critic I. A. Richards. He calls the literal meaning the *vehicle* of the metaphor, and the transferred meaning its *tenor*. So with the violet the vehicle is 'a kind of flower', and the tenor 'a sweet girl'. If you call a man a pig (meaning that he is greedy), the vehicle of the metaphor is 'an animal of the genus *Sus*' and the tenor is 'a greedy person'. The terminology can also be applied to allegory, which is a kind of extended metaphor: in John Bunyan's *Pilgrim's Progress* (1678), the vehicle of the allegory is 'a journey (from the City of Destruction to the Celestial City)', and the tenor is 'the Christian life'.

Metaphor can help a poet to achieve condensation, to pack much meaning into little space. Wyatt's *heart's forest* evokes very economically a sense of the darkness and danger of the inner life. Keats's *dewy wine* suggests the rich and intoxicating fragrance of the musk-rose. Metaphors can also shape a reader's attitudes. In Shakespeare's *Henry V*, a character describes the danger of an attack on England by the Scots if the English send an expedition to France:

> For once the eagle England being in prey,
> To her unguarded nest the weasel Scot
> Comes sneaking, and so sucks her princely eggs.

We hardly need to be told that it is an Englishman speaking. England attacking France is an eagle, the majestic king of birds. Scotland attacking England is a weasel, a small nocturnal animal (*Mustela nivalis*) which is a ferocious killer. We are clearly being invited to approve of the English, and to disapprove of the 'sneaking' Scots. The use of metaphor to shape our attitudes is by no means confined to poetry: it is particularly common in oratory and in advertising.

Metaphor can also work indirectly, by introducing ideas apparently unrelated to what the poet is saying. The vehicle of a metaphor must be analogous to the tenor in some way, but there may also be ways in which it is very different from it, so that it introduces associations into the poem unrelated to the tenor. Consider the famous opening of T. S. Eliot's 'Love Song of J. Alfred Prufrock' (1917):

> Let us go then, you and I,
> When the evening is spread out against the sky
> Like a patient etherised upon a table.

The third line is not indeed a metaphor but a simile, since it is introduced by the preposition *Like*; simile operates in much the same way as metaphor, but the comparison is made explicit, whereas in metaphor it is implied. Eliot's comparison is a startling one. The evening is 'spread out against the sky'; this suggests the evening light in the west, stretching over a considerable portion of the sky (but not all of it), and appearing to be nearer to the viewer than the sky is, but nevertheless pressed close against it. Then Eliot goes on to compare the evening to a patient under a general anaesthetic (*etherised*), while the sky is the operating-table on which the patient lies. The comparison suggests the stillness and inertness of the evening. At the same time, *etherised* ('subjected to the influence of the anaesthetic ether') reminds the reader of an older sense of the word *ether* — 'the clear sky, the upper regions of space beyond the clouds' — which bears very closely on the appearance of this particular evening sky. But at the same time the comparison to a patient under an anaesthetic can bring in associations which have nothing to do with the evening sky, such as surgery, illness, white clothes, face-masks, sterile instruments, death; some of these may be quite irrelevant, but some may contribute to the poem as a whole.

A metaphor may consist of a single word, like Keats's 'dewy *wine*', or it may extend over a whole sentence, as when, in Shakespeare's *Richard III*, Queen Margaret says to her enemies:

> What? were you snarling all before I came,
> Ready to catch each other by the throat,
> And turn you all your hatred now on me?

Although the word is not used, Margaret is saying that her enemies are dogs. In the following fine poem attributed to Sir Walter Ralegh (1552–1618), a single metaphor is sustained throughout:

> What is our life? a play of passion,
> Our mirth the music of division,
> Our mothers' wombs the tiring-houses be,
> Where we are dressed for this short comedy,
> Heaven the judicious sharp spectator is,   5
> That sits and marks still who doth act amiss,

Our graves that hide us from the searching sun
Are like drawn curtains when the play is done,
Thus march we playing to our latest [last] rest,
Only we die in earnest, that's no jest.   10

The life of man is compared to a stage-play, in which the brilliant melodic passages (*music of division*) played by the theatre's orchestra are our diversions or entertainments (*mirth*). The wombs in which our souls take on human flesh and form are the dressing-rooms (*tiring-houses*) where the actors dress up for their parts. God (*Heaven*) is the critical (*sharp*) spectator of the play, observing which actors perform their parts badly (*amiss*). Finally, the curtains drawn at the end of the play are the graves in which we are concealed from the light at the end of our lives. Thus we all march *playing* to our final rest, death. The word *playing* is rich in associations. Primarily it means '(play-)acting', but can also mean 'amusing ourselves', 'sporting', 'behaving frivolously', 'taking part in a game', 'gambling', 'springing or darting about'; and these other meanings reverberate in Ralegh's poem. Up to this point, the poem has dealt with the resemblances between human life and a stage-play, but in the final line the poet wrily calls attention to a difference: on the stage, characters only pretend to die, but we really die, that's no *jest* (meaning both 'joke' and 'something only pretended, a theatrical performance').

The sustained metaphor suggests vividly the transience and vanity of human life. Life, from birth to death, is like the two or three hours of a stage-play; and human beings, priding themselves on their rank or possessions or endowments, are like actors dressed up in fine clothes for an hour or two. The metaphor enables the poet to express strong feelings about human life without actually mentioning them: because of the obliquity of his approach, the emotions seem to arise directly from the images presented.

In general, *talking about* your feelings is not the best way of communicating them: you are more likely to be successful if you offer your hearer events, objects, images, from which the emotions can flow. The perils that arise if instead you contemplate yourself and your feelings can be seen in the following lines of Percy Bysshe Shelley (1792—1822):

> Oh lift me from the grass!
> I die! I faint! I fail!
> Let thy love in kisses rain
> On my lips and eyelids pale.
>
> ('The Indian Serenade')

The second line in particular, where the poet's attention is focused on himself, is singularly ineffective: it seems to be straining after effect, and at the same time is so self-centred as to border on the ludicrous. By contrast, Ralegh's use of metaphor communicates powerful feelings, yet keeps the poet distanced from them.

Poems in which a single image is sustained throughout are most likely to be found in the Renaissance period, but there are also more recent examples. Wilfred Owen's sonnet 'Anthem for Doomed Youth' sustains a comparison between the events of the battlefield and the religious rites for those killed. In 'For he was a shrub among poplars' by the Nigerian poet Christopher Okigbo (1932—67), the aspiring creative man struggling for survival is compared to a shrub growing in an equatorial forest. In some poems, the two-sidedness (vehicle and tenor) is not made explicit all the way through, but is nevertheless implied. In 'Bullocky', by the Australian poet Judith Wright (1915—), the pioneer cattle-drover (*bullocky*) is equated with Moses, and the whole poem implies a comparison between the history of modern Australia and the journey of the Israelites from Egypt to the Promised Land.

Rhetoric

Metaphor was one of the so-called Figures (sometimes called 'figures of speech') discussed in the handbooks of classical rhetoric; and some knowledge of rhetoric is useful for a reader of earlier English poetry.

Rhetoric was the art of oratory, and the rhetorical handbooks of ancient Greece and Rome were designed to train

people in the art of public speaking. Even in antiquity, however, the Rhetorics influenced the writing of poetry, and
in Renaissance England they were thought of as guides to
poets rather than orators. A rhetorical tradition derived from
ancient Rome had persisted throughout the Middle Ages, but
in the Renaissance, with the rise of the new humanist education based on the Greek and Latin classics, the full content of
the ancient rhetorical handbooks was recovered. The new
style of education reached England in the early sixteenth
century, and the first humanist handbooks of rhetoric
written in English appeared around the middle of the century.
The influence of rhetoric on English poetry became very
powerful in the last quarter of the sixteenth century, and
persisted, with some attenuation, to the end of the nineteenth.

The five branches of Rhetoric

The classical handbooks divided their art into five branches:
Invention, Disposition, Elocution, Memory, and Pronunciation.

Invention was the process of finding suitable material for
the oration or poem. This was done by the use of 'topics' or
'places', sets of categories which the writer went through to
get ideas. One popular set was that of the Latin author
Cicero: definition, division, the name, conjugates, genus,
species, similarity, difference, contraries, adjuncts, consequences, antecedents, incompatibles, causes, effects, comparison. English schoolboys in the sixteenth and seventeenth
centuries were trained to take a subject and find material by
considering it from the point of view of each of these sixteen
categories; and anybody writing on a subject (like Sidney
writing about poetry) is likely to define it, divide it into its
parts, discuss the significance of its name, and so on.

When the material had been found, it had to be arranged,
and this was the business of Disposition. The classical handbooks discussed the best order for handling different parts of
a subject, and laid down a standard five- or six-part plan for
an oration. This plan had some effect on English prose-
writing, but its influence on poetry was negligible. The poets

were more likely to be influenced by Poetics, handbooks on poetry (also derived from classical sources) which could discuss such things as the structure of a play or an epic poem.

Elocution was not what we mean by that word, but rather *style* in the broadest sense. When the material had been discovered and arranged, Elocution taught the writer how to 'clothe' it (to use a favourite neo-classical metaphor) in suitable words. One of the subjects handled in the Elocution section was the Figures, and in the Renaissance handbooks this became the dominant topic.

Memory was the technique of memorising your oration. Pronunciation was the art of delivering it — voice-production, gesture, theatrical business. When rhetoric came to be thought of as something for poets rather than for public speakers, these two branches fell into the background.

The Figures

The Figures, on the other hand, became the dominant part of an English rhetorical handbook. Indeed, in the sixteenth and seventeenth centuries there are books devoted entirely to the subject, in which as many as 150 different figures may be discussed, all defined, categorised, and illustrated.

In Rhetoric, a figure is defined as a departure from everyday usage for artistic effect (though in fact this definition is unsatisfactory, since most of the things called figures can occur in ordinary speech). The Renaissance handbooks divide the figures into two main types, Tropes and Schemes.

Tropes are figures in which there is some kind of substitution or transfer of meaning; that is, there is a vehicle and a tenor. Obvious examples are metaphor and allegory, but they also include irony (in which you say the opposite of what you mean), pun, metonymy, proverb, and many others. If you are puzzled by the inclusion of proverbs, consider an example: 'Birds of a feather flock together' has the tenor 'People of similar outlook and attitudes will be found associating with one another'.

Schemes are figures in which there is no such transfer of meaning. They are subdivided into Grammatical Schemes and Rhetorical Schemes.

In Grammatical Schemes the writer allegedly breaks the rules of the language. He may use a non-normal form of a single word, as when Spenser, for the sake of rhyme, uses *hether* and *gether* (for *hither* and *gather*). He may break off a sentence and leave it unfinished, as King Lear does:

> I will have such revenges on you both
> That all the world shall — I will do such things —
> What they are yet I know not . . .
> (King Lear, II.4.279–81)

He may insert a parenthetical sentence, as John of Gaunt does:

> This land . . .
> Is now leas'd out — I die pronouncing it —
> Like to a tenement or pelting farm.
> (Richard II, II.1.57–60)

He may omit a conjunction, as in the following line of Donne's:

> Nor hours, days, months, which are the rags of time.
> ('The Sun Rising')

Alternatively, he may insert more conjunctions than are necessary. He may use non-normal word-order: for example, the object may for emphasis be placed at the beginning of the sentence, as in Milton's account of the fall of Satan:

> Him the Almighty Power
> Hurl'd headlong flaming from th'Ethereal Sky
> (Paradise Lost, I.44–5)

Or the adjective may be placed after its noun instead of before it, as in Shakespeare's *meadows green* (Sonnet 33) and Milton's *A Dungeon horrible* (*Paradise Lost*). All these things were categorised as Grammatical Schemes.

In Rhetorical Schemes there is no such violation of linguistic rules. They cover a wide variety of things, but there are three main types: the production of verbal patterns by means of repetition; whole modes of procedure, such as imprecation or consolation; and set pieces, such as the elaborate description of a person or place, or a comparison.

The figures thus cover an enormous range of different things, from the choice of a single word to the mode within which a whole work operates. In the late Elizabethan period, poets made liberal use of figures of all kinds, but especially popular were the Rhetorical Schemes which produced verbal patterns by repetition. The following is an example from Shakespeare's *As You Like It*:

> If ever you have looked on better days:
> If ever been where bells have knolled to church:
> If ever sat at any good man's feast:
> If ever from your eyelids wiped a tear,
> And know what 'tis to pity, and be pitied . . .
> (II.7.113–17)

The words *If ever* are repeated at the beginning of four successive lines. Orlando, the speaker, has burst in on Duke Senior and his followers, sword in hand, believing them to be brigands; but he has now realised his mistake, and the repetitions in this speech make it a formal and ceremonious conjuration, in contrast to the blunt violence of his language when he first entered. The Duke, in his reply to Orlando, continues the pattern by repeating Orlando's very phrases, thus suggesting the harmony and sympathy which have now been established between the speakers.

The patterns can be more complicated, for example by having repetition at the end as well as at the beginning, or by consisting of such arrangements as A-B-B-A, or A-B, B-C, C-D, and so on. Such complex patterns are found in Spenser and in early Shakespeare. Later writers tend to use less obvious devices, but nevertheless the figures have been a continuing influence in English poetry.

Form and content

A training in rhetoric encouraged writers to think of form

and content as separable, since they were handled by different branches of the art: the finding of material was the business of Invention, while the finding of words to 'clothe' the material was the business of Elocution. This fitted in with the common view of the function of poetry (current from the sixteenth to the eighteenth century) as being to teach and delight, or to teach by pleasing: the teaching was carried out by the content, the substance of the poem, while the delighting was given by the form, the beautiful words it was put into. It was not until the time of Samuel Taylor Coleridge (1772—1834) that this view was seriously challenged, and a new outlook arose, which looked upon form and content as inseparable: if the form is changed, the content is changed too, something different is being said. On the old view, the relationship between form and content is a mechanical one; but the newer view uses instead the model of an organism: the relationship is like that between the shape and the substance of an apple, or a tree; the form grows, as it were, from inside. The 'organic' rather than the 'mechanical' view of poetry has been commonly held since the early nineteenth century.

Rhetoric and self-expression

The rhetorical handbooks recognised three types of oration: the deliberative, a political speech made in the Senate or popular assembly to persuade people on affairs of state; the forensic, made in the law-courts to persuade the judges in a law-suit; and the occasional, addressed to an individual on a particular occasion, usually in praise or celebration, though sometimes in dispraise. So the orator operated in certain recognised modes which called for persuasion or praise.

Poets, too, thought of themselves as working in established modes, and finding material and style in ways suggested by their rhetorical training. These modes included praise and persuasion: praise of a patron or a monarch, persuasion of a woman to love. The love-persuasion poem is a common type, seen in Marlowe's 'Come live with me and be my love', Jonson's 'Come my Celia', Herrick's 'Gather ye rose-buds', Waller's 'Go lovely rose', Marvell's 'To his Coy Mistress', and many more. These very different poems are the products of a single tradition, each poet making something rather different of it.

A poet who works within an established mode is unlikely to conceive of his work as self-expression. Indeed, the idea that poetry is self-expression is rather recent, dating from the time of the Romantics. Earlier poets were more likely to think of themselves as operating within established modes (praising, persuading, denigrating, satirising, meditating, and so on), using established genres (epic, ode, pastoral, and so on), and then to look for material and to elaborate on their themes in the ways suggested by their rhetorical training. At the same time, the poet might well try to give a distinctive twist to the traditional form: working in an established mode is by no means incompatible with originality.

Poetic Structure

Poems can have many different kinds of structure. An obvious type is narrative structure; though in narrative poems there are often, in addition to the obvious line of the story, other structural devices, such as repeated themes, parallelism of incident or character, and thematic image-clusters. Such devices are characteristic of long narrative poems, like *The Canterbury Tales* and *Paradise Lost*. Shorter poems often have a narrative element, in that they present an incident or experience; usually, however, this is not presented for its own sake, but leads on to some reflection or insight or revelation.

So in Wordsworth's 'Resolution and Independence', the poet, in a state of melancholy and depression, walks on the moors, where he meets and converses with an old leech-gatherer. The dignity and strength of character of the old man make such a powerful impression on the poet that he has a visionary experience of him pacing 'About the weary moors continually'. When he comes back to earth and completes his conversation with the leech-gatherer, he recognises the latter's moral strength compared with himself, and realises that this experience will give him greater strength for the future.

In an even shorter poem, 'Old Man' by Edward Thomas (1878–1917), the poet watches a girl who, every time she goes in or out of the house, takes a leaf from the aromatic shrub Southernwood ('Old Man', or 'Lad's Love') which grows by the door, and shrivels and sniffs at it. He wonders how much she will remember of that bitter scent, and of the setting where she smelt it. He himself loves the plant, but cannot remember when he first encountered it; and as he sniffs the leaves and tries to recall this lost piece of the past, he is desolated by a sense of loss and of the passing of time, 'an avenue, dark, nameless, without end'.

On the other hand, a poem may simply create a mood or an atmosphere, which constitutes its unity. Tennyson's 'Lotos-Eaters' creates powerfully the languid atmosphere of the land of the Lotos-Eaters and the world-weary mood of the crew of Odysseus who arrive there; and this mood and atmosphere are the main aim of the poem (though there is also a slight narrative element).

Alternatively, a poem may have a logical unity: it may conduct an argument, or pretend to, as do many of Donne's poems. There are also other kinds of logical structure: Renaissance students were trained in logic as well as rhetoric, and were taught (for example) to frame definitions, and to divide things into their logical parts; and these processes could be used as structural devices by poets. A poem attributed to Ralegh begins as follows:

> Now what is love, I pray thee tell.
> It is that fountain and that well
> Where pleasure and repentance dwell,
> It is perhaps that sauncing bell [sanctus bell]
> That tolls all in to heaven or hell,
> And this is love, as I hear tell.

And so the poem continues for another four stanzas, each beginning by asking what love is, and then giving a series of witty definitions of it. The whole poem is constructed round the process of defining.

In later poetry especially, there may be no continuous narrative or logical line, and the structure may consist of a pattern of contrast or of complementation, as in 'The Clod and the Pebble', a poem by Blake:

> 'Love seeketh not itself to please,
>   Nor for itself hath any care,
>   But for another gives its ease,
>   And builds a Heaven in Hell's despair.'
>
> So sung a little Clod of Clay,
>   Trodden with the cattle's feet,
>   But a pebble of the brook
>   Warbled out these metres meet:
>
> 'Love seeketh only Self to please,
>   To bind another to its delight,
>   Joys in another's loss of ease,
>   And builds a Hell in Heaven's despite.'

The poet presents two contrasting views of the nature of love, but makes no comment or judgement on them (though he does leave the reader to ponder on the choice of the Clod and the Pebble as spokesmen for these views). The structure of the poem suggests that antithesis is part of the nature of things, that conflicting concepts of love are inherent in the universe.

Keats's 'To Autumn'

In the Blake poem, the structural principle is quite plain. In some poems the underlying structure is less apparent, though it will emerge for the careful reader. Consider the ode 'To Autumn', by John Keats (1795–1821). The first of its three stanzas deals with fruitfulness, ripeness, maturity:

> Season of mists and mellow fruitfulness,
>   Close bosom friend of the maturing sun;
> Conspiring with him how to load and bless
>   With fruit the vines that round the thatch-eaves run;
> To bend with apples the moss'd cottage-trees,   5
>   And fill all fruit with ripeness to the core;

To swell the gourd, and plump the hazel shells
With a sweet kernel; to set budding more,
And still more, later flowers for the bees,
Until they think warm days will never cease,   10
For Summer has o'er-brimm'd their clammy cells.

This evokes wonderfully the relaxed warmth and 'mellow fruitfulness' of early autumn. Notice how concrete and physical it is: the loading of the vines with fruit; the branches of the trees bending under the weight of apples; the swelling gourd; the expressiveness of *plump* used as a verb, and of *clammy cells* (the comb overflowing with honey in the coolness of the hive). The stanza contains no main verb: it consists of one sentence built round the participle *Conspiring*, which takes the place of a finite verb; dependent on *Conspiring* are a series of infinitives (*load, bless, bend, fill, swell, plump, set*). There are a few finite verbs (*run, think, will cease, has o'erbrimm'd*), but they are all in subordinate clauses, and these clauses are not even directly dependent on *Conspiring*, but rather on infinitives. The effect of this unconventional sentence-structure is to suggest a continuing state of affairs, a situation rather than action. Things do indeed happen, but within a framework of sameness and stability, so that we feel that 'warm days will never cease'.

The stanza deals with natural things (trees, fruit, nuts, bees), but is not about *wild* nature: it implies a domesticated nature, nature in the service of man. The things mentioned are all used by man (grapes, apples, the gourd, hazel nuts, honey); the bees, with their honeycomb, are hive-bees, not wild bees; and human habitation is made explicit by the *thatch-eaves* (overhanging edge of a thatched roof) and by the *cottage-trees* (apple-trees growing in the garden of a humble country dwelling). Moreover, the cottage-trees are *mossed* (have moss growing on them), which suggests long and settled human habitation. The human context is made explicit in the second stanza:

Who hath not seen thee oft amid thy store?
Sometimes whoever seeks abroad may find
Thee sitting careless on a granary floor,

> Thy hair soft-lifted by the winnowing wind;   15
> Or on a half-reap'd furrow sound asleep,
>   Drows'd with the fume of poppies, while thy hook
>   Spares the next swath and all its twinèd flowers:
> And sometimes like a gleaner thou dost keep
>   Steady thy laden head across a brook;   20
>   Or by a cyder-press, with patient look,
>   Thou watchest the last oozings hours by hours.

Here Autumn is personified as a series of human figures, male and female, and they are all to do with harvest. Autumn sits idly on the floor of a granary, where the grain is stored. The *winnowing wind* reminds us of the process by which the grain has been separated out: after being threshed, the corn is winnowed, that is, exposed to the wind so that the chaff is blown away. Next, Autumn is a reaper, sleeping in the field by his work, with his sickle (*hook*) lying beside him. Then Autumn is a gleaner, gathering the corn left by the reapers and carrying it on her head. Finally, Autumn is a cider-maker, watching the apple-juice trickle out of the press. In this stanza there is as little sense of movement as in the first, even though it purports to deal with human work: the general effect is of stillness, even somnolence. Autumn is *sitting*, not bustling about. The reaper is asleep in the middle of his work; and the soporific effect is reinforced by the poppies which grow among the corn, and whose *fume* makes the reaper drowsy (the juice of poppies has narcotic qualities). The cider-maker just sits for hours watching the press. Only the gleaner is moving, and even she is a slow-moving figure in a still harvest landscape. The overall feeling is of relaxed and indolent well-being.

   Notice the use Keats makes of the line-break. In lines 13–14, the break comes between a verb (*may find*) and its object (*Thee*); the effect is to throw a strong stress on to *Thee*, emphasising the fact that the figure which we might take for a mere country labourer is indeed Autumn himself. Even more striking is the effect in lines 19–20, where the break at *keep/Steady* (with successive stressed syllables) seems to enact physically the balanced motion of the gleaner as she steps into or across the brook with a load on her head.

The third stanza is about the sounds of autumn:

> Where are the songs of Spring? Ay, where are they?
>   Think not of them, thou hast thy music too, —
> While barrèd clouds bloom the soft-dying day,   25
>   And touch the stubble-plains with rosy hue;
> Then in a wailful choir the small gnats mourn
>   Among the river sallows, borne aloft
>   Or sinking as the light wind lives or dies;
> And full-grown lambs loud bleat from hilly bourn;   30
>   Hedge-crickets sing; and now with treble soft
> The red-breast whistles from a garden-croft;
>   And gathering swallows twitter in the skies.

The sounds are those of birds and animals — gnats, lambs, hedge-crickets, the robin, swallows. Except for the lambs, these are wild creatures, not domestic ones; and non-domesticated aspects of nature are also introduced by the clouds, the willow-trees (*sallows*) by the river, the wind, the skies, and perhaps the *hilly bourn* (which may mean 'hill-stream', but perhaps rather means 'field-boundary on a hill'). But the domesticating hand of man also appears in the stanza, with the *stubble fields* (fields where the corn has been reaped and the stubs left standing in the ground), the lambs, the garden-croft. The sounds are all thin and rather high-pitched, and in the case of the gnats are specifically said to be sad (*wailful*, *mourn*). There is none of the sense of luxury and relaxed ease found in the first two stanzas, and there is even a suggestion of restlessness (the cloud of gnats rising and falling, the gathering swallows).

Each stanza of the poem, then, has a clear theme: Stanza 1 is about ripening and fruitfulness; Stanza 2 is about the harvest; and Stanza 3 is about the sounds of autumn. But what is the relationship between these three stanzas? How does the poem hang together, and what is it getting at? If we look at the poem as a whole, we see that there is a movement in time: Stanza 1 is set at the beginning, Stanza 2 in the middle, and Stanza 3 at the end of autumn. In Stanza 1 we are only just at the end of summer: it is Summer which has filled the cells of the honeycomb (11); the days are still warm

(10); and flowers keep on budding (8—9). The sole warning word, planted strategically in the first line, is *mists*. In Stanza 1 things are still ripening, but in Stanza 2 they have ripened: the reaper is cutting the corn, and the apples have been picked and are being made into cider. In Stanza 3 the harvest is over: the corn has gone from the fields and only the stubble remains (26); the lambs are fully grown (30); and winter is approaching, for the swallows are *gathering* (33) in preparation for their migration southwards to warmer climates. So the poem moves from the relaxed warmth and richness of the end of summer to the astringency and chill of approaching winter, to which the melancholy sounds of Stanza 3 are appropriate.

Moreover, this movement from late summer to early winter reminds us of the whole seasonal cycle; indeed, the poem explicitly refers to summer in line 11 and to spring in line 23, and in its final line alludes unmistakably to the approach of winter. The poem thus evokes the whole seasonal cycle — germination, growth, maturity, decay, death, rebirth — and it does so with a marvellous concreteness and richness. Man depends on the seasonal cycle, as we see in Stanzas 1 and 2; but he does not control it, as we are reminded in Stanza 3: winter will come, whatever man does. Moreover, although the poem does not make this explicit, man has his own cycle of birth, maturity, and death, which we feel as analogous to that of the seasons; so the poem is surely also about the condition of man. Its main emphasis is on maturity, ripeness, the coming to fulfilment; but, equally clearly, it points back to the spring of youth and forward to the winter of old age and death; and its attitude is one of calm acceptance.

Readers from outside Europe, who may be accustomed to a quite different seasonal pattern, should note the typically English seasons implied in the poem (and in many others to be discussed later). Spring (March to May) is the season of growth and rebirth, bringing a sense of refreshment and joy and new life after the deadness and hardships of winter. Summer (June to August) may be hot, but never unpleasantly so, and is usually sufficiently wet for the vegetation to remain green, and even lush. Autumn (September to November) is the period of harvest and of leaf-fall; the weather may be mild and summer-like, it may be wild and windy. Winter (December to February) is the period of cold, when vegetation is dead and most trees are bare of leaves; frost and snow and storms are likely.

Thematic structure

Some poems have neither a logical nor a narrative structure, but rather a musical one, in which a number of themes are interlaced and developed, in a manner analogous to that of, say, a symphony. A famous example is T. S. Eliot's *The Waste Land* (1922). This has no narrative structure as a whole, though it does include numerous incidents and characters. It consists of five apparently independent sections, each of which deploys certain themes, which may reappear in other sections. The themes include fertility rituals, and the myths associated with them; the Tarot pack of cards; rainless desert; water as the bringer of death and the bringer of life; death and resurrection; sex and its debasements; and contrasts between modern industrial civilisation and various civilisations of the past. All these contribute to the main theme of the poem: the decay of Western civilisation, with its resultant spiritual aridity and need for spiritual regeneration.

Poetry and Meaning

Some people have denied the importance of meaning in poetry. It has been argued, for example, that poetry achieves its effects solely by means of its *sounds*, and that meaning is irrelevant. This view is difficult to sustain. Poetry in a language of which we are completely ignorant has hardly any effect on us, especially if the language is unrelated to our own. If we hear such poetry read aloud, some vague kind of emotion may indeed be communicated; but this is due to the energy and feelings of the reader, who understands what he is reading. In any case, poetry in an unknown language rapidly becomes very boring: a lover of poetry can with great pleasure listen to a reading of *Paradise Lost* or *The Prelude*, but only if he understands English; otherwise he will probably be asleep before the end of Book I.

This is not to deny that the sounds of poetry *contribute* to its effect. Some poets have taken great care with the sound-patterns of their writing. Such is Tennyson, who produces intricate and sonorous patterns of vowel-sounds, and who is fond of onomatopoeic effects, as in the famous lines

> The moan of doves in immemorial elms,
> And murmuring of innumerable bees.
>
> (*The Princess* VII.206)

There we do indeed seem to hear the sound of doves and bees. But the effect would be pointless if we did not know what the lines meant.

Other people have emphasised the irrational and 'magical' elements in poetry, suggesting that it operates on us at subconscious levels rather than through the surface meaning. It may indeed be true that poetry affects us at a level below that of consciousness; and it is certainly true that some passages of poetry have a quite breathtaking effect on us which we find difficult to explain, and really do seem magical. But how do they have this effect? The poem, surely, has no direct Hot Line to our unconscious; it must operate through the meanings of its words.

Let us agree, then, that the meaning of a poem is central to our experience of it, and that when we read it we must be concerned to understand what it is saying. But at the same time we must recognise that 'meaning' is not a simple thing. The meaning of a word or phrase includes the things it suggests as well as the things it states, its connotations as well as its denotations. A passage may even suggest things which are the direct opposite of what it is apparently saying: in the opening speech of Shakespeare's *Henry IV Part 1*, the King looks forward to the end of civil war and the coming of a period of peace in England:

> No more the thirsty entrance of this soil   5
> Shall daub her lips with her own children's blood,

No more shall trenching war channel her fields,
Nor bruise her flowrets with the armèd hoofs
Of hostile paces.

And so he goes on for another ten lines. The speech is apparently about peace, but what the audience in fact hears and is impressed by is a series of images of battle — blood, trenching war, armed hoofs; and the fact that the King puts the words *No more* before them does very little to nullify their effect. So the speech creates an atmosphere of war, suggesting that the play is not going to be about peace but about civil discord.

Moreover, the meanings in a poem can be rich and complex: as we have seen, the use of metaphor especially can pack associations and suggestions into a small space, and these are all part of the poem's meaning. So too are the stylistic implications of a word or phrase — whether it is formal or colloquial, standard or regional, current or outdated. In 'Lines on a Young Lady's Photograph Album' (1955), a poignant poem by Philip Larkin (1922–), the poet looks through the girl's album, fascinated and disturbed by the pictures from her past, which he had not shared; and the very pastness of it all hurts him:

Or is it just *the past*? Those flowers, that gate,
These misty parks and motors, lacerate
Simply by being over; you
Contract my heart by looking out of date.   30

The misty parks suggest nicely the faded and amateurish old monochrome photographs; but the beautifully chosen word is *motors,* which is almost an archaism. In the earlier years of this century, *motor* was commonly used as a colloquial shortening of *motor-car,* but has since been displaced in this sense by *car.* So Larkin's *motor* suggests the old-fashioned kind of cars seen in these old photographs, in which the girl too looks 'out of date'.

Poems can also be ambiguous, or contain self-contradictions. There may be implications lurking below the surface which contradict the surface-meaning; in this case, what the poem 'says' is neither just the surface meaning nor the submerged meaning, but something which relates to both.

Submerged meaning: a Shakespeare sonnet

As an example of meaning below the surface, consider Shakespeare's Sonnet 94, which begins as follows:

> They that have power to hurt, and will do none,
> That do not do the thing they most do show,
> Who moving others, are themselves as stone,
> Unmovèd, cold, and to temptation slow:
> They rightly do inherit heaven's graces,   5
> And husband nature's riches from expense,
> They are the Lords and owners of their faces,
> Others, but stewards of their excellence.

Ostensibly the poet is praising men of a certain kind (and by implication the young man that the sonnet is addressed to) — men who are in control of their passions, who do not yield to temptations, who do not squander their sexual energies (*nature's riches*), who do not use their power to hurt others. Such men, the poet says, 'rightly do inherit heaven's graces'. But this ostensible meaning is undercut by the associations of some of the words in the passage, especially *stone* (3) and *cold* (4); for *stone*, which seemingly refers to self-control and resistance to temptation, also suggests insensibility, hardness of heart, even cruelty; and *cold*, which nominally refers to an absence of sensuality, also suggests a lack of affection or warmth of feeling. The implications of these two words therefore contradict the praise which the poet appears to be giving; and, when we have noticed this, we shall also notice that the praise of lines 2 and 7 is rather double-edged, since it could imply hypocrisy. The attitude of the poem towards such men is therefore not simple, and its ambivalence becomes explicit in the remainder of the sonnet:

> The summer's flower is to the summer sweet,
> Though to itself it only live and die,   10
> But if that flower with base infection meet,

The basest weed outbraves his dignity:
For sweetest things turn sourest by their deeds,
Lilies that fester, smell far worse than weeds.

Here the poet gives us an extended comparison. The young man (the change to the singular shows that one person specifically is now being referred to) is like a flower in summer, which is sweet even if it is unpollinated and lives only for itself (like those who *husband nature's riches*); but if the flower becomes infected, it is less beautiful than the basest weed. The word *infection* can refer to moral corruption as well as to disease, and the poet clearly has doubts about the young man's character and 'deeds'. The whole sonnet expresses the poet's doubleness of feeling about the young man, who is (he fears) both beautiful and corrupt; and this conflict of feelings is superbly expressed in the final line by the startling juxtaposition of *Lilies* and *fester*.

'Sailing to Byzantium'

A curious example of submerged meaning occurs in the final stanza of Yeats's marvellous poem 'Sailing to Byzantium' (1927), for it seems possible that the poet was unaware of it. The poem revolves round the contrast between Nature and Art. Nature is the realm of the transitory, of flux and change, of birth, procreation, and death; it is the world of the body, of sex, of instinct, youth. Art is the realm of the soul, of the intellect, of Platonic absolutes, eternal and unchanging, outside time. The symbol for this eternal world of art and intellect is the ancient city of Byzantium (now Istanbul), with its superb mosaics, churches, and works of art.

In the first stanza, the poet, now an old man, turns his back on the world of Nature, of youth, sex, and fertility:

That is no country for old men. The young
In one another's arms, birds in the trees,
— Those dying generations — at their song,
The salmon-falls, the mackerel-crowded seas,
Fish, flesh, or fowl, commend all summer long   5
Whatever is begotten, born, and dies.

At the literal level, the *country* (1) is Ireland; but what it represents (in contrast to Byzantium) is youth, sex, nature (young people making love, birds singing in the trees, the fecundity of the oceans); and, even though the poet says it is not for him, it is evoked with remarkable power and passion. The sense of flux is given by *dying generations* (3): here *generations* means 'offspring', 'progeny' and also 'age-groups', 'successive groups of descendants'; but it also reminds us of the process of sexual generation by which the offspring are produced. Each generation of birds is producing young, and is also in the process of dying to make room for them in the world: it is a universe where everything 'is begotten, born, and dies' (6). The *salmon-falls* (4) are the waterfalls where the salmon, in their migration from the sea, actually leap up the falls on their way upstream. The purpose of this journey is for the salmon to breed in the head-waters of the river where they themselves were born; and *salmon-falls* suggests very concisely the sexual energy of the salmon as they leap over the barrier on the way to their breeding-ground. A similar conciseness and concreteness, achieved by the use of a compound adjective, is seen in *the mackerel-crowded seas* (4), which gives a wonderful sense of the teeming fertility of fish in the sea.

The poet, then, has a strong feeling for the world of nature, but he regrets that people ensnared in it are deaf to the world of the mind:

> Caught in that sensual music all neglect   7
> Monuments of unageing intellect.

The 'sensual music' is the world of nature and generation just described. Entrapped in that music, everybody neglects (*all neglect*) monuments of the human intellect (art, philosophy, and so on), which are eternal (*unageing*).

The word *unageing* bears on what immediately follows, for in the second stanza we see that the force which impels the poet to turn to the realm of the eternal is his resentment at old age:

> An agèd man is but a paltry thing,
> A tattered coat upon a stick, unless   10
> Soul clap its hands and sing, and louder sing
> For every tatter in its mortal dress.

An old man is merely a scarecrow ('tattered coat upon a stick'), unless the soul rejoices; *clap its hands and sing* suggests the action of a child, and gives a sense of innocence, simplicity, and unselfconscious energy. The ragged coat of the scarecrow is the man's body, his *mortal dress*; and the more decrepit the body is, the louder the soul must sing. The only way it can learn to sing is by studying the great works that the soul of man has produced:

> Nor is there singing school but studying   13
> Monuments of its own magnificence.

To study these monuments, works of art and of the intellect, the poet has left the country of the salmon-falls, and come to Byzantium:

> And therefore I have sailed the seas and come   15
> To the holy city of Byzantium.

Sailing to Byzantium is thus an allegory for the turning away from the body and nature to the soul and art. And, just as the first stanza conveys a rich sense of the fecundity of nature, so this second stanza communicates an enormous intellectual excitement, as in the vivid images of the old man as a scarecrow and the soul clapping its hands and singing. In both stanzas, the energy of the rhythms, the speech-like quality of the language, the expressive concreteness of the images (even about the soul), and the vigorous working of the intellect (as in the wit of *Those dying generations*) convey an intense sense of passionate thought.

In the third stanza the poet is in Byzantium, and addresses the *sages standing in God's holy fire*. The holy fire is that of eternity, and the poet compares it to the *gold mosaic of a wall*. He is, it seems, contemplating one of the great Byzantine wall-mosaics, depicting human figures, which provides an apt symbol for the eternity of art. He asks the sages to come from the holy fire and be the singing-masters of his soul. But, although he has turned from the transient to the eternal, he still has a body as well as a soul, and he asks the sages to release him from it:

> Consume my heart away; sick with desire   21
> And fastened to a dying animal
> It knows not what it is; and gather me
> Into the artifice of eternity.

The dying animal is his own body. The heart stands for the emotional and instinctive life, and he wishes the sages to consume it away and to gather him into eternity. Eternity is an *artifice*: it is like an artefact, which continues to exist after the artist has died; the poet wishes to be gathered into the world of the permanent, which is also that of art. So while Stanza 1 deals with nature and instinct, and Stanza 2 with art and the soul, Stanza 3 presents the tension between the two in the poet's mind, his anguished sense of himself as both soul and dying animal. He may say that he has turned from the body to the soul, but his heart is still *sick with desire*.

Being gathered into the artifice of eternity means escaping completely from the body by dying; for the word *gather* occurs in Biblical phrases which have become proverbial, such as *to be gathered to one's ancestors* 'to die'. So the escape from Nature is by death; and in the fourth and final stanza the poet plays with the idea of metempsychosis, the migration of the soul into a different body:

> Once out of nature I shall never take   25
> My bodily form from any natural thing,
> But such a form as Grecian goldsmiths make
> Of hammered gold and gold enamelling
> To keep a drowsy Emperor awake;
> Or set upon a golden bough to sing   30
> To lords and ladies of Byzantium
> Of what is past, or passing, or to come.

When the poet is dead (*out of nature*) he will not take the form of anything natural, but of an exquisite work of art, such as an artificial bird. So the movement from Stanza 1 is complete: we have, it seems, escaped from the sensual music to a monument of the soul's magnificence. But what does the artificial bird sing about? It sings to lords and ladies about 'what is past, or passing, or to come' (32): in other words about time, about the world of transience and change. In the very last line of the poem we are back in the world of flux, and not 'out of nature' at all: art, even if it seems permanent, is about this transient world. The poet has turned from the sensual music to another aspect of human experience, and in the process the decay of the human body has been accepted; regretted, certainly, as the force of the first stanza makes clear; but the resentment of the second and third stanzas has been transcended.

It is in the fourth stanza that the submerged meaning occurs. To any devotee of Hans Christian Andersen (1805–75), the references in the stanza to a drowsy emperor, and to an exquisite artefact which sings to lords and ladies, brings irresistibly to mind the story of the Nightingale, which Yeats certainly knew as a child. In this story, an Emperor of China is so enchanted by the singing of a nightingale that he invites it to come and live in his palace; it accepts, and is treated as a favoured member of the household, and in return delights the court by its singing. One day, the Emperor receives as a gift an exquisitely made artificial nightingale, with diamonds, rubies, and sapphires; it can also sing, though, unlike the real nightingale, it has only one song. The courtiers are delighted at this new toy, which they think superior to the real nightingale. They try to make the two sing together, but this is not a success, so they turn back to the artificial nightingale; whereupon the real nightingale flies out of an open window and does not return. The court are indignant at what they consider the ingratitude of the nightingale, and it is proclaimed a traitor; but in any case, they say, the artificial nightingale is better. After a year, however, the mechanism of the artificial nightingale breaks down, and it proves impossible to mend it; so now it can no longer sing. Five years later, the Emperor is seriously ill; his life is despaired of, and all his courtiers leave his bedside and go off to greet the new heir. The Emperor sees Death standing at the foot of his bed, and in his agony cries out for music; but the broken nightingale stands silent on a shelf. Then, on a branch outside the window, the real nightingale appears, alone faithful to the Emperor; it sings a ravishing song, the Emperor revives, Death disappears.

This story, too, is obviously about Nature and Art: and there are characters in it who assert that the artificial is superior to the natural. There can be no doubt, however, about which is preferred: it is the real nightingale which is the hero of the story. So in Andersen's story Nature triumphs over Art; and this story is embedded beneath the surface of a Yeats stanza which ostensibly is saying the opposite. This does not undermine the effect of the poem; indeed, it reinforces our sense of the tension in the poem between opposing feelings, a tension round which the whole poem is built.

Tradition and Expectation

We do not read poetry in a void. When we encounter a poem, we read it with certain expectations, because of other English poetry we have previously read: expectations about the metres and rhythms that poetry employs, about poetic diction, about the themes that poetry handles, and how it handles them. The new poem will not necessarily fulfil all these expectations, but they are part of the context in which we understand it.

If the poem comes from an earlier age, we shall also read it with some knowledge of the language and the beliefs of its time. In the present century there has been an influential school of thought which has denied the relevance of any knowledge external to the poem: it is a verbal structure, there on the page in front of us, and that is all we need to know. We do not even need to know who wrote it, or when it was written. Indeed, it has even been suggested that such knowledge is positively undesirable and that the perfect material for practical criticism is an anonymous poem of unknown date. But this is not the way in which, in practice, we read poetry: normally, we *do* know who wrote the poem, and what else he wrote, and what century it dates from; and without such information we may misread it. At the simplest level, we may misinterpret the meaning of words in the poem: language changes continually, and in Shakespeare there are hundreds of words used in senses that no longer exist. The stylistic value of words also changes with time: expressions which were once colloquial may now be literary or archaic, and conversely expressions which once seemed literary or even pompous may now be everyday usage. To read Shakespeare well, we have to learn the English of his age, just as we have to learn Latin to read Virgil and French to read Baudelaire.

We also read poetry with a knowledge of certain poetic traditions. In the past there have been accepted poetic genres (lyric, ode, epic, satire, pastoral, and so on). There have also been popular themes of poetry, and traditional ways of treating them. When we read a poem, we do so within the context of these traditions, which influence our response. The poem, indeed, may not conform to tradition: it may flout it, or mock it; but in that case we shall not understand what it is doing unless we know the tradition.

The remainder of this book will therefore discuss some of the common types of English poetry, such as lyric, and epic, and ballad, and some of the themes frequently handled, such as love, and nature, and public affairs. Within each section, the treatment will be chronological, giving a broad account of the development during the past four or five hundred years, but dwelling on particular authors or poems which are central to the tradition, or which are especially rewarding for the modern reader.

2 *Lyric and Ode*

Lyric as Song

Originally a lyric was a poem which was set to music for performance as a solo song. The word is now commonly used of poems with similar characteristics, even if they have never been set to music. It is usually confined to short poems which have no narrative element (though they may present a situation). A lyric therefore tends to be the expression of a mood or an emotion, and is often written in the first person.

In the sixteenth century, the link between lyric poetry and music was still strong: lyrics were the words of songs. Such lyrics occur in Shakespeare's plays, like the following from *As You Like It* (*c.* 1599), which was set to music by Thomas Morley (1558—1603):

> It was a lover and his lass,
>   With a hey, and a ho, and a hey nonino,
> That o'er the green cornfield did pass,
>   In spring time, the only pretty ring time,
>   When birds do sing, hey ding a ding ding,   5
>   Sweet lovers love the spring.
>
> Between the acres of the rye,
>   With a hey, etc.,
> These pretty country folks would lie,
>   In spring time, etc.   10
>
> This carol they began that hour,
>   With a hey, etc.,
> How that a life was but a flower,
>   In spring time, etc.

And therefore take the present time,   15
    With a hey, etc.,
For love is crownèd with the prime,
    In spring time, etc.

Like most lyrics, this poem is stanzaic, and for obvious reasons: in songs, the music repeats, and so demands a repeating pattern in the words. For the same reason, the rhythms of the poem are relatively simple and regular, with few departures from the iambic pattern. The number of syllables is identical in corresponding lines in each stanza; this is not, indeed, essential in a stanzaic song, since the music can be varied slightly from stanza to stanza (for example, by dividing one note into two); but it certainly makes it easier for the words to be fitted to the tune. This particular lyric also has a refrain: line 2 and lines 4–6 are repeated in each stanza, so that each stanza contains only two new lines while having three lines of refrain. Parts of the refrain are meaningless: 'With a hey, and a ho, and a hey nonino' simply expresses a mood of carefree celebration, while 'hey ding a ding ding' represents birdsong. Refrains are common in sixteenth-century lyrics; when the poems are read aloud, they often sound ridiculous, but when the poems are sung they become perfectly acceptable.

The subject-matter of the poem is simple. It begins as if it were going to be a narrative poem, but in fact there is no story. The poem simply evokes a mood of carefree gaiety: it is a celebration of youth and love and spring. The intellectual content is slight, a fact that is reinforced by the extensiveness of the refrain, with its repetitiousness and its nonsense-phrases. The refrain does contribute, however, to the atmosphere of springtime joyousness. The poem is typical of sixteenth-century song-lyrics in its lack of complexity and in its evocation of a simple mood or feeling. This feeling, however, may be extremely intense, as it is in some of Wyatt's lyrics, like 'Forget not yet', 'And wilt thou leave me thus?', and 'My lute awake'.

Simple lyrics of this kind are often regarded as the purest form of poetry, because they lack features which poetry can share with other types of literature (the novel, drama), such as plot, character, and dialogue. In such lyrics, consequently, form plays a large part, and much of the reader's pleasure may come from the neatness and elegance of the poem.

Seventeenth-Century Lyric

In the age of Shakespeare we see the beginnings of the divorce between lyric poetry and music, and during the seventeenth century it becomes increasingly common for poets to write lyrics which are not intended for singing. Freed from the demands of song, lyrics can be less regular in rhythm, and can offer greater intellectual content. But some poets continue to write songs, so that there is a double tradition, and two poets in particular are influential: Ben Jonson (1572–1637) and John Donne (1573–1631). Most seventeenth-century poets are influenced by one or other of these, and many by both.

Ben Jonson

Jonson's lyrics are still song-like, in that they have smooth and simple rhythms. The following example is indeed a song, from Jonson's play *The Silent Woman* (*c.* 1609):

> Still [always] to be neat, still to be dress'd,
> As [as if] you were going to a feast;
> Still to be powder'd, still perfum'd:
> Lady, it is to be presum'd,
> Though art's hid causes are not found,   5
> All is not sweet, all is not sound.
>
> Give me a look, give me a face,
> That makes simplicity a grace;
> Robes loosely flowing, hair as free:
> Such sweet neglect more taketh [charms] me,   10
> Than all th'adulteries [adulterations] of art.
> They strike mine eyes, but not my heart.

This has smooth rhythms, and its parallel balanced phrases (in the first, third and sixth line of each stanza) give it a graceful neatness. But beneath the elegance there is a sharp intellect at work. The poem rejects an artificial style of feminine beauty in favour of a simple and natural one. And the exercise of the poet's mind is seen in the wit of *art's hid causes* (5). This suggests undiscovered underlying laws of nature, *art* meaning something not far different from our *science*; but Jonson drily applies the phrase to the woman's use of cosmetics, *art* then meaning 'practical skill': the woman uses her make-up so cleverly that we cannot see the reasons (*causes*) for her use of it, but we presume that underneath her perfume and powder 'All is not sweet, all is not sound'.

John Donne

Donne's lyrics are less song-like: they have less regular rhythms, often being colloquial in movement; they can be weighty in content, with intricate argument and the use of wide-ranging philosophical and scientific knowledge; they use startling comparisons (so-called 'metaphysical images'); and they are often highly dramatic. These characteristics are seen in *Songs and Sonets,* which do not include any sonnets in our sense of the word but which are a collection of love-poems probably written between about 1593 and 1612. As an example we can look at 'A Valediction: forbidding mourning', which is much smoother in rhythm than many of Donne's poems but which is nevertheless strikingly different from lyrics written for singing.

The poem is one of parting, and was perhaps addressed by Donne to his wife when he went abroad in 1611. The poet begins by telling his mistress that their parting should be a quiet one, not marked by violent demonstrations of emotion:

> As virtuous men pass mildly away,
>   And whisper to their souls, to go,
> Whilst some of their sad friends do say,
>   The breath goes now, and some say, no:

> So let us melt, and make no noise,   5
>   No tear-floods, nor sigh-tempests move,
>   'Twere profanation of our joys
>   To tell the laity our love.

Their parting is to be like the peaceful death of a virtuous
man, the soul leaving the body almost imperceptibly; this
suggests that their parting is itself a kind of death, that they
belong together like body and soul. There are to be no
floods of tears or tempests of sighs (a reference to the extravagant expressions of much conventional poetry). Their love
is a religion, of which they are the priests: and it would be
profanation to disclose its mysteries to those who were not
initiates (*the laity*).

The third stanza compares earthly events with celestial
ones:

> Moving of th'earth brings harms and fears,
>   Men reckon what it did or meant,   10
>   But trepidation of the spheres,
>   Though greater far, is innocent.

Earthquakes cause damage and frighten people, but the
quaking of the heavenly spheres, which is much greater, is
harmless (*innocent*). In traditional astronomy, which was still
accepted by nearly all educated people in Donne's time,
the earth was surrounded by a nest of concentric invisible
spheres, which carried the 'planets' (the Moon, Mercury,
Venus, the Sun, Mars, Jupiter, and Saturn) and the 'fixed
stars'; the rotations of these spheres accounted for the movements of the heavenly bodies. The 'trepidation of the
spheres' was a movement of the ninth of these spheres which
was used to explain the astronomical phenomenon now
known as the precession of the equinoxes. Donne is saying
that their love is a heavenly one; its disturbances are harmless
and almost imperceptible to others, whereas the upsets of an
earthly love are obvious and harmful.

The contrast between earthly and heavenly love is continued in the next two stanzas:

Dull sublunary lovers' love
(Whose soul is sense) cannot admit
Absence, because it doth remove   15
Those things which elemented it.

But we by a love, so much refin'd,
That our selves know not what it is,
Inter-assurèd of the mind,
Care less, eyes, lips, and hands to miss.   20

Sublunary means 'below the sphere of the moon'. Of all the spheres, that carrying the moon was the one nearest to the earth. Beneath the sphere of the moon was the realm of mutability: everything there was composed of the four elements (earth, air, fire, water) and underwent continual change. But above the sphere of the moon were the heavens, which were composed of a fifth element (the quintessence, or ether), and which were perfect and unchanging. Such, Donne implies, is the love between himself and his mistress, whereas ordinary earthly (*sublunary*) lovers are imperfect and inconstant. Such earthly love, whose essential animating force (*soul*) is the senses, cannot survive a parting of the lovers, because this removes the things of which it was composed (*elemented*). In contrast, the poet and his mistress are betrothed to one another (*Inter-assured*) spiritually, and are less concerned about bodily absence.

Because their two souls are united, they are not really separated even when absent from one another:

Our two souls, therefore, which are one,
Though I must go, endure not yet
A breach, but an expansion,
Like gold to airy thinness beat [beaten].

This is one of Donne's celebrated metaphysical images, described by Samuel Johnson as 'the most heterogeneous ideas . . . yoked by violence together'. The souls of the parted lovers are compared to a piece of gold beaten out into very fine leaf, which extends a long way but remains in one piece. (*Expansion* must be pronounced as four syllables, with stresses on the second and fourth.) The image introduces associations of purity (because gold has to be pure to be beaten out in this way), and of richness, incorruptibility, and nobility (traditional qualities of gold). It also suggests the spiritualisation of the physical, the apparently solid gold becoming something of 'airy thinness' (like the soul).

The poem ends with perhaps the most famous of Donne's metaphysical images:

If they be two, they are two so   25
   As stiff twin compasses are two,
Thy soul the fix'd foot, makes no show
   To move, but doth, if th'other do.

And though it in the centre sit,
   Yet when the other far doth roam,   30
It leans and harkens after it,
   And grows erect, as that comes home.

Such wilt thou be to me, who must
   Like th'other foot, obliquely run;
Thy firmness makes my circle just,   35
   And makes me end, where I begun [began].

Unity-in-separation is conveyed by the comparison of the lovers' souls to a pair of compasses, and the image is given immediacy by *stiff* (26), which makes us feel the physical effort of adjusting them. The woman is the stationary foot in the centre, while the poet is the foot that moves out across the map; the word *fix'd* (27) also refers to the woman's constancy, as does *firmness* (35). The image suggests their union on a higher plane: the compass-legs are used for drawing on two-dimensional paper, but are joined in the third dimension, above the paper. It also shows the sympathetic connection between the lovers: neither leg can move without a corresponding movement in the other leg; especially expressive is *leans and harkens after it* (31), giving the reaching-out of the woman's soul towards her parted companion.

In the final stanza, the compasses are used for drawing a circle: the firmness of the central foot ensures that the outer foot draws it perfectly. The woman exercises moral and emotional control over her partner, so that his behaviour is impeccable (the circle was considered a 'perfect' figure); and he will return to her, his journey ending where it began.

In this lyric we have moved a long way from the simple song. The rhythms are often speech-like, as in *admit/Absence* 14–15). There is an intricate argument, drawing on specialised knowledge (such as that about the precession of the equinoxes). There are surprising and ingenious images, sometimes (like that of the compasses) developed at length. But weight of intellectual content and ingenuity of imagery do not preclude feeling: the poem is charged with emotion, and reminds us of one critic's characterisation of Donne's poetry as 'passionate paradoxical reasoning'.

Robert Herrick

The influence of Jonson is seen in the lyrics of Robert Herrick (1591–1674): for example, his 'Delight in Disorder' is clearly indebted to Jonson's 'Still to be neat'. He was also influenced directly by the classical poets on whom Jonson had modelled himself, especially Horace and Catullus. From Horace comes one of his favourite themes, the transience of beauty and the need to catch the passing hour, seen in such anthology pieces as 'Gather ye rosebuds', 'To Blossoms', and 'To Daffodils'. These lyrics are exquisitely written, with economy of expression and felicity of phrasing. Compared with Jonson's lyrics, however, they are literary: they read like the work of a recluse, a man withdrawn from the hurly-burly of real life, whereas Jonson, even at his most polished, has his feet firmly on the ground, and his writing rooted in real speech.

The influence of Donne is absent from Herrick: there are no metaphysical images or dramatic colloquial lyrics. Nevertheless, Herrick can surprise us with a witty phrase, as in 'Upon Julia's Clothes':

> Whenas [when] in silks my Julia goes [walks],
> Then, then (methinks) how sweetly flows
> The liquefaction of her clothes.

Next, when I cast mine eyes and see
That brave [splendid] vibration each way free;   5
O how that glittering taketh [charms] me!

Each stanza contains one striking word, which takes the reader by surprise. In the first it is *liquefaction*: this gives the liquid-like motion of the silk as Julia moves, and the way in which surface-details disappear (as if melted) because of the movement. It also suggests that Julia's shape is seen under the clothes: if they become liquid, they become moulded to her form. In the second stanza, the word is *vibration*, which to the modern reader is perhaps an anticlimax after the remarkable effect of *liquefaction*. To the original readers, however, *vibration* was probably the more striking of the two, because it was a brand-new word, Herrick's own invention (taken from the Latin): the poem was published in 1648, while the earliest recorded example of the word in the *Oxford English Dictionary* is 1656. When the word did come into common use in the 1660s, it was often used of a swinging motion, like that of a pendulum, and this is a possible meaning in the poem: Julia's skirt (which would of course reach to the ground) swings freely in all directions (*each way free*) as she walks. But the verb *to vibrate* was often used in Herrick's time to mean 'to emit light (especially with a sparkling lustre)'; so *vibration* might also mean 'sparkling, shining', as is suggested by *glittering* in the next line.

But why does the second stanza begin with the word *Next*? This suggests that something new happens, not that the poet just continues admiring Julia's clothes. The obvious thing to happen is that the lady's clothes are removed, as is suggested by *free*: in the first stanza she was *in* silks, but now she takes them off. If this were the case, we should expect the poet now to be admiring Julia herself, not her clothes, whereas *glittering* seems more appropriate to the silks than to her. For the original readers, however, the word could perhaps have applied to either, since *to glitter* could be used of persons in the sense 'to make a brilliant appearance or display'. The idea that Julia undresses fits well with the air of sexual excitement in the second stanza, but is not made explicit: the poet leaves it as a suggestion, something below the surface. Whatever interpretation is accepted, this charming little poem shows that even the non-metaphysical Herrick can use language in a novel and witty way.

The Cavalier Poets

The influence of Jonson is also seen in the 'Cavalier Poets', the aristocratic writers who supported King Charles I against Parliament, described later by Pope as 'The mob of gentlemen who wrote with ease'. The best-known of them are Thomas Carew (1595–1640), Sir John Suckling (1609–42), and Richard Lovelace (1618–57). Like Jonson, they look back to the classical lyrical poets; unlike him, they are occasionally gifted amateurs, cultivating upper-class urbanity and grace.

Lovelace is the most song-like of them; his best-known lyrics, 'To Althea, from Prison' and 'To Lucasta, going to the Wars', combine the themes of love and contemporary political events. Carew is the one who shows most clearly the influence of Donne as well as that of Jonson: he has the urbanity and grace of the cavalier, but also an intellectual wit which reminds us of the metaphysical poets, as in the opening stanza of 'A Song':

> Ask me no more where Jove [God] bestows,
> When June is past, the fading rose:
> For in your beauty's orient deep [radiant depths],
> These flowers as in their causes, sleep.

The poet asks a philosophical question: where does the beauty of the rose go to when the flower fades? He answers that the flowers 'sleep' in the lady's beauty, as if in their 'causes'. He is drawing on Aristotle's doctrine of four different kinds of cause (material, formal, efficient, purposive). The cause in question is the formal cause: the lady's beauty contains the essential quality of roses.

Andrew Marvell

The more direct influence of Donne is seen in Andrew

Marvell (1621–78), one of the finest poets of the century. Marvell's poetry has the ingenuity and metaphysical wit of Donne, the elegance of the Cavalier Poets, and a neatness, lucidity, and poise which are later to characterise the work of Pope. As a brief example of his work, let us consider the last four stanzas of 'The Definition of Love'. In the first four stanzas, the poet tells us that his love is the product of despair and impossibility, not of hope. Even so, he might achieve his love, were it not that Fate always intervenes. Fate sees that there are two perfect loves, whose union would end her power. The poem continues:

> And therefore her [Fate's] Decrees of Steel
> Us as the distant Poles have plac'd,
> (Though Love's whole World on us doth wheel)
> Not by themselves [one another] to be embrac'd.   20
>
> Unless the giddy Heaven fall,
> And Earth some new Convulsion tear;
> And, us to join, the World should all
> Be cramp'd into a Planisphere.
>
> As Lines so Loves oblique may well   25
> Themselves [one another] in every Angle greet:
> But ours so truly Parallel,
> Though infinite can never meet.
>
> Therefore the Love which us doth bind,
> But Fate so enviously debars,   30
> Is the Conjunction of the Mind,
> And Opposition of the Stars.

In the first of these stanzas, the poet compares the lovers to the north and south poles of the universe of spheres: they are central to the whole world of love, which rotates (*doth wheel*) around them, but are inexorably held apart; unless, the poet adds in the next stanza, the whole universe suffers a disaster and is crushed flat (in which case it would be possible for the two poles to be together). The surprising and witty word is *planisphere*: this is the name for a map formed by the projection of a sphere on to a plane; so if the universe of spheres were compressed (*cramp'd*) until it was flat, it would form a planisphere. There were indeed planispheres in which the two poles were touching, as can be seen from a quotation from 1594 cited by the *OED*:

Astrolabe . . . is called of some a Planisphere, because it is both flat and round, representing the Globe or Sphere, having both his [its] Poles clapped flat together.

The kind of astrolabe here referred to was a planisphere representing the circles of the heavens (with a graduated rim and sights for taking altitudes); the *Poles* are therefore the celestial poles, round which the heavens rotate, not the poles of the earth. It is pretty clear that Marvell too means the celestial poles, for the giddy heavens have to fall to bring them together.

In the third stanza Marvell moves to a new image: the lovers are like two parallel lines, which can never meet. The key-word is *oblique,* which refers to both lines and loves: oblique lines are slanting ones, while oblique loves are morally defective ones. The poet thus suggests that it is the very perfection of their love that makes it impossible for them to be united.

In the final stanza the poet returns to astronomy, or more properly astrology. Astrologers believed that a person's destiny was determined by the positions of the heavenly bodies: the lovers cannot be united because of the *Opposition of the stars.* But both *Conjunction* and *Opposition* are used in a double sense. In the primary contrast between them, *conjunction* means 'union', or more specifically 'marriage', while *opposition* means 'hostile action, antagonism'. But both words also had a technical astronomical meaning: two planets were in conjunction when they were in the same part of the heavens (the same Sign of the Zodiac), and in opposition when they were in exactly opposite parts of the heavens (in Signs 180° apart). It is the compression achieved by these double meanings, together with the neatness of the antithesis, that makes the lines sound both witty and final.

The poem is bubbling with intellectual excitement, but

this is held in control by the strictness of the form and the neatness of the expression. The relative shortness of the lines (all four-foot) means that rhymes occur fairly frequently; and the rhyme-words are invariably important and heavily stressed ones. This emphasis on the rhyme-words contributes to the neatness of the poem, and perhaps also to our sense of the inexorability of Fate and the inevitability of the situation.

The poem illustrates a common characteristic of lyrics: we are not told the story behind the situation. In a novel, or short story, or narrative poem, we would be told why it was impossible for the lovers to be united (incompatibility of age or of social class, parental opposition, the fact that one part-ner is already married, and so on). But in Marvell's lyric there is no mention of this at all: the poet is concerned to explore the feelings aroused by the situation, not to examine the situation itself or to give us its history.

John Milton

The influence of Jonson and of Donne permeates seventeenth-century lyric, but a few writers are relatively untouched by it, and notably Milton, who develops a lyric style of his own. As an example, let us take one of the songs from *A Mask pre-sented at Ludlow Castle* (commonly called *Comus*) (1637):

> Sweet Echo, sweetest Nymph that liv'st unseen
>   Within thy airy shell
>   By slow Meander's margent green [green bank],
>   And in the violet-embroider'd vale
>   Where the love-lorn Nightingale   5
> Nightly to thee her sad Song mourneth well.
> Canst thou not tell me of a gentle Pair
>   That likest thy Narcissus are?
>   O if thou have
>   Hid them in some flow'ry Cave   10
>   Tell me but where
> Sweet Queen of Parley [speech], Daughter of the Sphere,
> So mayst thou be translated to the skies,
> And give resounding grace to all Heav'n's Harmonies.

This is sung by the Lady, who is lost in the forest, and hopes that she may be heard by her two brothers (the *gentle Pair* of line 7). It is mythological in theme, being addressed to Echo, a Greek nymph who was punished by Hera (queen of the Gods) for her chattering: she was made unable to speak, except that she could repeat the final syllable of anything said to her. She loved the beautiful youth Narcissus, but he rejected her, and she wasted away until only her voice remained (which is why she lives *unseen*). She is perhaps said to live in an *airy shell* (2) because certain kinds of conch, when placed to the ear, produce a sound like that of the sea. The *Meander* (3) was a winding river in Phrygia.

The Lady asks Echo whether she has seen her brothers: if she will tell her where they are, the Lady wishes that the nymph may be carried up to Heaven without dying (*translated to the skies*), where she will add resonance to the celestial music. In these last two lines, the reference is Christian, for *translated* is used in a technical religious sense: the poem rises from the charming fancies of Greek mythology to the majesty of the Christian Heaven, and there is a corresponding change of style in the final line, with its greater length (six feet) and its resonant effect.

The poem is delicately and exquisitely phrased. But it has neither the wit and ingenuity of Donne, nor the down-to-earth quality that lies beneath the elegance of Jonson, nor the stylish urbanity of the Cavalier Poets. The distinctive quality of the poem is perhaps its *mellifluousness*. This is not just a matter of smooth rhythms, but also of the actual sounds of the words, especially the vowel-sounds, and the cunning ways in which they are arranged. This is clear in such a line as 'Nightly to thee her sad Song mourneth well' (6): the sequence of vowel-sounds has no special relevance to the meaning, but is extremely pleasing aurally, and also gives a kind of physical pleasure to the speaker when the line is read aloud. Pronunciation has of course changed since Milton's time, but the effect in present-day pronunciation is in fact very similar to that in seventeenth-century pronunciation. In the earlier pronunciation, the aural effects are if anything more marked; in particular, all the rhymes in the poem were exact ones.

The absence of wit and the delight in sound-effects make

the poem decidedly different from the other seventeenth-century lyrics we have examined. It has more in common with Spenser, and with the lyrics of some nineteenth-century poets (Keats, Tennyson) who were influenced by him.

Eighteenth-Century Lyric

The lyrical traditions which dominated the seventeenth century had petered out by the beginning of the eighteenth. After the Restoration of Charles II in 1660, we still find secular poetry written in the metaphysical style, for example by Abraham Cowley (1618—67), but such poetry was by then old-fashioned, not suited in style to the attitudes and outlook expressed: Cowley's poetry is like new wine in old bottles. Jonson's poetry was still much admired, but the seriousness underlying his wit had given way to the raffishness of such writers as John Wilmot, Earl of Rochester (1647—80). In the Restoration period there are indeed a few fine songs by John Dryden (1631—1700), but these represent an extremely small part of his poetic output.

During the greater part of the eighteenth century, lyric poetry was a negligible force in English literature. The dominant poet of the first half of the century, Pope, wrote practically no lyric poetry at all. The fashionable metre was the heroic couplet, and poetry was on the whole public and often satirical, rather than personal and lyrical. Songs continued to be written, but usually by minor poets. There is some change around the middle of the century, with the work of Thomas Gray and of William Collins (1721—59): neither of them makes much use of the heroic couplet, and both of them write mainly odes; neither writes many shorter lyrics, but among them is Collins's exquisite 'How sleep the brave' (which in fact he calls an ode).

Robert Burns

In the last quarter of the century appeared a major poet in

whom the lyrical strain was again strong. Robert Burns (1759—96) was not an English poet but a Scot, and one who wrote in Scottish English (*Scots*), and drew on a long literary tradition quite different from the one in which Gray and Collins had been versed. For centuries England and Scotland were separate, independent kingdoms: the union of their crowns did not take place until 1603, and the union of their parliaments not until 1707. Not unnaturally, Scotland developed a standard literary language of its own, based on the educated speech of the Scottish lowlands (the Highlands being predominantly Gaelic-speaking until the nineteenth century). From the late Middle Ages there was a substantial literature in Scots, the high points being the poetry of Robert Henryson and William Dunbar in the late fourteenth and early fifteenth century. In the seventeenth century the Scots literary language disappeared, supplanted by the standard southern form of the language, but many Scots poets continued to produce literature in their own dialects. The father of the Scots dialect-literature movement was Allan Ramsay (1686—1758), who wrote a great deal of poetry and a pastoral drama. The movement continues to this day, and Burns is to be seen, not as an isolated phenomenon, but as one of the high points in a long literary tradition.

Burns wrote many kinds of poetry, including rollicking narrative such as 'Tam o' Shanter', accounts of Scottish country life such as 'The Cotter's Saturday Night', and brilliant satire such as 'Holy Willie's Prayer'. A large part of his output, however, is lyrical: in his collected works there are 300 poems classified as 'Songs and Ballads'. Burns's lyrics really are songs, often written for existing tunes; sometimes they are his own adaptations of the words of popular songs current in his time. Many of them are still sung, and by Englishmen as well as Scots. As an example of a Burns lyric, let us look at one of his popular anthology-pieces:

> My love is like a red red rose
> That's newly sprung in June:
> My love is like the melodie
> That's sweetly play'd in tune.

So fair art thou, my bonnie lass,   5
  So deep in love am I:
And I will love thee still, my dear,
  Till a' [all] the seas gang [go] dry.

Till a' the seas gang dry, my dear,
  And the rocks melt wi' the sun: 10
And I will love thee still, my dear,
  While the sands o' life shall run.

And fare thee weel [well], my only love,
  And fare thee weel awhile!
And I will come again, my love,   15
  Tho' it were ten thousand mile.

Here we are back to song lyric, with relatively slight intellectual content, expressing strong and simple emotion. The
poem is a straightforward declaration of affection, relying a
good deal for its effect on hyperbole (the seas going dry and
the rocks melting) and on repetition, which is almost hypnotic
in its effect. There are explicit affirmations (as in lines 6 and
11), together with the evocative comparisons of the girl to a
rose (1–2) and a melody (3–4): these get their effect, not by
any special or detailed ways in which she is like these things,
but simply from the general loveliness of the rose and the
melody. The final stanza introduces a poignant note of parting, which is itself made into a reaffirmation of the poet's
commitment, again by means of hyperbole ('ten thousand
mile'). These hyperbolical expressions in the poem get their
effect from the simple way in which they are said, extravagant ideas being expressed in homely language. The overall
effect of the poem is of a flow of pure feeling, but feeling
under control.

    In its personal declaration of emotional attachment the
poem is unlike most eighteenth-century poetry: we do not
find such declarations in the poetry of Pope, or Gray, or
Johnson. This contrast stems from differences in tradition
and audience. The southern poets were writing for a polite
metropolitan audience, for whom poetry was public statement rather than private feeling; while Burns was not only a

regional poet, but also a popular one, writing about and for the ordinary country people of Scotland. And, while the English poets were part of a political and cultural élite, Burns was a rebel against the conventional pieties of his time, and his poetry makes more than one tilt at the Scottish Establishment. It is true that he was lionised for a time by polite Edinburgh society, but his poetry is not metropolitan, and draws its strength from everyday Scottish speech. Burns wrote a few poems in the standard southern language, but these are undistinguished; the strength of his poetry lies in its rootedness in Scottish rural life and in colloquial Scots speech.

William Blake

Lyric again becomes a major strain in southern English poetry with the coming of the Romantic poets at the end of the eighteenth century: Blake's first volume was published in 1783, and by the end of the century he had produced much of his major work; while Wordsworth's first volume of poetry was published in 1793, and Coleridge's in 1796.

In bulk, most of Blake's work consists of long poems, the various 'prophetic books', but his finest work is found in his shorter poems, especially the *Songs of Innocence and Experience* (1789–94). Although Blake calls them songs, they are not words for music, as Burns's are: in Blake we see clearly the movement away from music, the development of a purely literary lyrical poetry divorced from song. We also see the return to lyrical poetry of a substantial intellectual and moral content.

We have already looked at the opening stanza of Blake's 'London'; as an example of his lyrics let us take the whole poem:

> I wander thro' each charter'd street,
> Near where the charter'd Thames does flow,
> And mark in every face I meet
> Marks of weakness, marks of woe.

In every cry of every Man,   5
In every Infant's cry of fear,
In every voice, in every ban,
The mind-forg'd manacles I hear.

How the chimney-sweeper's cry
Every black'ning church appals;   10
And the hapless soldier's sigh
Runs in blood down palace walls.

But most thro' midnight streets I hear
How the youthful harlot's curse
Blasts the new-born infant's tear,   15
And blights with plagues the marriage hearse.

The poem has a heavy insistent rhythm, which is reinforced by the use of repetition, like *mark, Marks, mark* (all heavily stressed) in Stanza 1. The rhythm suggests the dead mechanical movements of the people in the streets of London, but also has an ominous ring, a hint of prophetic doom.

   The poem gives us the poet's vision of London in his time, in the early phases of the Industrial Revolution. The streets through which he wanders are *charter'd* (1): that is, they are privileged, given special rights by a royal charter (as most English cities are). This is ironical, for, while certain citizens of London may enjoy privileges, this is not the case with the people in the streets that the poet is observing; and he underlines the irony by saying that the River Thames too is chartered. But a charter was also a written contract, especially for the conveyance of landed property, so the poet is also saying that London is a mass of private property, tied up in legal contracts. In contrast to the charters are the *faces* of the people — a word with which the poet insists on their humanity. And in every face the poet marks ('observes') marks ('signs') of weakness and sorrow. In the second stanza the universality of these signs is emphasised by the insistent repetitions (*In every . . . every . . . In every . . . In every . . . in every*). The word *ban* (7) can mean both 'a curse, imprecation' and 'an official prohibition, interdict'.

   In and through the marks of weakness and of woe the poet

hears the *mind-forg'd manacles* (8), an expression which is highlighted at the centre of the line by its three successive stressed syllables. People are in chains, but in chains of their own creation, forged by their minds. External authorities (the church and the palace of the following stanza) bind and oppress people, but people contribute to their own servitude by internalising the commands of authority. True freedom, the poet implies, begins with the internal freedom of the individual, the liberation of the self.

The third stanza deals with the evil effects of established institutions, both religious (the church) and secular (the palace). The *chimney-sweeper* (9) refers to the common practice of employing small children to climb up inside chimneys to clean them: little boys were cheaper than long brushes. For a century there was an outcry against this barbarous practice, but it was not finally stamped out until 1875. The cry of the chimney-sweeper discomfits or dismays (*appals*) the Church, because it calls attention to the discrepancy between the Church's teachings and the reality around it. The Church is turning black (*black'ning*) because, like all buildings in industrial England, it is coated with soot from the chimney-smoke: the Church cannot escape the blight put on everything by industrialism; and there is also a suggestion that the Church is morally corrupt. The secular authority, the palace, is responsible for wars, which claim the blood of the unfortunate (*hapless*) soldier.

Worst of all is sexual corruption. In the final stanza the poet hears the curse of the young prostitute, that is, one for whom sex has become a commodity to be sold on the market. The verb *to blast* (15) could mean 'to blight, to sap the beauty or promise of', but it also had a stronger meaning, 'to strike with the wrath of heaven'. The infant whose tear is thus blasted may be that of a woman whose husband has made use of the prostitute: in a society where the institutionalised forms of sexual behaviour are marriage and prostitution, the latter may have a baleful effect on the children of marriage. But the infant may equally well be that of the prostitute herself: in an age lacking effective birth-control techniques, a prostitute was likely to have unwanted children, and to curse them. The baleful effects of prostitution on marriage are evoked in the final line of the poem: the *plagues* can be infectious diseases, or more generally afflictions and calamities; but the word also meant 'a visitation of divine anger or justice, punishment by God'. The final word in the line, *hearse,* is unexpected and startling: the coach in which the married couple ride is suddenly turned into a funeral-carriage; or their marriage-bed is turned into a coffin. (The word *hearse* means 'a carriage constructed for carrying the coffin at a funeral', but formerly also meant 'bier, coffin, tomb, grave'.) It is the unexpected collocation of *marriage* with *hearse* that gives the line its remarkable shock-effect.

In this poem we have moved a long way from the song-lyrics with which we started. The intellectual content is weighty, and the poem is a critique of the society of its time. There is neither the wit nor the urbanity of the seventeenth-century lyric, and in their place we have powerful moral and emotional commitment, and a poetic vision which seems to see into the heart of things.

Romantic and Victorian Lyric

With the coming of the great English Romantic poets, of whom Blake is the first, lyric becomes one of the dominant forms of poetry, and continues to be so throughout the nineteenth century. There are indeed many other kinds of poetry in the period — long narrative poems, satires, dramatic monologues, and so on; but the lyrical strain is powerful in every poet of any standing, so that a full study of nineteenth-century lyric would be very extensive. All that can be attempted here is an outline sketch.

The general trend during the century is for the lyric to get thinner in content: the intellectual substance decreases, sound-effects play a larger part, and there is a tendency, especially late in the period, for poetry to escape into a dream-world.

Wordsworth

The great Romantic poets of the earlier part of the century are more robust. William Wordsworth (1770—1850) above all has his eye firmly on the real world. His cultivation of everyday language and everyday topics makes some of his poetry seem pedestrian, but the apparent ordinariness can blossom into moments of intense emotion, or of sudden insight, or of mystic vision. In 'The Solitary Reaper' the poet listens to a girl singing in the fields in the Scottish highlands; he wonders what she is singing about (obviously her song is in Gaelic), and the simplicity of the language suddenly blooms into a haunting and unforgettable phrase:

> Will no one tell me what she sings? —
> Perhaps the plaintive numbers flow
> For old, unhappy, far-off things,
> And battles long ago.   20

In 'Strange fits of passion have I known', the poet rides one evening towards the cottage of his beloved Lucy, watching the moon sinking towards it; the poem ends thus:

> My horse moved on; hoof after hoof
> He raised and never stopped:
> When down behind the cottage roof,
> At once, the bright moon dropped.
>
> What fond and wayward thoughts will slide   25
> Into a Lover's head!
> 'O mercy!' to myself I cried,
> 'If Lucy should be dead!'

This captures a highly personal experience: the poet has been unconsciously identifying Lucy with the moon, and when the moon disappears behind the roof he has a sudden intense pang of fear.

The moments of mystic vision are produced by the contemplation of Nature, as in 'The Simplon Pass':

> The immeasurable height
> Of woods decaying, never to be decayed,   5
> The stationary blasts of waterfalls,
> And in the narrow rent, at every turn,

Winds thwarting winds bewildered and forlorn,
The torrents shooting from the clear blue sky,
The rocks that muttered close upon our ears,   10
Black drizzling crags that spake by the wayside
As if a voice were in them, the sick sight
And giddy prospect of the raving stream,
The unfettered clouds and region of the heavens,
Tumult and peace, the darkness and the light —   15
Were all like workings of one mind, the features
Of the same face, blossoms upon one tree,
Characters of the great Apocalypse,
The types and symbols of Eternity,
Of first, and last, and midst, and without end.   20

Characteristically, the poem combines a firm grasp on physical reality with a visionary experience in which the physical
universe melts away. The Alpine scenery is given with superb
concreteness of detail: the decaying woods, the waterfalls
apparently still, the confusing variations of wind-direction,
the torrents shooting out of the blue sky, the giddiness of the
heights (notice the physical impact of 'the *sick* sight'), the
black drizzling crags. But even as we take in this wonderfully
realised mountain-landscape, we see that there is more than
meets the eye: the rocks mutter, the crags speak by the wayside, and finally the whole scene becomes a revelation of
hidden things (*Apocalypse*), in which the physical objects are
perceived as expressions of an underlying eternal spirit.

Coleridge

Coleridge is perhaps more celebrated as a critic than as a
poet, but he did produce a small number of distinguished
poems, of which the most famous is *The Rime of the Ancient
Mariner* (1797–8). Among his shorter poems, the most
rewarding are the so-called 'conversation poems' — meditative
blank-verse poems written in a low-key conversational style.
Such is 'Frost at Midnight' (1798), a poem of 74 lines which
opens as follows:

The Frost performs its secret ministry,
Unhelped by any wind. The owlet's cry
Came loud — and hark, again! loud as before.
The inmates of my cottage, all at rest,
Have left me to that solitude, which suits   5
Abstruser musings: save that at my side
My cradled infant slumbers peacefully.
'Tis calm indeed! so calm, that it disturbs
And vexes meditation with its strange
And extreme silentness. Sea, hill, and wood,   10
This populous village! Sea, and hill, and wood,
With all the numberless goings-on of life,
Inaudible as dreams! the thin blue flame
Lies on my low-burnt fire, and quivers not;
Only that film, which fluttered on the grate,   15
Still flutters there, the sole unquiet thing.
Methinks, its motion in this hush of nature
Gives it dim sympathies with me who live,
Making it a companionable form,
Whose puny flaps and freaks the idling Spirit   20
By its own moods interprets, every where
Echo or mirror seeking of itself,
And makes a toy of Thought.

The tone is meditative and intimate, the language unaffected and speechlike. In form, the poem gives the impression of simply following the natural movements of the poet's thought. He begins by evoking his immediate surroundings: the cottage at midnight with everybody else asleep, the frost active but silent outside, the poet meditating with his child in the cradle beside him. The effect of silence and stillness is powerfully built up, and is even reinforced by the things that break it: the repeated cry of the small owl sounds loud in the calm and windless night. The poet's thought then moves out from the cottage to the village outside, and the surrounding landscape. The repetition-with-a-difference of *Sea, hill, and wood* (10—11) suggests the ever-varying richness of nature and of the 'numberless goings-on of life' (12). But all these things are now still and silent, 'Inaudible as dreams' (13). The word *dreams* brings the poet back to himself musing by the almost-dead fire, with a film of soot fluttering on the grate; and the inward movement continues as the poet turns in on himself, identifying the fluttering film with the unpredictable movements of the mind, the 'idling Spirit' (20) which looks everywhere for analogues of itself.

The first section of the poem is set in the poet's present. In the second section he moves into the past. The move is produced by the fluttering film of soot, a phenomenon which was believed to presage the arrival of a stranger (guest, visitor). The poet recalls how as a boy he was away from home at school, and would dream of his 'sweet birth-place, and the old church tower'; often, seeing the omen of a 'stranger' in the fire, he would wait in keen expectation, his heart leaping up every time the door half-opened,

> For still I hoped to see the *stranger's* face, 41
> Townsman, or aunt, or sister more beloved,
> My play-mate when we both were clothed alike!

The thought of his sister produces the modulation into the third section of the poem, in which his mind turns to the future: the memory of his childhood with her moves his attention to the child sleeping in the cradle beside him. He looks forward to a future for this child quite different from his own:

> For I was reared
> In the great city, pent 'mid cloisters dim,
> And saw nought lovely but the sky and stars.
> But *thou*, my babe! shalt wander like a breeze
> By lakes and sandy shores, beneath the crags 55
> Of ancient mountain, and beneath the clouds,
> Which image in their bulk both lakes and shores
> And mountain crags.

From the sense of confinement in the school, and then 'pent' in the great city, we here open out into the expansive vista of lakes and shores and mountain crags, with an exhilarating sense of freedom and large-scale variety: the repetitions, once again, suggest the ever-changing richness of nature, the lakes and mountain crags and shores seeming to mirror and echo and repeat one another.

In a final section, the poet prophesies that the child will rejoice in nature in all its moods and manifestations:

> Therefore all seasons shall be sweet to thee,   65
> Whether the summer clothe the general earth
> With greenness, or the redbreast sit and sing
> Betwixt the tufts of snow on the bare branch
> Of mossy apple-tree, while the nigh thatch
> Smokes in the sun-thaw; whether the eave-drops fall   70
> Heard only in the trances of the blast,
> Or if the secret ministry of frost
> Shall hang them up in silent icicles,
> Quietly shining to the quiet Moon.

This is exquisite in its observation and in its delicacy of phrasing, as in the description of the robin singing between the 'tufts of snow' on the bare branch of the mossed apple-tree, while from the nearby (*nigh*) thatched roof the vapour rises as the sunshine thaws the snow. In the last three lines we come full circle, and are back with the *secret ministry of frost* with which the poem began; but to this is now added the lovely image of the 'silent icicles,/Quietly shining to the quiet Moon'. This is not only beautiful in itself, but also shows that there has been a change in the poet: we have come back to the same place, but with a difference, for the moon is a symbol of illumination, mental and spiritual. The poet's mind, beginning in the cottage with frost at midnight, has ranged in space and time, recalling the past and looking into the future, and now returns to its starting-point with an enhanced feeling of joy and peace and understanding, wonderfully expressed in that final image of the icicles and the moon. And now the reader understands that the secret ministry of the frost, its silent unhelped operation, with which the poem opened, is analogous to the operations of the poet's mind; and not until the end of the poem do we see exactly what work the frost performs.

Tennyson

The outstanding lyric poet of the Victorian age was Tennyson. In his work, however, we already see the narrowing of poetry: a reduction in intellectual content, a tendency to inhabit a dream-world. This happens in Tennyson despite his determined efforts to write public poetry and to grapple with the intellectual and social problems of his day, particularly the conflict between science and religion. In *In Memoriam* (1850), a sequence of over one hundred lyric poems on the death of his friend Arthur Hallam, he wrestles with the problems of religious doubt, and the apparent discrepancy between a God of Love and 'Nature, red in tooth and claw'. But these parts of *In Memoriam* are unimpressive, and the really moving poems are those expressing personal grief and loss, like 'Dark house, by which once more I stand'.

In general, Tennyson's best poems are set in distant ages, bathed in an atmosphere of romantic enchantment: in 'Tithonus', 'Oenone', 'Ulysses', and 'The Lotos-Eaters' it is legendary and heroic ancient Greece; in 'Morte d'Arthur' it is the romantic and chivalrous Middle Ages. Tennyson was aware of the danger of poetry becoming an ivory tower, and two of his better-known poems, 'The Lady of Shalott' and 'The Palace of Art', deal explicitly with withdrawal from the real world into a world of private fantasy or of pure art, and its disastrous consequences. What is interesting about these poems is that their effects contradict their overt moral: in both of them, it is the escape-world which is brilliantly realised, rather than the disaster.

The most effective of the shorter lyrics deal with personal loss, like the following song from the narrative poem *The Princess* (1847):

> Tears, idle tears, I know not what they mean,
> Tears from the depth of some divine despair
> Rise in the heart, and gather to the eyes,
> In looking on the happy Autumn-fields,
> And thinking of the days that are no more.   5

Fresh as the first beam glittering on a sail,
That brings our friends up from the underworld,
Sad as the last which reddens over one
That sinks with all we love below the verge;
So sad, so fresh, the days that are no more.   10

Ah, sad and strange as in dark summer dawns
The earliest pipe of half-awakened birds
To dying ears, when unto dying eyes
The casement slowly grows a glimmering square;
So sad, so strange, the days that are no more.   15

Dear as remembered kisses after death,
And sweet as those by hopeless fancy feigned
On lips that are for others; deep as love,
Deep as first love, and wild with all regret;
O Death in Life, the days that are no more.   20

This poem shows Tennyson's delight in pure sound, and his
tendency to give intense expression to a simple emotion. The
deep nostalgia, the despair at the lost past, is contemplated,
not analysed or judged. In structure, the poem is a series of
comparisons, each introduced by *as*. Each of the four unrhymed stanzas is built round a single image or idea, becoming
progressively more intense and hopeless. In the first stanza,
tears 'gather to the eyes' simply from contemplation of the
present autumn scene (with its Keatsian hint of maturity and
approaching winter) and memory of the past. In the second,
the sail on the horizon belongs to the ship of birth and then
of death; it suggests the mysterious places from which we
come and to which we go, with which we have no communi-
cation except when we make the voyage ourselves; the word
underworld could simply mean 'the Antipodes', but it was also
used to mean the abode of the dead in classical mythology.
In the third stanza, a dying person hears early morning bird-
song as the window slowly becomes visible in the dawn. It
might be thought that death should be the climax of the
poem, but the poem is about memories, and the final stanza
gives us the even greater intensity of the *memory* of the dead,
'remembered kisses after death'. But the days that are no

more are also *sweet* (17), even if the sweetness is that of unfulfilled desire; the poet is enjoying the nostalgia as well as grieving for what is lost.

Late Victorian lyric

In later Victorian times, poetry became increasingly remote from life. This was not simply a matter of themes, but also of language: poetry was dominated by a highly conventional diction, remote from everyday speech. There were poets who resisted its influence, notably Hopkins, but he was completely ignored in his own time. Even a poet as powerful and original as Yeats was dominated for many years by the conventional late-Victorian poetic style, as can be seen in the following example, 'He tells of the perfect beauty', from his third volume of poetry, published in 1899:

> O cloud-pale eyelids, dream-dimmed eyes,
> The poets labouring all their days
> To build a perfect beauty in rhyme
> Are overthrown by a woman's gaze
> And by the unlabouring brood of the skies: 5
> And therefore my heart will bow, when dew
> Is dropping sleep, until God burn time,
> Before the unlabouring stars and you.

The poet contemplates the woman's beauty, which overthrows ('surpasses') the work of the poets, who strive to build 'a perfect beauty in rhyme' (3). Similarly the birds, 'the 'unlabouring brood of the skies', outdo the poets, without effort: they have a simple spontaneous beauty, like the lilies of the field (which are brought to mind by the Biblical turn of phrase in line 5). The poet's heart will therefore bow in worship before the stars (another example of 'unlabouring' beauty) and before the woman, until the end of the universe ('until God burn time').

The effect of the poem, however, is not one of simple spontaneous life and beauty: it gives the impression of a very deliberate artist working in precious stones rather than in flesh and blood. Neither the woman nor the birds and stars become actual in the poem: notice the plurals in the opening lines, which leave the reader momentarily in doubt whether the poet is addressing one specific person. In fact he seems more interested in the perfect beauty in rhyme than in the woman, as is suggested by such phrases as *when dew/Is dropping sleep* (6–7), with its deliberate, rather precious quality. The phrase is not demanded by the ostensible theme of the poem, but in fact is quite in harmony with its real interests. These are revealed by the key-words which establish the atmosphere of the poem: *cloud-pale, dream-dimmed, beauty, unlabouring, sleep.* They produce the typically dreamy and vague atmosphere of late-Victorian poetry, with its incantatory, semi-magical quality. We are not far from the world of the aesthetes, where our servants will do the living for us.

Twentieth-Century Lyric

In the present century, even more than in the nineteenth, the short lyric has been the predominant type of poetry. There have been longer poems, such as Eliot's *Waste Land* (1922) and *Four Quartets* (1936–42), and there have been attempts to revive the poetic drama. But long narrative or autobiographical poems have gone out of fashion, and poets have concentrated overwhelmingly on short poems handling personal experience. It is indeed the cultivation of the personal in poetry, as opposed to the public, which has led to the dominance of the lyric, a process which began with the Romantics.

The poetic revolution

Early in the century there occurred one of the periodic revolutions in poetic style, and the old late-Romantic type of poetry was displaced. A crucial time was the First World War, when settled convictions were violently disturbed. The change in poetry, however, had begun before the work of the war-poets. It is seen in Yeats. A comparison of 'He tells of the perfect beauty' with 'Sailing to Byzantium' shows how much his poetry changed between 1899 and 1928, from a dreamy aestheticism to a taut, witty, passionate colloquial-lism. The change can be seen coming in the volume he published in 1904, and is quite plain in the volume of 1910, as in 'The fascination of what's difficult', with its emotional urgency, its use of everyday language, and its marvellous Donne-like rhythms. In the same volume, Yeats reflected on the change, in a short poem ironically titled 'The coming of wisdom with time':

> Though leaves are many, the root is one;
> Through all the lying days of my youth
> I swayed my leaves and flowers in the sun;
> Now I may wither into the truth.

The romantic poetry he wrote in his youth had been lies, but it had been vigorous and flourishing, like a tree in the sun. And now that his poetry deals with truth instead of lies, he reflects bitterly, it is too late: the tree has withered, he has reached his winter. Fortunately he was mistaken, for far from withering he blossomed into the marvellous creative period, from about 1914 to 1933, in which his finest poetry was written.

T. S. Eliot

Above all, however, it was the work of T. S. Eliot, both in poetry and in criticism, which broke the old moulds and gave English poetry a fresh start. In his early poetry, collected in the volume *Poems 1909–25* (1925), he went back behind the Romantics to the seventeenth century, to the metaphysi-cal poets and the Jacobean dramatists; to their influence was added that of the French Symbolist poets of the nineteenth century, especially Jules Laforgue. The dreamy solemnity of late-Romantic poetry was replaced by wit and irony; and instead of the poetic clichés of the former age we find a flex-ible poetic style which can range from the colloquial to the majestic, and reflect a wide range of moods and feelings.

Much of this early poetry of Eliot's can hardly be called lyric, because he cultivates impersonality, and rarely speaks in his own voice: many of the poems are clearly spoken by a 'character' who is different from the author. One of those that can reasonably be classified as lyric is 'Whispers of Immortality'. This is a poem of eight stanzas, in two contrasted groups of four. The first half of the poem deals with the attitudes to death of Webster (the Jacobean dramatist) and Donne:

> Webster was much possessed by death
> And saw the skull beneath the skin;
> And breastless creatures under ground
> Leaned backward with a lipless grin.
>
> Daffodil bulbs instead of balls   5
> Stared from the sockets of the eyes!
> He knew that thought clings round dead limbs
> Tightening its lusts and luxuries.
>
> Donne, I suppose, was such another
> Who found no substitute for sense;   10
> To seize and clutch and penetrate,
> Expert beyond experience,
>
> He knew the anguish of the marrow
> The ague of the skeleton;
> No contact possible to flesh   15
> Allayed the fever of the bone.

The manner is informal, almost casual: notice for example the apparently artless *I suppose* inserted parenthetically in line 9. The theme is not simply Webster's and Donne's obsession with death, but the nature of their sensibility, in which intellect and feeling are intimately fused: Donne *knew* the anguish of the marrow (13), the verb meaning both 'experienced' and 'had cognisance of'. And Webster knew that 'thought clings round dead limbs' (7). At the same time, the intensity of their imaginations was such that they experienced physically 'the fever of the bone' (16). There is an element of sensuality in these poets' imaginings of death: the 'lusts and luxuries' of thought are tightened (made more intense, compressed, fixed more firmly) when it 'clings round dead limbs' (7–8).

The second half of the poem follows with no transitional passage or explanation, simply being juxtaposed. It moves to the modern world, and presents a quite different kind of sensuality:

> Grishkin is nice: her Russian eye
> Is underlined for emphasis;
> Uncorseted, her friendly bust
> Gives promise of pneumatic bliss.   20
>
> The couched Brazilian jaguar
> Compels the scampering marmoset
> With subtle effluence of cat;
> Grishkin has a maisonette;
>
> The sleek Brazilian jaguar   25
> Does not in its arboreal gloom
> Distil so rank a feline smell
> As Grishkin in a drawing-room.
>
> And even the Abstract Entities
> Circumambulate her charm;   30
> But our lot crawls between dry ribs
> To keep our metaphysics warm.

Grishkin is described, tongue-in-cheek, as *nice* (17), meaning that she is attractive in appearance; in many other senses of the word, obviously, she is not nice at all. The sexual pleasure that she seems to proffer is characterised by the witty phrase *pneumatic bliss* (20): here *pneumatic,* with its association with car-tyres, implies that the bliss is purely physical, as well as suggesting the amplitude of Grishkin's 'friendly bust'. There is also a learned pun: the Greek word *pneuma* meant both 'wind, breath' and 'spirit, soul', and the English word *pneumatic* has two technical meanings related to these: in physiology it means 'respiratory, pertaining to breathing', and in philosophy it means 'relating to spirit, spiritual'. The suggestion of spirituality is ironical, since it is plainly a quality lacking in Grishkin and in any relationships with her. The whole stanza is parallel to the first stanza of the poem, Webster's 'breastless creatures' being contrasted with Grishkin's 'friendly bust'.

In the next two stanzas, Grishkin is compared to the Brazilian jaguar: she is feline (in appearance, movement, smell), and (it is implied) she is a hunter. Grishkin is an animal, but one which operates in the drawing-room and in the maisonette. The use she makes of her maisonette is left to our imagination.

In the final stanza, the Abstract Entities (the kind of thing that philosophers deal with) circumambulate ('walk around') Grishkin's charm. This suggests a distance, even a barrier, between the physical and the metaphysical; but there is also a sly hint that even philosophers hang around Grishkin in the drawing-room. In the last two lines the poet makes his only overt comment on what he has presented, and even here with the slightly oblique *our* (not *my*); his fate (*lot*) is to crawl between dry ribs (like those contemplated by Donne and Webster), not to circumambulate the well-fleshed bust of Grishkin: he rejects the physical in favour of the metaphysical. But in the first half of the poem the physical and the metaphysical had been united, in the sensibilities of Donne and Webster. In the second half they are disjoined, Grishkin representing physical experience, while the poet himself, in the last two lines, represents an intellectual one.

The contrast between past and present is common in Eliot's poetry, and often, as here, it is achieved by a juxtaposition of scenes or persons or events. The purpose of the contrast is often to reveal the vulgarity and spiritual aridity of modern life. In many of his early poems Eliot evokes the modern urban scene in all its squalor and banality. Even more than the physical setting itself, it is the crumbling of traditional moral values that Eliot is concerned about; and, as in 'Whispers of Immortality', he finds modern sexual behaviour especially distasteful.

After Eliot

Eliot more than anybody else cleared the way for the poets

that followed, by liberating English poetry from outworn modes. The most successful poets of the century have not indeed been imitators of Eliot, but it was his achievement that enabled them to find voices of their own, many different voices. The greatest of them, Auden, has a great variety of styles and a brilliant technical virtuosity. In William Empson there is complex intellectual wit. The Welsh poet Dylan Thomas (1914–53), by contrast, produced a new kind of Romantic poetry, influenced by surrealism: highly-charged emotionally, full of Freudian and Biblical imagery, enormously energetic, but marked by extremely personal linguistic tricks. In the 1950s arose a group of poets, of whom the most prominent is Philip Larkin, who insisted on common-sense and prosaic virtues in poetry, and rejected large-scale theoretical systems in favour of an everyday empiricism. Among more recent poets, the outstanding figure is Ted Hughes (1930–), with his outstanding power to grasp physical appearances and movements, and his often disturbing treatment of human and animal violence. And these are merely a few of the better-known names among a host of talented practitioners of the predominantly lyrical poetry of our age.

In the United States, too, post-war poetry has been dominated by the short personal lyric, from Wallace Stevens (1879–1955) and Allen Tate (1899–1979) to younger writers such as Sylvia Plath (1932–63). In other parts of the English-speaking world, however, the dominance of lyric has been less absolute, and long autobiographical and narrative poems have continued to be written. Nevertheless, the lyric has played a large part in these countries too, and constitutes a substantial portion of the output of such prominent poets as Derek Walcott in the West Indies, Nissim Ezekiel (1924–) in India, and Judith Wright and A. D. Hope (1907–) in Australia. In these countries, too, Eliot has been a liberating influence: in India, for example, it was Eliot's work which enabled the poets of the post-Independence years, led by P. Lal (1931–) of Calcutta, to break away from the late-Victorian style and produce poetry in a modern idiom. In his volume *Charge! They Said* (1966), Lal has an elegy on Eliot, 'who taught us the use of words'.

The Ode

In the general category of lyric are usually included a number of sub-categories. One is the Sonnet, which we have already discussed. Another is the Ode, a form widely practised by English poets from the time of Spenser to that of Tennyson.

An ode is a fairly long lyric poem, dignified in style and serious in subject. It is normally stanzaic, and usually the stanzas are long and complex (though some odes are in simple four-line stanzas). The main inspiration for the English ode, the Greek poet Pindar, used an extremely complex metrical structure. Each section of the ode was in three parts: the Strophe, a long and complicated stanza; the Antistrophe, with an identical pattern; and the Epode, with a different and usually simpler stanza. An ode could consist of a number of such three-part groups, in which case the Epodes all had to have the same pattern, whereas the Strophe-Antistrophe stanzas were different in each group. The strict Pindaric pattern is found in two of Gray's odes, 'The Bard' (1757) and 'The Progress of Poesy' (1757) (though Gray uses rhymed stanzas, whereas classical Greek poetry was unrhymed). This is unusual, however, and most English odes simply repeat a single stanzaic pattern.

Some English odes, on the other hand, are irregular, with no repeating stanzaic pattern. The irregular ode was introduced by Abraham Cowley, and was used by several later poets, including Dryden in his 'Song for St Cecilia's Day' (1687) and 'Alexander's Feast' (1697), and Wordsworth in his 'Intimations of Immortality' (1807). In such odes there are stanzas of varying length and rhyme-scheme, according to the mood and subject-matter at each point.

Most of Pindar's surviving odes are in celebration of athletic victories. English odes are often celebratory, and are usually addressed to a person or to a personified abstraction (Duty, Evening), or composed in honour of some occasion (St Cecilia's Day, Cromwell's return from Ireland). Usually they follow Pindar in using an elevated style, but alongside the influence of Pindar was that of the Latin poet Horace, whose *Carmina* were considered to be odes. The Horatian style is more meditative and more low key than the Pindaric, and with more variety of mood. English odes in the Horatian manner, like Pope's 'Ode to Solitude' (*c.* 1700), are usually regular, with short stanzas; it is the higher-pitched Pindaric odes that are likely to be irregular.

The history of the English ode begins with Spenser. He did not himself apply the word to any of his poems, but his two magnificent poems in celebration of marriages, 'Prothalamion' (1596) and 'Epithalamion' (1595), have all the characteristics of stanzaic odes. Ben Jonson wrote a dozen odes, mainly Horatian, of which the most famous is 'Ode to Himself' ('Come leave the loathed stage'). Milton's earliest masterpiece (1629) was his ode 'On the morning of Christ's Nativity', with its technical virtuosity, its triumphant rhythms, and its charming baroque images. One of the great poems of the mid-seventeenth century is Marvell's 'An Horatian Ode upon Cromwell's return from Ireland' (1650). Dryden's two odes in honour of St Cecilia's day (1687 and 1697) are of the high-pitched irregular type, and both aim at simulating a variety of emotional effects. In the first, 'A Song for St Cecilia's Day', he takes in turn a number of musical instruments, and simulates the kind of emotion produced by each. In 'Alexander's Feast', the musician Timotheus produces a succession of different emotional effects in his audience by the songs he sings. Pope's 'Ode for Music, on St Cecilia's Day' (*c.* 1708) is a poor imitation. Later in the eighteenth century, Gray practised the ode as his favourite form. His most successful ones are perhaps the playfully humorous 'Ode on the death of a favourite cat, drowned in a tub of goldfishes' (1748), and the 'Ode on a distant prospect of Eton College' (1747), which is felicitously phrased and genuinely moving, despite a surfeit of personified Passions. Collins, too, wrote many odes, and his most exquisite work is 'Ode to Evening' (1747), with its fine observation, delicate phrasing, and beautiful evocation of mood and atmosphere; it is written in stanzas, but is unrhymed.

With the Romantic poets, the ode is given a more personal flavour. Often, like the traditional ode, it handles a public theme, but with some personal problem or experience of the poet's implicated; in other cases it may be purely personal.

Wordsworth's 'Intimations of Immortality' ode advances views about the soul, and about the way in which children, as they become adults, lose the 'celestial light' which had once glorified everything they saw; but above all it is about Wordsworth's own experience of Nature in childhood and later. Coleridge wrote a number of odes on public themes ('To the departing year', 'France'), or addressed to abstractions ('To Tranquillity'), or in honour of individuals ('Ode to Georgiana, Duchess of Devonshire'), but these works are at best undistinguished. One of Coleridge's odes, however, is a masterpiece: 'Dejection: an Ode', written in 1802. This is in the manner of Coleridge's conversation-poems, and is on a personal theme: the poet's own loss of emotional responsiveness, and his attempt to come to terms with this and to achieve inner harmony.

Shelley, 'Ode to the West Wind'

Shelley had strong political views, much influenced by William Godwin (1756–1836): he believed in human perfectibility; he looked forward to the achievement of an anarchist society, in which there were no institutions and no power-relations; he was opposed to violence; and he believed that the perfect society would be achieved when people saw the truth and their chains just melted away. The propagation of his ideas was therefore of prime importance, and he wrote a good deal of directly political poetry. But, besides being a highly political poet, Shelley was also a very personal one: indeed, his political views rest on an extreme form of individualism. The liberation which he desired included sexual liberation, and much of his poetry is love-poetry; even when it is not, it often has strong sexual undertones. The combination of a political theme with the self-centredness of the personal poet is seen in his finest ode, 'Ode to the West Wind' (1820).

The poet begins by addressing the West Wind, and calling upon it to hear him:

> O wild West Wind, thou breath of Autumn's being,
> Thou, from whose unseen presence the leaves dead
> Are driven, like ghosts from an enchanter fleeing,

Yellow, and black, and pale, and hectic red,
Pestilence-stricken multitudes: O thou,   5
Who chariotest to their dark wintry bed

The wingèd seeds, where they lie cold and low,
Each like a corpse within its grave, until
Thine azure sister of the Spring shall blow

Her clarion o'er the dreaming earth, and fill   10
(Driving sweet buds like flocks to feed in air)
With living hues and odours plain and hill:

Wild Spirit, which art moving everywhere;
Destroyer and preserver; hear, oh, hear!

We begin with a vivid picture of the fallen autumn leaves, in all their variety of colours, being driven by the wind; the word *hectic* (4) evokes the violent colour of a feverish flush, but also contributes in a more general way to the sense of violent uncontrolled movement. The comparison of the leaves to ghosts running away from a magician (3) illustrates a poetic habit of Shelley's; whereas other poets are likely to give physical counterparts to immaterial things, he often moves in the opposite direction: he compares the material to the non-material. This sometimes has a weakening effect on his poetry, since he dissolves the concrete world into intangible things; but in this instance it is very effective, suggesting as it does the mysterious power and invisibility of the violent autumn wind.

We move from the leaves to the seeds, and here the theme of rebirth enters the poem. The wind is carrying the seeds (winged ones, like those of a sycamore tree), as if in a chariot, to the places in the earth where they will lie until Spring comes, bringing new birth and new growth. In the passage on the coming of Spring, we see another of Shelley's poetic habits: the tendency of an image or comparison to take on a life of its own, to become a centre of interest in its own right quite apart from its nominal function in the poem. In line 11, the idea of Spring driving sweet buds expands into a comparison with the driving of flocks (of sheep, presumably);

but whereas sheep feed on grass, the buds have to feed 'in air', and it is difficult to see what this contributes to the poem.

In the first section, the poet addresses the wind as it operates on the earth. He continues his apostrophe in the second and third sections of the poem, but in the second the wind is in the sky, and in the third it is over the sea. Having thus appealed to the wind in its threefold manifestations to hear him, in the fourth section the poet expresses his wish to it:

> If I were a dead leaf thou mightest bear;
> If I were a swift cloud to fly with thee;
> A wave to pant beneath thy power, and share   45
>
> The impulse of thy strength, only less free
> Than thou, O uncontrollable! If even
> I were as in my boyhood, and could be
>
> The comrade of thy wanderings over Heaven,
> As then, when to outstrip thy skiey speed   50
> Scarce seemed a vision; I would ne'er have striven
>
> As thus with thee in prayer in my sore need.
> Oh, lift me as a wave, a leaf, a cloud!
> I fall upon the thorns of life! I bleed!
>
> A heavy weight of hours has chained and bowed   55
> One too like thee: tameless, and swift, and proud.

At this point the appeal is a personal one: the poet is in difficulty and distress, and wishes to be lifted from the thorns of life by the wind, like a wave, a leaf, a cloud (again the wind in its threefold aspect). Fine though it is, the passage does illustrate one way in which English poetry had lost by the time of the Romantics: the wit and irony which had been common in the poetry of the seventeenth century, and persisted well into the eighteenth, have vanished. A poet is dangerously lacking in a sense of irony when he can seriously describe himself as 'tameless, and swift, and proud' (56); and there is a danger that the reader, confronted by this piece of self-dramatisation, may simply laugh.

In the final section of the poem, the appeal to the wind becomes a political one, though couched in personal terms. He asks the wind to become his spirit:

> Drive my dead thoughts over the universe
> Like withered leaves to quicken a new birth!
> And by the incantation of this verse, 65
>
> Scatter, as from an unextinguished hearth
> Ashes and sparks, my words among mankind!
> Be through my lips to unawakened earth
>
> The trumpet of a prophecy. O, Wind,
> If Winter comes, can Spring be far behind? 70

This looks back to the opening section of the poem: the leaves and seeds which the wind was carrying into the earth until Spring should come are now the words of the poet, which will spread through the world and bring about a wakening among mankind. But the expression is typically self-centred: '*my* dead thoughts', '*my* words', '*my* lips'. The poet, however, does not expect an immediate rebirth: Winter has to be endured before Spring comes; and this foreboding lies behind the poet's distress, and his appeal to the wind to strengthen him.

Keats's Odes

John Keats (1795–1821) is the supreme master of the ode in English, and his five great odes ('Ode to a Nightingale', 'Ode on a Grecian Urn', 'Ode to Psyche', 'To Autumn', and 'Ode on Melancholy') (1820) are the peak of his poetical career. His odes are not celebratory, or public in theme. He may choose a topic apparently remote from his own immediate concerns, like the Grecian Urn; but the Odes are nevertheless intensely personal, and record the poet's achievement of emotional maturity. They were written after his brother Tom had died of tuberculosis, and when Keats himself had begun to fear that he too would die young, and they record his struggle to accept his situation. They have a wonderful concreteness and sensuous richness in their evocation of the poet's experience.

We have already looked at 'To Autumn', the culminating masterpiece. Let us also look briefly at 'Ode to a Nightingale'.

'Ode to a Nightingale'. The poem is built round conflicting impulses: the desire to enjoy the world, and the desire to escape from it; the desire to live, and the desire to die. These desires adopt disguises, so that what at one moment seems to be a life-wish appears at the next to be a death-wish. The conflict is seen in the first stanza: the nightingale, the 'light-wingèd Dryad of the trees', represents summer, joy, effortless song; but the poet's response to it is described in terms of deadening drugs — opiate, hemlock, sinking towards Lethe; and yet these feelings are said to be due to an excess of happiness. In the second stanza the poet wishes to drink wine, and here too there is a doubleness of feeling: the wine can be something that enhances life, evoking 'Dance, and Provençal song, and sunburnt mirth', but it is also a means of escape, so that the poet may 'leave the world unseen'. The third stanza describes the world from which the poet wishes to escape, the 'weariness, the fever, and the fret', the world of ageing and loss of beauty. In the fourth and fifth stanzas, the poet escapes from this world, not by drunkenness, but 'on the viewless wings of poesy': in imagination, he flies to the nightingale, and describes with wonderful richness and tenderness the dark wood where it is singing, with the scents of the bushes and flowers, and the 'coming musk-rose, full of dewy wine'. Here, clearly, escape has become something positive and creative.

But the poet is still held by conflicting feelings, and in the sixth stanza he expresses a wish to die. There is something slightly luxuriant about this: death is *easeful* and *rich*, and the poet is enjoying the idea of dying. But he also recognises the disadvantages of dying: he would be a mere clod of earth, and would be unable to hear the nightingale's dirge for him. These conflicting feelings appear in the paradoxical phrase 'Now more than ever seems it *rich to die*', which encapsulates the central tension of the poem.

The thought of the nightingale singing over his dead body leads the poet to think, in the seventh stanza, about the dead to whom the bird has sung in the past; and he asserts its immortality: the voice that he is listening to tonight was heard 'In ancient days by emperor and clown'. The fallacy is obvious: it is the nightingale species that has continued, not the individual, and the same is true of man. The poet is clutching at straws: in the world of flux and death, he is trying to find something exempt, and defies logic to do so. It could indeed be argued that it is the *song* of the nightingale which is not subject to death, and that in that case the contrast is between the eternity of art and the transience of human life, as in 'Ode on a Grecian Urn'. But in fact the assertion of the nightingale's immortality is just another attempt by the poet to *escape* from his predicament, and this becomes clear at the end of the stanza: after the emperor and clown, and the Biblical story of Ruth, we move on to the purely fantasy-world of fairyland, with its

> magic casements, opening on the foam
> Of perilous seas, in faery lands forlorn.   70

But the very last word of the stanza breaks the spell. Unfortunately, the popularity of the poem has caused 'faery lands forlorn' to become something of a cliché, and we no longer realise how surprising the last word is. It is drawn into the poem by alliteration and by its archaic Spenserian associations; but, having arrived, it introduces a note of desolation which reveals the futility of the attempted escape to the world of magic and faery. The poet is brought up short by the word, which in the final stanza of the poem takes him back into the world of reality. He recognises that even 'fancy' is a deceiver, who cannot relieve us of the burdens of life; and, as the song of the nightingale fades gradually into the distance, the poet, still bemused by the imaginative experience he has been through, returns to the light of common day.

Later odes

After Keats, the ode gradually went out of fashion. Tennyson published only four odes among his voluminous works, including two written for public occasions, 'Ode on the Death of the Duke of Wellington' (1852), and 'Ode sung at the Opening of the International Exhibition' (1862). In the present century, the ode has become very rare, despite the general predominance of lyric poetry, presumably because it is felt to be too formal in an age of personal poetry. The occasional ode can be found, for example in Auden, but on the whole the form has withered away.

3 *Narrative Poetry*

Geoffrey Chaucer (*c.* 1343–1400)

Before the rise of the novel in the eighteenth century, narrative poems were common, and often had features which we
now associate with prose fiction – plot, character, dialogue,
description, humour, situation, scene. Not that narrative
poems always depicted life in the realistic way common in
novels: in the Middle Ages especially, many narrative poems
were allegorical, and were peopled by personified abstractions rather than by human beings; others were dream-poems,
beginning and ending in the real world but with their main
substance consisting of a dream by the poet. Several of
Chaucer's early poems were dream-poems; and early in his
career he also translated from the French one of the famous
allegorical poems of the Middle Ages, *Le Roman de la Rose*,
though only fragments of the translation have survived.

'The Canterbury Tales'

Chaucer is one of the great masters of narrative poetry, and
the culmination of his poetic career is *The Canterbury Tales*,
written during the last quarter of the fourteenth century. The
plan of the poem is explained in its 'General Prologue': a
group of people on a pilgrimage to Canterbury meet in the
Tabard Inn in Southwark, and agree to travel together; they
also agree that, to pass the time on the journey, each pilgrim
shall tell two stories on the way to Canterbury and two more
on the way back. The body of *The Canterbury Tales* consists
of the stories told by the pilgrims, but the full plan is by no
means completed: twenty-six pilgrims are described in the

'General Prologue', and to these must be added the poet himself (the first-person narrator who takes part in the pilgrimage), and the Host of the Tabard Inn, and two or three other pilgrims who appear later; so the complete plan must involve about 120 stories. In fact there are only twenty-four stories, not all of them complete, and it is clear that the work was unfinished when Chaucer died around 1400.

In addition to the tales, there are a number of link-passages, in which there are conversations between the pilgrims, and decisions about who shall tell the next tale. Some of these are very substantial, notably the prologues to their tales spoken by the Wife of Bath and by the Pardoner, both of which become brilliant full-scale autobiographies.

The tales are of many different kinds: they include a long romantic tale of love and chivalry ('The Knight's Tale'); a slyly ironic beast-fable ('The Nun's Priest's Tale'); tales of hilarious bawdry ('The Miller's Tale', 'The Reeve's Tale'); a serious religious tale of martyrdom ('The Prioress's Tale'); a traditional catalogue of the fall of illustrious men ('The Monk's Tale'); a superb moral tale about three drunkards who went out in search of death ('The Pardoner's Tale'); and sundry tales of womanly constancy, marital infidelity, magic, justice, love, and chivalry. To the modern reader, the most accessible tales are the comic ones, but a knowledge of the age, its attitudes and conventions, brings an appreciation also of the more serious and slow-moving ones, such as 'The Knight's Tale'.

Plot. Chaucer is a master of plot. Sometimes he uses a highly stylised and patterned plot. In 'The Knight's Tale', the story both begins and ends with a funeral and a wedding. The two lovers, Palamon and Arcite, are given similar and parallel speeches and actions, so that a symmetry runs all through the tale; at the same time, they are distinguished in that they worship different gods, and this receives emblematic expression at the crisis of the poem: the lovers are to fight in the lists for the hand of fair Emelye, and early in the morning they both pray, one in the temple of Venus and the other in the temple of Mars, while Emelye prays in the temple of Diana.

A different kind of plot is seen in 'The Miller's Tale', which brilliantly combines two traditional themes. This tale is a *fabliau*, a popular medieval French form. A *fabliau* was a short story dealing with lower-class or citizen life (often in a satirical way) and aiming at ribald humour. One popular theme was the successful tricking of a husband (especially an old and jealous one) by his wife and her lover. Another was the turning of the tables: a character is tricked or deceived in some way, but then succeeds in getting his own back on his opponent. These two themes are combined in 'The Miller's Tale'. Alison and her lover Nicholas fool her husband, the carpenter John, into believing that a great flood is at hand, from which they must save themselves by spending the night in three tubs hanging in the roof, fully provisioned and with an axe to cut the ropes when the flood reaches them. As soon as John is asleep in his tub, Alison and Nicholas climb down and go to bed together. The second theme concerns Absolon, the dandyish parish-clerk, who also loves Alison. While she and Nicholas are abed, Absolon comes and taps on the window and asks her for a kiss; in the dark she plays an unsavoury trick on him, putting her backside out of the window for him to kiss. This cures Absolon of his love, and he determines to get his own back. He goes to a nearby smithy and gets a red-hot coulter, and then comes back to Alison's window and again asks for a kiss. Nicholas tries to play the same trick on him, and as his reward is smitten on the behind with the red-hot iron. It is here that the two themes coalesce: Nicholas shouts 'Help! water! water! help!'; the carpenter wakes up and hears these shouts, cuts the rope of his tub with the axe, and comes crashing down to the floor, bringing an unexpected end to the lovers' plot and making himself the laughing-stock of the town.

Pace. Chaucer is a master of pace. When Nicholas tells his story of the flood to John, the pace is slowed down, and the final revelation of the imminent peril is tantalisingly held back. By contrast, at the climax of the story, when John cuts the ropes and falls, things happen very quickly and suddenly. There is similar variation of pace in 'The Nun's Priest's Tale', Chaucer's version of the story of the Cock and the Fox: the pace is frequently slowed down by amusing digressions, such as the cock's long lecture to his wife on the significance of dreams; but when the fox has seized the cock, and everybody comes out shouting and running in pursuit, things move very fast, and there is a sense of enormous speed and activity.

Character. In Chaucer, and indeed in earlier literature generally, we do not find profound psychological studies of characters of the kind that the novel has accustomed us to. In some of the more romance-like tales, the characters are very slightly sketched, and are not always realistic. But Chaucer is superbly skilled in character-description, as can be seen in the accounts of the various pilgrims in the 'General Prologue'. He seizes on details of appearance, behaviour, clothing, habits, and mannerisms which combine to form a vivid picture of an individual person. Similar character-sketches are found in some of the tales; the following are extracts from the description of Alison in 'The Miller's Tale':

Fair was this yongė wyf, and therwithal
As any wezele hir body gent and smal [graceful and slender].
A ceynt [girdle] she werdė barrėd al of sylk,
A barmclooth [apron] as whit as mornė mylk,
Upon her lendės [loins], ful of many a goorė.   5
Whit was hir smok, and broyden [embroidered] al bifoorė
And eek [also] bihynde, on hir coler aboutė
Of col-blak silk, withinne and eek withoutė.
The tapės of hir whitė voluper [cap]
Were of the samė sute [kind] of her coler,   10
Hir filet [headband] brood of sylk and set ful hyė,
And sikerly [certainly] she had a likerous [lecherous] yė.
Ful smale ypullėd [plucked] were hir browės two,
And tho [they] were bent and blake as is a slo.
She was ful moorė blisful on to see   15
Than is the newė pere-jonettė [early pear] tree,
And softer than the wolle is of a wether.
. . .
. . .

But of hir soong, it was as loude and yernė [lively]   25
As any swalwė sittyng on a bernė [barn].
Therto she koudė skippe and makė gamė,
As any kyde or calf folwyng his damė [mother].
Hir mouth was sweete as bragott or the meeth [mead]
Or hoord of apples leyd in hey or heeth [heather].   30
Wynsynge [skittish] she was as is a joly colt,
Loong as a mast and uprighte as a bolt.
A brooch she baar [bore] upon hir lowė coler,
As brood as is the boos [boss] of a bokeler [buckler].
Hir shoes were lacėd on hir leggės hyė.   35
She was a prymėrole [primrose], a piggėsnyė [darling, pet],
For any lord to leggen [lay] in his beddė,
Or yet for any good yeman to weddė.

There is some disagreement about Chaucer's versification, but
the general view is that in his poetry the final *-e* is usually
pronounced as a syllable (probably sounding like the *e* of
present-day *father*); and in the passage above an accent is
placed over an *e* to show that it is to be pronounced. The *-e* is
not pronounced when it occurs immediately before a vowel,
as in 'kyd*e* or calf' (28); moreover, in many words spelt with
initial *h* there was no /h/ in the pronunciation, so that they
too began with a vowel and caused the elision of a preceding
e; an example is *hir* (2).

The picture of Alison is built up by splendid concrete
details. There is not much about her actual physical appearance, though we do learn that she is tall (32) and straight-
backed (like a crossbow bolt) (32). We learn more about her
clothes, about which she is plainly fastidious. The sophisticated smartness of her dress is brought out by a black and
white contrast: the apron, smock, and cap are white, while
her collar and her cap-tapes are coal-black. Her eyebrows are
also black, and are plucked so that they are narrow (*smale*).
The high-laced boots (35) were no doubt modish, as perhaps
was the large brooch on her collar (33–4); but the statement
that the brooch was as broad as the boss of a buckler (round
shield) suggests that she has overdone it, that the brooch is
too extravagantly and ostentatiously large. The use of silk for
her girdle (3), her collar (7–8), and her headband (10) also

suggests extravagance, and the material would not have been considered suitable for the wife of a carpenter, even a rich one. The overall effect of the clothes is to suggest a fashionable smartness, but also an aspiration above her proper social sphere.

Alongside these details is a series of comparisons, mainly with natural things, which produce a rather different effect. The apron is as white as morning milk (4); Alison's eyebrows are as black as a sloe (14); she is more delightful to look at than an early-fruiting pear-tree (15—16), and softer than the wool of a sheep (17); she sings like a swallow sitting on a barn (25); her mouth is as sweet as bragget (a drink made of honey and ale fermented together) or as mead, or apples stored in hay or heather (29—30); she is a primrose (36). The comparison to bragget and mead suggests an intoxicating quality as well as sweetness, but the general effect of the comparisons is one of naturalness and rustic wholesomeness, which is in sharp contrast to the urban sophistication of the clothes. Alison is a country girl aspiring to city smartness.

Other comparisons suggest an animal-like quality in Alison. She is as graceful and slender as a weasel (2); but the reader knows that a weasel is also a ferocious killer. She skips about like a kid or a calf (27—8), and is as skittish as a colt (31). The comparison to these young animals suggests legginess and frisky liveliness, and also a certain degree of irresponsibility and absence of morality: her naturalness includes a disregard for human prohibitions.

The description of a character is only the first stage: the character is then put into action, and is given dialogue to speak, and it is above all the dialogue which brings characters to life. In some tales, like 'The Knight's Tale', the dialogue is rather stylised, in conformity with the general ritual manner of the tale; but in more realistic tales the dialogue is lively, colloquial, and racy.

The Epic

An epic is a long narrative poem which celebrates the achievements of heroic figures of history or legend. Early epics were orally performed, and passed on by oral tradition; some were also composed orally, or assembled from earlier poems which had been so composed. Poems which can be described as epics are found in many cultures and languages: examples from the present century include the 'Ozidi' of the Ijo people of Nigeria, the 'Anggun Nan Tungga' of Sumatra, and the performances of the Serbo-Croat epic minstrels in what is now Yugoslavia. For the literature of Western Europe, however, the significant and influential epics are those of ancient Greece and Rome, especially Homer's *Iliad* and *Odyssey* and Virgil's *Aeneid*.

Homer and Virgil

The two ancient Greek poems attributed to Homer, perhaps dating from the ninth century BC, are 'primary' or 'traditional' epics. That is, they go back to an age when literature was oral, and when heroic poetry was sung, or chanted with musical accompaniment, by a bard at the court of a king or nobleman. Virgil's poem, on the other hand, is a 'secondary' or 'literary' epic, produced in a literate age (the first century BC) and designed to be read; it closely imitates the Homeric epics.

The *Iliad* deals with the siege of Troy by the Greeks, the quarrel between Achilles and Agamemnon, and the killing by Achilles of the Trojan hero Hector. The *Odyssey* recounts the adventures of the Greek hero Odysseus on his voyage back home from the siege of Troy, and his final arrival in time to rescue his wife from the attentions of a crowd of suitors. The *Aeneid* gives a legendary account of the founding of Rome by the Trojan hero Aeneas, who escapes from Troy when it is sacked by the Greeks.

These three epics have characteristics which were much imitated by later writers of heroic poems. The style is high and formal, remote from everyday speech. The central character is a great hero, and the fate of a whole people hangs on his deeds; these deeds, and those of many other of the characters, are superhuman. The Gods play a part in the poem, and intervene in the action. The narrative begins, not with the earliest events, but in the middle, and the earlier events are related later, in the form of narratives by one character to another: in the *Aeneid*, the poem begins with Aeneas and his men being driven by a storm on to the coast of Africa; the earlier events (the fall of Troy and Aeneas's escape) are then related by Aeneas to Dido, queen of Carthage.

'The Faerie Queene'

In the Renaissance, the epic was considered to be the highest form of literature, and poets who wanted their national literature to rival that of Greece and Rome were likely to write epic poetry. One such attempt is Spenser's incomplete poem *The Faerie Queene*, published in the 1590s. This poem, however, bears little resemblance to Homer or Virgil: it is influenced rather by the romantic type of epic which had arisen in Italy, and also by medieval allegorical poetry. It is set in the time of King Arthur, and one of Arthur's knights is the central character of each of its books; Spenser intended to write twelve books, but completed only six and the fragment of a seventh. The central knight of each book represents some virtue: Holiness, Temperance, Chastity, and so on; and this virtue is the main theme of the book. Many of the characters are personifications of various kinds, and there is a great deal of allegory — moral, religious, political.

The allegorical figures are of more than one kind. Some are just types, examples of people with the virtue or vice in question: in Book II, Braggadocchio is simply an example of a boastful coward. Others are personifications of the vice or virtue in question: in Book II, Furor is not a man suffering from intemperate rage, but a personification of the vice: the person who suffers from the vice is Phedon, who is beaten and wounded by Furor, just as, in Bunyan's prose allegory *The Pilgrim's Progress* (1678), Giant Despair is not a despairing man, but the quality of despair which afflicts the pilgrims. Some of Spenser's characters are inconsistent, at one time being type-figures, at another personifications. The central character of Book II is Sir Guyon, who represents temperance. Sometimes he is a temperate man, feeling temptation but resisting it, as when in Canto XII he resists the allure of naked maidens in a fountain, feeling lust but overcoming it. But at the end of the same canto he throws a net round

Acrasia, the wicked enchantress, and destroys her palace and her gardens: and here he is a personification, the virtue temperance overcoming the vice intemperance. In addition, the poem contains magicians, marvels, giants, palmers, elfin knights, allegorical beasts, and much more besides. We are a long way from the world of the *Iliad*.

The narrative, too, is unlike that of classical epic, being of the 'interweaving' kind. In each book, Spenser keeps several narrative strands going; none of them is dealt with completely at one time, but instead there is frequent switching from one strand to another.

'Paradise Lost'

Later English writers of epic remained closer to the classical pattern, and one of them, John Milton, produced a master-piece. His *Paradise Lost* (1667) is the one outstanding example of the genre in English.

Milton intended for many years to write a great epic poem, and prepared himself carefully for the task. He considered various possible subjects, including the wars of King Arthur against the Saxons, but finally chose a Biblical theme, the Fall of Man. According to traditional Christian interpretations of the Bible, the first man and woman, Adam and Eve, were perfect and sinless, but were tempted by Satan to disobey God, who then drove them from the Garden of Eden (Paradise). This is the central episode of *Paradise Lost*. The poem also includes an account of a previous fall, that of Lucifer and his angels, who had rebelled against God and been thrown by him out of Heaven into Hell; Lucifer became Satan, and tempted Eve in order to gain revenge on God. Lest Satan should be left apparently triumphant, the poem also contains extensive predictions of the future history of the world after the Fall, including the other two great events in the Christian story, the coming of Christ and his redemption of man through his crucifixion, and the Last Judgment, when God will descend in glory to the earth and all men shall be judged.

The poem, which runs to over 10,000 lines of blank verse, is divided (like the *Aeneid*) into twelve books, and the material is arranged in ways suggested by the classical epics. We do not begin with the rebellion of the angels and the wars in Heaven: at the opening of the poem these have already taken place, and are related later, in Books V and VI, when the angel Raphael narrates them to Adam. In Books I and II, the fallen angels, encouraged by Satan, recover from the stupor in which they lie in the burning lake of Hell, and build themselves a palace, in which their leaders meet in council. They agree to continue their war against God, and Satan sets off from Hell alone to find the Earth, of which they had heard predictions before their fall. In Book III the scene moves to Heaven; God sees Satan flying towards the earth, and foretells his success in seducing mankind; the Son of God (Christ) offers himself as a ransom for the redemption of mankind. The remaining books take place in the Garden of Eden. In Book IV, Satan spies on Adam and Eve. In Books V and VI, the angel Raphael warns Adam about the necessity for obedience to God, and the danger from Satan; he recounts the rebellion of Lucifer and his followers, the consequent wars in Heaven, and the defeat of the rebellious angels. In Book VII he tells Adam about the creation of the world, which happened after the fall of Lucifer, and in Book VIII Adam tells Raphael about his own experiences in Eden since his creation. In Book IX the Fall takes place: Satan, disguised as a serpent, persuades Eve to eat the fruit of the Tree of Knowledge, which God has forbidden; when she tells Adam, he eats it too, in order to share her fate. In Book X, the Son of God descends to Paradise and passes sentence on Adam and Eve; Sin and Death, who had been stationed at the gates of Hell, come to the earth. In Books XI and XII, the Arch-angel Michael comes with a band of Cherubim to turn Adam and Eve out of Paradise, but first tells Adam the future history of the world, including the redemption of man by Christ, and the Last Judgment.

Milton takes over other features of classical epic. Like Homer and Virgil, he opens the poem with a brief statement of its main theme and an appeal to the Muse for inspiration. He gives a catalogue of the fallen angels, as Virgil and Homer give catalogues of heroes. Like them, he uses 'epic similes', that is, extended comparisons in which the 'vehicle' is elaborated and has features with no parallel in the 'tenor': such is the comparison of Satan lying on the Lake of Hell to a whale in the Sea of Norway, to which a benighted sailor moors his skiff, thinking it an island (I.201−10); and the comparison of Satan's shield to the moon as seen through Galileo's telescope (I.284−91). The epic similes in *Paradise Lost* enable the poet to introduce features of the everyday world, which are notably lacking in Heaven, Hell, and Paradise, where the action of the poem takes place. Finally, Milton adopts the high heroic style expected in an epic poem.

The style of 'Paradise Lost'. The style of the poem is an elevated one, remote from the colloquial; it uses many words of Latin derivation, and often departs from normal English word-order for rhetorical effect. The sentences are often long, with many dependent clauses, so that the reader has to hold the sense open over a considerable number of lines, waiting for the final closure before the meaning is complete. The long sentences give dignity, and a sense of sustained argument. The following example comes early in Book I; the poet has stated the theme of the poem, and now asks who had incited Adam and Eve to be disobedient to God:

> Who first seduc'd them to that foul revolt?
> Th'infernal Serpent; he it was, whose guile
> Stirr'd up with Envy and Revenge, deceiv'd   35
> The Mother of Mankind, what time his Pride
> Had cast him out from Heav'n, with all his Host
> Of Rebel Angels, by whose aid aspiring
> To set himself in Glory above his Peers,
> He trusted to have equall'd the most High,   40
> If he oppos'd; and with ambitious aim
> Against the Throne and Monarchy of God
> Rais'd impious War in Heav'n and Battle proud
> With vain attempt. Him the Almighty Power
> Hurl'd headlong flaming from th'Ethereal Sky   45
> With hideous ruin and combustion down
> To bottomless perdition, there to dwell
> In Adamantine Chains and penal Fire,
> Who durst defy th' Omnipotent to Arms.

This is the kind of thing that Milton does exceptionally well: the large-scale cosmic event, seen at a distance. Neither the rhythms nor the diction nor the word-order remind us at all of everyday speech; rather it is magniloquent, oratorical. A typical departure from the normal word-order is *Him the Almighty Power/Hurl'd* (44–5), where for emphasis the object of the sentence is placed at the beginning. Notice too the characteristic device of varying the adjective–noun patterns: *Th'infernal Serpent* (34), *The Mother of Mankind* (36), *Rebel Angels* (38), *the Throne and Monarchy of God* (42), *impious War in Heav'n and Battle proud* (43), and so on. Sometimes the adjective comes before the noun, sometimes after; sometimes a noun modifies another noun; sometimes there is a preposition-phrase; and the changes are rung on these features as a deliberate stylistic device.

The vocabulary of the passage inevitably contains many ordinary words, but there is a substantial sprinkling of Latin or French loan-words, such as *seduc'd, infernal, Ethereal, combustion, perdition, Adamantine*. This is part of the high epic style, which has to avoid anything 'mean'. Words derived from Latin are sometimes used in their etymological sense instead of (or in addition to) their current English one. So *infernal* (34) has both its original meaning 'belonging to the lower regions' and its more recent English meaning 'devilish, hellish'.

Rhythmically, the passage is relatively simple if compared with Donne or mature Shakespeare. The departures from the iambic pattern are few and fairly obvious, and the movement of the verse is smooth and apt for declamation. Milton's rhythmical effects are large-scale ones, operating over a whole paragraph. His characteristic device is to play line-length against phrase-length: the phrases vary in length, so that pauses inside the line occur at different places. This becomes plain if you go through the passage marking the pauses with a pencil; as a refinement, try marking heavy pauses with two strokes, and light pauses with one stroke. In the opening line of the passage there is no pause inside the line but there is a strong pause at the end, so that the line stands out in isolation. In the lines that follow, the pause never comes at the end of the line but at varying points inside it; emphasis is given to *deceiv'd* (35), which stands by itself at the end of a line, and to *aspiring* (38), which is separated by the line-ending from the *To* which follows. The most remarkable effect, however, is the astonishing sense of falling given in lines 44 to 49: there is no pause at all between *Him* in line 44 and *perdition* in line 47, and we seem to be overbalancing at the end of each line, especially line 46, where *down* is separated from its following preposition. Not until *Fire*, at the end of line 48, is there a pause at the end of a line: Satan is no longer falling, but has hit the bottom. In the final line of the passage, as in the first, the sense-unit coincides exactly with the line-length: the episode is concluded, and some kind of stability restored. The whole passage has enormous energy: the narrative drives on purposefully, and the rhythms are full of life and power.

The danger in the style of *Paradise Lost* is that it cannot descend: the poet is on a high horse, and cannot dismount. When he needs to talk about prosaic everyday things, the style may be unsuitable. In Paradise, Adam and Eve eat and drink, but food is seldom called food: it is *nourishment, alimental recompense, viands, ambrosial fruitage,* and the contrast between the mundane subject-matter and the high style can sometimes border dangerously on the comic.

In some of the later parts of the poem, the weakness of the style is not pomposity, but flatness. Michael's narration to Adam in Books XI and XII sometimes becomes pedestrian, even when he is handling topics which we know were close to Milton's heart. Such passages, however, form a relatively small part of the poem; and in the central and crucial episodes the writing is magnificent. Passages that spring to mind are the whole of Books I and II, the invocation to light at the beginning of Book III, the description of Adam and Eve in Paradise in Book IV, the quarrel between Adam and Eve after the Fall in Book IX, their subsequent reconciliation in Book X, and the moving end of Book XII when Adam and Eve leave Paradise.

'And justify the ways of God to men'. In stating the theme of *Paradise Lost,* Milton says that his aim is to 'justify the ways of God to men'. His central argument is that God gave man free will, and that man alone was responsible for the Fall.

Not all readers have been convinced by the argument: Blake said that 'Milton was a true poet and of the devil's party without knowing it'; Shelley considered that Milton's Satan was morally superior to Milton's God. (In such discussions, we have to remember that we are dealing with characters in a poem: we are not discussing God and Satan, but two characters who are given those names in *Paradise Lost.*) Many readers have found Satan, especially in Books I and II, a heroic figure in his courage and unwavering defiance in defeat.

But many recent critics have argued that such reactions are misguided, and that the attitudes presented by the poem are completely orthodox, Satan being absolutely evil. Moreover, it is argued, Adam represents a different kind of heroism, a Christian heroism which is superior to military valour.

Part of the difficulty is that Milton makes all his characters talk and behave like human beings, and it is difficult not to react to them as we react to human beings. So we see Satan, not as the principle of absolute evil, but as a wicked man who nevertheless has some admirable qualities. There may therefore be a gap between Milton's intentions and the effect he actually achieves. It is noticeable that his comments on characters do not always correspond to what he in fact shows us. An example of this is the fallen angel Belial, who in the great debate in Book II argues for peace and quietism. Before the speech, Milton comments that Belial's 'thoughts were low,/To vice industrious, but to Nobler deeds/Timorous and slothful'; and after the speech there is a similar disparaging comment, saying that Belial had 'Counsell'd ignoble ease, and peaceful sloth'. But this view is not supported by what Belial actually says; in one place, for example, he argues that, if the fallen angels provoke God, he may destroy them completely:

> And that must end us, that must be our cure,
> To be no more; sad cure; for who would lose,
> Though full of pain, this intellectual being,
> Those thoughts that wander through Eternity,
> To perish rather, swallow'd up and lost
> In the wide womb of uncreated night,
> Devoid of sense and motion?

> (II.145—51)

This is not ignoble sloth, but an assertion of life, of the will to live (and to live the life of the intellect), despite all the pain that living entails.

Similarly, there is sometimes a discrepancy between what Milton says about Adam and Eve, and the way the reader reacts to what they do and say, for example when Adam decides to share Eve's fate (IX.896—999). Most serious of all, Milton introduces God as a speaking character, and one moreover who frequently makes speeches of self-justification: he always seems to be on the defensive, to be making a case. This inevitably provokes the reader into counter-arguments, especially as God often seems a vindictive and tyrannical figure.

Inevitably, too, Hell seems a more interesting place than either Heaven or Paradise. Hell, Milton says, is 'A Universe of death . . . for evil only good' (II.622—3). But, while Satan is away on his expedition to earth, we see the fallen angels in Hell indulging in athletic games and mock battles, singing enchanting songs to the harp, arguing about philosophy, and organising expeditions of exploration (II. 528—629). In Paradise it is difficult for Milton to make life seem interesting, since there is so little that Adam and Eve can do, except a little unnecessary gardening. In the absence of other interests, sexual feeling comes to play a dominant part in Paradise, and it is not surprising that Adam's fall is finally due to his sexual passion for Eve, which he allows to overcome his reason. This, however, does somewhat blur the distinction between Adam unfallen and Adam fallen, since his yielding to Eve at the Fall seems a natural continuation of his normal behaviour.

Mock Heroic and Satiric Epic

Because of the high prestige of the epic form in the neo-classical period, and the magnificent achievement of *Paradise Lost,* quite a few epic poems were written in the eighteenth century, but none of them is distinguished. There are however two remarkable poems by Pope which can be classed as variants of the form: *The Rape of the Lock* (1712) is a Mock Heroic poem, while *The Dunciad* (1742—3) is a satiric epic.

'The Rape of the Lock'

In a Mock Heroic poem, the author takes a commonplace or insignificant episode or theme, and treats it in the grand epic manner, for comic effect. This is what Pope does in *The Rape of the Lock*. The poem arose from a contemporary episode: Lord Robert Petre stole a lock of hair from the head of Arabella Fermor, and this caused a quarrel between the two families. Pope's poem aims to reconcile them by making a joke of the whole affair, and suggesting that a great fuss is being made about something relatively insignificant. The poem is thus not a parody: its aim is not to discredit epic poetry, or make a joke of it. The joke is rather against the fine ladies and gentlemen of London society, and the burlesque of epic a means to this end.

The poem is in five cantos, and incorporates many of the themes and conventions of epic. It begins with a statement of the subject and an appeal to the Muse. It has supernatural characters (often called the 'machinery' of an epic): the heroine, Belinda, is guarded by a band of sylphs, who add great delicacy and charm to the poem. There is a journey — but only in a boat on the Thames. There is a visit to the underworld — to the Cave of Spleen. After the stealing of Belinda's lock by the Baron, there is a great epic battle — between the men and the women. In the battle the lock disappears, and the poem ends with it being carried up to the heavens, where it becomes a comet and there perpetuates Belinda's name. All this is done in a high epic style, though, since it is Pope, it is in neat and witty couplets, not in blank verse. Particularly delightful are the ordinary everyday episodes related in high poetic style — Belinda doing her toilet, the game of cards, the drinking of coffee.

Pope makes frequent use of bathos (anticlimax). In Canto II, Ariel, the leader of the sylphs, tells his followers that some disaster is threatening Belinda, but he does not know what it is:

> Whether the Nymph shall break Diana's Law,   105
> Or some frail China Jar receive a Flaw,
> Or stain her Honour, or her new Brocade,

Forget her Pray'rs, or miss a Masquerade,
Or lose her Heart, or Necklace, at a Ball;
Or whether Heav'n has doom'd that Shock must fall. 110

This series of anticlimaxes suggests that Belinda, and great London ladies in general, have strange values: being unchaste (breaking Diana's law) is on a par with breaking a china vase; getting a stain on her new dress is as serious a matter as staining her honour. And the crowning disaster is that her pet dog (Shock) must fall. The humour, however, is good-natured: there is no sharp critical edge to it, and the atmosphere of the poem is one of gaiety and enjoyment.

'The Dunciad'

The Dunciad lacks the immediate and obvious charm of *The Rape*, and is less easily accessible to the modern reader, but it is a greater poem. It too is Mock Heroic, with all the apparatus of the conventional epic, but it is also satire: it uses humour as a weapon to attack opponents, and to arouse in the reader feelings of scorn and disgust at them. The target is what Pope calls the Dunces — the contemporary poets and critics to whom he is hostile, and whom he considers to be stupid and ungifted. Most of these figures are mere names to the modern reader, which is one reason why the poem is less accessible.

The poem is in four books, and is presided over by a supernatural character of Pope's own invention, the goddess Dullness, to whose empire all the dunces of London belong. She crowns Colley Cibber king of dullness, and holds games in his honour, in the manner of classical epic; the games, however, are decidedly unsavoury ones. The hero also visits the underworld, where he has a vision of the past and future triumphs of dullness.

The poem has enormous power and energy, but the reader often feels that there is something petty about it: Pope is venting his personal malice, denigrating people he dislikes. Moreover, as Johnson pointed out, Pope seemed to believe that poverty was in itself contemptible, something to be ridiculed. Nevertheless, there is much more than mere malignity in the poem: there is a strong concern for civilisation, and a sense of its fragility. This especially comes out in the wonderful passage with which the poem ends, a vision of the empire of Night and Chaos overwhelming the world, destroying the arts, truth, religion, and morality, until universal darkness buries all.

Later Narrative Poetry

The period between the death of Pope and the coming of the Romantics is not notable for narrative poetry. Its best poetry is rather meditative, often with a strong elegiac strain. The one exception is George Crabbe (1754—1832), a narrative poet of considerable distinction.

Crabbe

In fact Crabbe's best work was written in later life, when the Romantic poets were already in full spate: *The Borough* was published in 1810, *Tales* in 1812, and *Tales of the Hall* in 1819. Poetically, however, he belongs to the eighteenth century: he writes in couplets, uses a good deal of eighteenth-century poetic diction, and holds to the Augustan values of decorum, moderation, common sense, and reason. *The Borough,* although it contains narrative passages, is not a narrative poem, but an extensive description of the people and life of Aldeburgh, Crabbe's native town in Suffolk. The *Tales,* however, are a series of narrative poems dealing realistically with contemporary life, the poetic equivalent of short stories. In his preface, Crabbe remarks that a series of tales, as compared with a single long poem, has

> greater variety of incident and more minute display of character, . . . accuracy of description and diversity of scene: in these narratives we pass from gay to grave, from lively to severe, not only without impropriety, but with manifest advantage.

This is a fair claim, and it can be added that Crabbe has a sharp insight into people's motivations and self-deceptions, and a steady moral vision. These tales are gems of minor English poetry.

Wordsworth

The Romantic poets produced a considerable number of narrative poems, and outstanding among them are those of Wordsworth. The more successful ones deal with humble and rustic life. Wordsworth had grown up in the Lake District, and after his disillusionment with the French Revolution he turned to English country life as a source of moral strength, as we have seen in 'Resolution and Independence'. The traditional pieties and values of the countryside are pitted against the rising tide of industrialism in the cities, with its utilitarian ethos and rootless populations. One of the finest of these poems is 'Michael' (1800), a blank verse narrative of about 500 lines.

Wordsworth's 'Michael'. 'Michael' is set in the Lake District, near Grasmere, and concerns an aged shepherd, Michael, his wife Isabel, and the darling son of their old age, Luke. The first half of the poem describes their frugal and industrious life while Luke is growing up, and the emotional link between Michael and the mountain pastures where he lives and works. Then, when Luke is eighteen, there comes a financial disaster, and, to avoid having to sell part of his fields, which he wishes to pass in due course to Luke, Michael sends his son to a prosperous kinsman in London, to repair their fortunes. The day before he goes, Michael takes him to a place where he has assembled a pile of stones to make a new sheepfold, and asks Luke to lay the first stone; the rest of the task will now fall upon Michael alone. Luke departs, and for some months he does well, but then he goes to the bad in 'the dissolute city', and is eventually obliged to flee abroad. Michael is too strong to collapse in the face of disaster, but the meaning has now gone out of his life:

There is a comfort in the strength of love;
'Twill make a thing endurable, which else
Would overset the brain, or break the heart: 450
I have conversed with more than one who well
Remember the old Man, and what he was
Years after he had heard this heavy news.
His bodily frame had been from youth to age
Of an unusual strength. Among the rocks   455
He went, and still looked up to sun and cloud,
And listened to the wind; and, as before,
Performed all kinds of labour for his sheep,
And for the land, his small inheritance.
And to that hollow dell from time to time   460
Did he repair, to build the Fold of which
His flock had need. 'Tis not forgotten yet
The pity which was then in every heart
For the old Man — and 'tis believed by all
That many and many a day he thither went,   465
And never lifted up a single stone.

The verse moves on in a steady even flow, quiet and undra-
matic. There is a remarkable absence of rhetorical or poetic
devices: there is hardly even a metaphor in the whole passage.
The effects are achieved by direct statements, which build up
into a rich and moving story. The references to Michael's
bodily frame and its unusual strength, and to the way he
went among the rocks, and looked to sun and cloud, and
listened to the wind, are all close echoes of phrases used
earlier in the poem, in the initial description of Michael; but
now these qualities merely serve to prolong a life which has
lost its centre. The passage shows the power that can be
achieved by plainness and simplicity, notably in the intense
pathos of the final two lines.

The sheepcote is never completed. Michael dies, and when
Isabel too dies a few years later, the lands are sold and pass
into a stranger's hand. The poem had begun with the pile of
stones (the unfinished sheepfold) seen by the stranger beside
the brook at Greenhead Ghyll, and it ends in the same way;
and this framework distances the whole story into the past.

Wordsworth's 'Prelude'. Although perhaps it is not strictly a narrative poem, we may briefly consider also *The Prelude*. In the Romantic poets, personal experience becomes the central material of poetry, and *The Prelude,* one of the great English poems of modern times, is autobiographical. It is a *spiritual* autobiography: it carries the subtitle 'Growth of a Poet's Mind', and is concerned with the poet's inner life, his mental conflicts, the way he developed into a poet. It was written between 1798 and 1805, but was not published until 1850. This published version had been extensively revised by Wordsworth in later life, and it was not until the present century that the original 1805 text was printed. The account which follows refers to the 1805 version.

The Prelude is a poem of about 8500 lines of blank verse, divided into thirteen books (fourteen in the 1850 version). It begins with an introduction addressed to Coleridge, in which Wordsworth rejoices that, after a long period of stress, he is now free to devote himself to poetry. He then gives an account of his childhood and schooldays in and near the Lake District, and of his life as a student at Cambridge. During a Cambridge vacation comes the first turning-point in his life, the moment when he realises that he is a 'dedicated Spirit' (IV.344), and poetry becomes his vocation. After a digression on the books he had read and what they meant to him, he continues his account of his life in Cambridge, his journey through the Alps, then his residence in London. Book VIII is headed 'Love of Nature leading to love of Mankind', and is the next turning-point: the poet describes how Nature had led him on

> By slow gradations toward human kind
> And to the good and ill of human life.
>
> (VIII.862–3)

Indeed, he now seemed to travel independent of Nature's help, as if he had forgotten her. He then has a period of residence in France, and describes the excitement and hope raised by the French Revolution:

> Bliss was it in that dawn to be alive,
> But to be young was very heaven.
>
> (X. 693–4)

But bliss is followed by disillusionment: later, back in England, it seems to the poet that the Revolution has gone astray, that France has embarked on wars of conquest and a new tyranny; and he has a period of despair and mental conflict. In books XI and XII comes the recovery; the poet's imagination is restored by recourse to Nature, and he regains his faith in mankind.

Wordsworth has obviously imposed a pattern on *The Prelude,* which is highly selective, and is shaped by his view of his own poetic development, the sequence being Love of Nature, Self-dedication to Poetry, Love of Nature leading to Love of Man, Involvement in the French Revolution, Disillusionment and Despair, Recovery with the aid of Nature.

The Prelude contains a good deal of reflection, philosophising, and moral utterance. Its strength, however, lies in its narrative passages, where the poet describes people, episodes, personal experiences. With the Romantic poets, childhood becomes a major theme of literature, and in *The Prelude* Wordsworth's account of his early years is especially vivid. Particularly memorable are two famous passages in Book I, one telling how he borrowed a boat without permission and rowed on Ullswater, only to be taught a lesson by Nature (372—427), the other describing the skating on the frozen lake (452—89). But the whole poem is full of splendid things.

Byron's 'Don Juan'

Byron was famous in his own time for his verse-romances, with their fatal Byronic heroes, but is now prized for his more conversational and satirical works, especially the long narrative poem *Don Juan*. It was unfinished when Byron died in 1824, and the incomplete poem consists of sixteen cantos, written in eight-line stanzas.

The hero of the poem is not the cynical libertine of tradition, but young, sensitive, and generous, a kind of child of nature living according to his impulses. Following an obscurantist education, he breaks out and has an affair with a married woman, Donna Julia; this has a comic fabliau-like climax, which results in Juan being sent on his travels. He is shipwrecked, and has a tender affair with Haidée, the daughter of a pirate; but when the pirate comes home he sells Juan into slavery. In Constantinople he is bought by one of the sultan's wives, and resists her advances. He escapes, and joins the Russian army fighting the Turks. He is seen by the Empress Catherine II and becomes her favourite and her lover. She sends him on an embassy to London, and it is during the visit to London that the poem breaks off. It seems that Byron intended Juan to visit Italy and Germany, and to end up in France during the Revolution; but it is the kind of poem that could go on indefinitely.

The purpose of the travel is satirical, and the centre of interest is often not Juan himself but the societies he visits and the people he meets. Everywhere there is a penetrating yet exuberant observation of human follies, pruderies, and hypocrisies. The satirical effects get greater scope from the double point of view, Byron's and Juan's. Juan has the satirical effectiveness of the innocent, who sees things as they are; Byron himself interposes with long digressions and comments.

The poem deals especially with sex, war, and politics. There is a wide range of material and attitudes: for example, the treatment of sex includes Juan's calf-love for Donna Julia, the idyllic affair with Haidée, the interlude in the Turkish harem, the sensuality of the Empress of Russia, and the hypocrisies of the English marriage-market. The satire on war comes mainly in the powerful description of the siege of Ismail in Cantos 7 and 8; but at moments the reader feels that the poet is *enjoying* the carnage: there is a destructive element in Byron's make-up. Much of the political satire comes in the Russian episode, but it also reflects on England (Russia's ally in the Grand Alliance). In England, it is mainly social satire: we see high society, with its heartlessness, boredom, futility, and hypocrisy. The satirical effects are achieved by ironical commentary, by clever juxtapositions of events and sayings, by shifts of tone and point of view. The method can be seen in miniature when Juan, arriving in England, muses on the law-abidingness and peacefulness of this country, only to have his meditations interrupted by four footpads — 'Damn your eyes, your money or your life'.

Like Chaucer, Byron uses digressions to create atmosphere

and suspense: he often gets his hero into a difficult position, and then leaves him in the air for pages while he digresses on some subject. The style of the poem is the one which Byron had developed in *Beppo* and *The Vision of Judgment*. It is colloquial, irreverent, often flippant, but able to rise and fall at will, though a more serious passage is always liable to be punctured by an anticlimax; there is a disrespectful familiarity, and the use for comic effect of puns, bathos, and humorous rhymes; there is something reckless about it, but it is a wonderfully flexible instrument. The whole work reminds us that Byron is an aristocrat who has become a radical and a rebel: the irreverence, impudence, and devil-may-care recklessness of the Regency lord are carried over into his radicalism; and he is better at destroying than at building.

After Byron

Many nineteenth-century narrative poems, including some by Scott and by Byron himself, are little more than adventure-stories with exotic settings — oriental, classical, medieval. The Middle Ages were particularly popular with later Romantic and Victorian poets, who often present a highly idealised picture of chivalry and knighthood. The legends of ancient Greece were also popular, notably with Keats, who early in his career wrote the long and rather sickly *Endymion* (1818), and later began a classical-style epic called *Hyperion* (1820). Only two books of *Hyperion*, and a fragment of a third, were completed; the style of the poem is rather obviously Miltonic, and Keats was apparently dissatisfied with it. He attempted to recast it, under the title *The Fall of Hyperion: a Dream,* and the opening section of this uncompleted revision is one of the most remarkable things he wrote. Of Keats's three middle-length narrative poems, all published in 1820, 'Lamia' is set in ancient Corinth, 'Isabella' in medieval Florence, and 'The Eve of St Agnes' in a medieval castle or manor-house. Of these three poems, the last is a considerable achievement.

'The Eve of St Agnes'. 'The Eve of St Agnes' has an extra-ordinarily rich sensuousness without being in any way cloying or oppressive. At the beginning of the poem, we not only

see the hare limping through the grass, and the 'frosted breath' of the Beadsman: we also feel the cold, most intensely. And throughout the poem all the reader's senses are brought into play: we see, and hear, and smell, and have tactile sensations, and even taste, and the impressions are conveyed vividly and exactly. Whether it is the 'sculptur'd dead', or Porphyro standing 'Buttress'd from moonlight', or Angela grasping his fingers in her palsied hand, or the elaborate casement in Madeline's bedroom, or the 'poppied warmth' of her sleep, or the tactile experience of her 'blanched linen, smooth, and lavender'd', or the delicates that Porphyro heaps up by her bed, or the flaw-blown sleet pattering on the window-pane — they are all given to us as experiences both rich and precise. The whole is held together by a simple romantic story, and then in the final stanza the whole episode is suddenly distanced, thrown back into a remote past — 'aye, ages long ago/These lovers fled away into the storm'.

Tennyson and after

Tennyson wrote a great deal of narrative poetry, and the settings varied widely, from contemporary England to classical Greece. He too, however, was much attracted to the Middle Ages, and wrote a cycle of stories on King Arthur and his knights, *The Idylls of the King*, published piecemeal between 1857 and 1885. It is a blank-verse poem in twelve books, and as a whole is rather solemn and long-winded, and often moralisingly didactic. It does, however, incorporate a short narrative poem, 'Morte d'Arthur', which Tennyson had published in 1842, and which is one of his finer works. Tennyson was deeply influenced by Keats, and 'Morte d'Arthur' has a Keatsian concreteness and sensuous vividness: we see the 'shining levels' of the lake, and hear the lapping of its waters and the whistling of the wind in the waterflags; we see the sword flashing and circling in the moonlight when Sir Bedivere finally throws it into the lake; we have a superb picture of Bedivere carrying the dying Arthur on his back, striding from ridge to ridge, 'Clothed with his breath, and looking, as he walked,/Larger than human on the frozen hills'. Moreover, the hand that catches the sword, and the queens in black who come to carry Arthur away in a barge, really do seem mysterious.

The Keats–Tennyson poetic tradition continues in the Pre-Raphaelite poets, notably Dante Gabriel Rossetti (1828–82) and William Morris (1834–96), though the writing in the later period is less muscular and more literary, and the general atmosphere more dream-like. The interest in the Middle Ages continues, and Morris's poetry includes the Arthurian 'Defence of Guenevere' (1858) and the long narrative poem *Sigurd the Volsung* (1877), a sign of the growing interest in Germanic mythology.

Recent narrative poetry

In Britain and the United States, long narrative and autobiographical poems have been out of fashion during the last half-century. In general, poets wishing to write something more extended than a lyric have either turned to poetic drama, as both Eliot and Auden did in the 1930s, or have written semi-dramatic poems like Auden's *For the Time Being* (1944) and *The Age of Anxiety* (1947), or have produced sequences of linked lyrics, like Day-Lewis's *The Magnetic Mountain* (1933) and Ted Hughes's *Crow* (1970) and the splendid *Mercian Hymns* (1971) of Geoffrey Hill (1932–).

In other parts of the English-speaking world, however, long narrative and autobiographical poems have been produced even in recent times. In the West Indies, Derek Walcott has published a fine autobiographical poem called *Another Life* (1973), in twenty-three 'chapters'. In Canada, Edwin John Pratt (1882–1964) has written heroic narrative poems, such as *The Titanic* (1935), *Brébeuf and his Brethren* (1940), *Dunkirk* (1941), and *Towards the Last Spike* (1952). In Australia, A. D. Hope has published *Dunciad Minor* (1970), a satiric epic in the manner of Pope. This is a joke-poem, complete with comic notes, but there is also a tradition of serious narrative poetry in Australia, as in *Captain Quiros* (1960) by James Philip McAuley (1917–).

In some countries, local narrative traditions have been influential, and English translations have been made. In India,

P. Lal has translated *The Mahābhārata,* publishing it in monthly parts. In Nigeria, the poet and scholar John Pepper Clark (1935–) has produced a version of *The Ozidi Saga* (1977), translated from the Ijǫ of Ǫkabou Ojobolo. This is a long epic-drama, the performance of which lasts seven evenings, with dance, music, mime, and ritual. The text which Clark translated was recorded at an actual performance. Clark has also written *Ozidi* (1961), a play of his own which draws on the same traditional material.

Dramatic Monologue

In a dramatic monologue, the entire poem is spoken by a single fictional character; it is spoken in a specific situation to some hearer, and the situation and the hearer have to be deduced by the reader from what the character says. In the course of the poem, the speaker reveals his character to the reader, and part of the poet's art lies in making the speaker give himself away without realising it.

The dramatic monologue has a long history, but it was in the Victorian Age that it became a highly developed and distinctive genre, especially in the hands of its most famous practitioner, Robert Browning (1812–89).

Browning

The dramatic monologue is Browning's favourite poetic form, and he offers us a wide variety of characters, some sympathetic and some not, from many different ages and backgrounds. The speaker may be completely egotistical and repulsive, as in 'My Last Duchess' (1842); or pathetically self-deceiving, as in 'Andrea del Sarto' (1855); or a sympathetic scamp, as in 'Fra Lippo Lippi' (1855).

The speaker in this last poem is the fourteenth-century Florentine painter Fra Filippo Lippi, who was a Carmelite monk. The situation is that he has just been stopped in the streets after midnight by the watch (the earlier equivalent of the police), who want to know what a monk is doing out at such an hour. The situation is established in the opening lines of the poem:

I am poor brother Lippo, by your leave!
You need not clap your torches to my face.
Zooks, what's to blame? you think you see a monk!
What, it's past midnight, and you go the rounds,
And here you catch me at an alley's end   5
Where sportive ladies leave their doors ajar?
The Carmine's my cloister: hunt it up,
Do, — harry out, if you must show your zeal,
Whatever rat, there, haps on his wrong hole.

This opening at once gives us the situation: from the highly colloquial manner, and the direct mode of address (*your, you*), we know that somebody is speaking; and then we see the torches being held to the speaker's face, and learn that he is a monk, that it is past midnight, and that he has been caught by the watch in what sounds like a red-light district.

In the continuation, we constantly feel the interplay between Lippi and the watch, as he manoeuvres to justify himself and get out of their hands: he protests at their violent behaviour; drops the name of his patron Cosimo of the Medici to impress them; adopts a mollified patronising air and hands out a quarter-florin for them to drink the health of his house; flatters the leader of the watch for the 'proper twinkle in his eye'. He explains how, after three weeks during carnival-time shut up painting nothing but saints, he had leaned from his window and seen girls scampering by, and, being only flesh and blood, had climbed down and gone after them. The leader of the watch shakes his head at this unbecoming behaviour from a monk.

In response, Lippi launches into an account of his life — how he had been an orphan starving on the streets of Florence, been taken in by the monastery, become a painter. This narrative leads on to a long exposition of Lippi's artistic philosophy. As an observant ragamuffin on the city streets, he had learnt to read people's characters in their faces and postures; and when he had begun drawing and painting, this is what he had gone for. But the Prior of the monastery objected to this naturalistic style:

Paint the soul, never mind the legs and arms!

But Lippi believes that you can only get at the soul through the body. The Biblical story of the creation of Eve teaches us the 'value and significance of flesh'; and we should rejoice at the wonderful physical universe that God created. But his superiors are critical, and Lippi has to clench his teeth and suppress his rage, and keep on painting, sometimes pleasing them, sometimes not. Is it surprising that he should occasionally break out, as tonight? He ends by giving an eloquent description of the next big picture he is going to paint, a vision of God surrounded by angels and saints; the painter himself will appear in it out of a corner, caught up into Heaven by mistake in his monk's things, his old serge gown and rope that goes all round; and he will be taken by the hand, and justified to God, by St Lucy, a sweet young slip of a thing who looks remarkably like the Prior's niece. The poem ends with a handshake and amicable parting.

Tennyson

Some of Tennyson's best poems are also dramatic monologues, though they do not adopt the colloquial style that is found in many of Browning's, and are less dramatic: we do not feel so sharply as in Browning the presence and responses of the person being addressed. In 'Tithonus' (1860) the speaker is the mortal man who was the lover of Aurora, goddess of the dawn; she had obtained for him the gift of eternal life, but had forgotten to specify that he should also have eternal youth. He is now an old man:

> A white-haired shadow roaming like a dream
> The ever-silent spaces of the East.

The poem is spoken to Aurora, and Tithonus begs her to recall her gift, and let him die. But he remembers a saying from his days on earth, 'The Gods themselves cannot recall their gifts', and Aurora's tears make him fear that this is true.

In 'Tithonus' the person addressed is clearly present in the poem, but in 'Ulysses' (1842) this is not so. At line 45 Ulysses addresses his mariners, and the rest of the poem is spoken to them. The earlier lines could be interpreted as also addressed to the mariners, but they could equally well be the speaker's own musings. Moreover, the mariners are not seen reacting to what is said. The poem is therefore a borderline case between meditation and dramatic monologue.

Ulysses is the Latin name for Odysseus, the hero of Homer's *Odyssey*. In Tennyson's poem he is now old, but is restless, and will not remain an 'idle king' among the barren crags of Ithaca:

> I cannot rest from travel: I will drink
> Life to the lees: all times I have enjoyed
> Greatly, have suffered greatly, both with those
> That loved me, and alone; on shore, and when
> Through scudding drifts the rainy Hyades   10
> Vext the dim sea.

But Ulysses wants something more than just travel: he has a yearning

> To follow knowledge like a sinking star,
> Beyond the utmost bound of human thought.

Travel-lust is a symbol for the unquenchable desire of man's spirit for knowledge and experience. Ulysses contrasts himself with his son Telemachus, who will be left to rule Ithaca, a task for which he is eminently fitted. Then he addresses his mariners, who have grown old with him, and calls them to join him in a final voyage, for it is not too late to perform some work of noble note. They cannot prophesy the outcome:

> It may be that the gulfs will wash us down:
> It may be we shall touch the Happy Isles,
> And see the great Achilles, whom we knew.
> Though much is taken, much abides; and though   65
> We are not now that strength which in old days
> Moved earth and heaven; that which we are, we are;
> One equal temper of heroic hearts,
> Made weak by time and fate, but strong in will
> To strive, to seek, to find, and not to yield.   70

It is not the outcome that matters, but the attitudes of the heroes, the determination to confront life to the very end.

Eliot

Three of Eliot's early poems are influenced by the dramatic monologue, though none of them conforms exactly to the type as seen in Browning. The opening line of 'The Love Song of J. Alfred Prufrock' (1917), 'Let us go then, you and I', might be addressed to a silent hearer, or to the reader, but is perhaps better understood as addressed by Prufrock to part of himself, so that the poem becomes soliloquy rather than dramatic monologue. It does however create a character: Prufrock is self-conscious, sensitive, ironic, vulnerable to the fears and embarrassments of life in polite society and yet acutely conscious of its vacuity: he has measured out his life in coffee spoons. In the poem we see Eliot's technique of omitting connecting passages, and of juxtaposing things unlike — the past with the present, the serious with the ludicrous, the beautiful with the grotesque. Prufrock's feelings find expression in images: the lonely men in shirt-sleeves (a reflection of his own different kind of loneliness); the pair of ragged claws scuttling across the floors of silent seas (his desire for the unselfconsciousness of the animal kingdom, and for a protective carapace); his vision of himself as an obtuse attendant lord to Prince Hamlet; the dream of escape to the world of the mermaids under the sea, a dream which is destroyed when 'human voices wake us, and we drown'. The method is akin to that of stream-of-consciousness in the novel: we share in Prufrock's shifting thoughts, moods, feelings.

'The Portrait of a Lady' appeared in the same 1917 volume as 'Prufrock', and is an even finer poem. It is not, however, strict dramatic monologue: the speaker of the poem is not the lady, but a young man whose encounters with her are described; and there is not one scene, but three successive ones, in December, in the summer when the lilacs are in bloom, and finally in October. Moreover, although the character of the lady is superbly conveyed by what she says, the interest of the poem lies equally in the embarrassed and uncertain responses of the young man who is the narrator.

Both these poems combine wit with a fundamental serious-ness. The third of these early monologues, 'Gerontion' (1920), is not witty, but it is the most powerful and moving of the three. The speaker is 'an old man in a dry month,/ Being read to by a boy, waiting for rain'. There is no sign of a hearer who reacts to what he says, so the poem is again soliloquy rather than dramatic monologue. The memories and meditations of the old man have no logical or narrative sequence, and build up, not to a character, but to a vision of a civilisation, its history and its decay. It points clearly for-ward to *The Waste Land* (1922).

Recent examples

The dramatic monologue continues to be influential. Con-siderable use has been made of it by the American poet Robert Lowell (1917—), for example in his volume *The Mills of the Kavanaughs* (1951). The Nigerian poet Wole Soyinka, in his 'Telephone Conversation', gives a new twist to the form by letting us hear one end of a telephone conversation (though some of the utterances from the other end are relayed to us by the speaker). The poem is not strictly a dramatic monologue, since it has a narrative element, but it is clearly influenced by the form. The poet is in a telephone-box in England, speaking to a landlady from whom he wishes to rent a room, and the landlady's attitudes and character emerge to the reader. The poem is an extremely amusing exposure of genteel suburban racialism.

A more substantial use of the form has been made by the Ugandan poet Okot p'Bitek (1931—). His *Song of Lawino* (1966) is a long poem in thirteen sections, and constitutes an extended dramatic monologue. The speaker, Lawino, addresses her husband Ocol, whom she attacks for his westernised habits and attitudes; the poem is a diatribe in favour of traditional African values and modes of behaviour. The sequel, *Song of Ocol* (1970), is her husband's mocking reply, which is rhetorically brilliant but which lacks Lawino's fire and passion.

Okot's poems are the first English-language poems of consequence in East Africa, and they have encouraged other

East Africans to follow his example, and in particular to write long poems.

The Ballad

All the poetry we have so far considered has been the product of a dominant social and cultural group in English society. This is even true of poetry in periods of social conflict, like the Civil Wars of the seventeenth century. Milton, a spokesman for revolutionary Puritanism, is in the opposite camp to Cavalier poets such as Lovelace. But Milton's poetry, with its dependence on the classical past and on neo-classical theory, is nevertheless part of an élite tradition of English literature.

But alongside such writing, there has always been a popular tradition of literature, produced by and for the ordinary people of England. It may have drawn on upper-class literature for material, but is clearly distinct from it in its attitudes and styles. It has taken many forms, for example proverbs, fireside stories, political lampoons, mummers' plays. One continuing form has been folk-song in its various manifestations. Folk-song is a variety of oral literature; but the popular tradition and oral literature are by no means synonymous. Some oral literature has not been an expression of popular culture: the Homeric epics, for example, are aristocratic works, produced for a military élite. Conversely, some popular literature has been in written form, like sixteenth-century jest-books and almanacs.

Oral literature

When we call something oral literature we can mean more than one thing. We may refer to *performance*: if a work is not normally read but heard (sung or recited) we may call it oral literature, irrespective of its origins. Or we may refer to *transmission*: if a work is passed from generation to generation by word of mouth, not by being written down, we can call it oral literature. Literature which is orally transmitted usually gets changed in the process of transmission, but this is not invariably so: in Somali literature, works by known authors are passed on orally, quite unchanged, from generation to generation. Or thirdly we may refer to *composition*: some works, such as the Serbo-Croat epics of Yugoslavia, and the Yoruba praise-poems (*oríkì*) of Nigeria, are actually composed by the performer at the moment of performance. A Yoruba *oríkì*-chant, a praise-poem addressed to an individual, is different every time it is performed, even by the same performer. It contains a number of recognisable units, and incorporates a great deal of standard material (proverbs, formulaic phrases, and so on); but the units which are chosen, the order in which they are performed, and the precise expression given to each, are all determined spontaneously by the performer while she performs.

English folk-songs are oral literature in the sense that they are *performed,* and in the sense that they are often *transmitted* orally (though folk-singers in fact often pick up songs from all sorts of sources, and do not necessarily confine themselves to ones they have received by oral tradition). English folk-songs, however, are not *composed* orally, as *oríkì* are. It is true that the song varies from performance to performance, and also is gradually changed in the process of oral tradition, but this is accidental and unconscious: the folk-singer is performing a song he knows, not inventing a new one. It is probable that some English folk-songs (though not all) were originally composed orally at some remote date in the past; but in the periods for which we have firm knowledge there is no evidence for oral composition.

Traditional ballads

Traditional ballads are folk-songs of a particular kind, namely short narrative ones, ranging in length from about twenty lines to about 150. Like other folk-songs, they have been transmitted orally from generation to generation, but periodically the words of particular ballads have been written down, so that we have texts of them from earlier periods. The oldest surviving text of a traditional ballad dates from the thirteenth century; quite a few are recorded in the fifteenth century, and thereafter large numbers. In the later eighteenth century, literary people became interested in the popular ballad, and in 1765 Bishop Thomas Percy published his *Reliques of Ancient English Poetry,* a collection of popular poems including many ballads. The definitive collection of traditional ballads is F. J Child's great five-volume work, *English and Scottish Popular Ballads* (1882–98), which records 305 different ballads. Child gives variant versions of each ballad, because a ballad, unlike an 'art-song', has no single definitive form, but changes in the course of transmission: pieces drop out, because a performer forgets them; pieces belonging to a different ballad get inserted; and variations of phraseology occur, even with a single performer. Child's collection is based on written texts, whereas Cecil Sharp (1859–1924), the great English collector of folk-songs, went round and took down the songs from the lips of their performers.

'The Wife of Usher's Well'

Many of the finest ballads are Scots, perhaps because the social conditions for their survival continued longer in Scotland than in England, where settled rural communities were disrupted by the Industrial Revolution as early as the eighteenth century. Our first example of a traditional ballad is 'The Wife of Usher's Well', which was first recorded in Sir Walter Scott's collection, *Minstrelsy of the Scottish Border* (1802–3). It begins as follows:

> There lived a wife at Usher's Well,
> And a wealthy wife was she;
> She had three stout and stalwart sons,
> And sent them o'er the sea.

> They hadna [had not] been a week from her,   5
> A week but barely ane [one],
> When word came to the carline wife [old woman]
> That her three sons were gane [gone, dead].

> They hadna been a week from her,
> A week but barely three,   10
> When word came to the carlin wife
> That her sons she'd never see.

'I wish the wind may never cease,
   Nor fashes [storms] in the flood,
Till my three sons come hame [home] to me,   15
   In earthly flesh and blood.'

The stanza used is extremely common in ballads, so much so
that it is often called 'ballad metre'. It is a four-line stanza,
alternately four-foot and three-foot, with the second and
fourth lines rhyming. Alternatively, it can be analysed as two
seven-foot lines, rhyming.

The ballad plunges straight into the story: there is no
scene-setting, description of the Wife's farmstead, account of
her circumstances or previous history, or anything of that
kind. The narrative leaps from point to point, without linking
passages: we leap from the sending away of the sons to the
Wife receiving news of their death; and then the Wife leaps
into speech, without any introduction ('She said', or anything like that). This leaping on from point to point in the
story is typical of the narrative movement of ballads. When
the ballad has leapt to a new point in the story, it may well
then move in a rather leisurely way, and in particular it may
make considerable use of repetition: Stanza 3 of 'The Wife of
Usher's Well' is almost identical with Stanza 2, with just a
few key-words changed to move the story forward. This is
called 'incremental repetition', and is common in the ballads.
This double characteristic of ballad narrative movement, the
leaping on and the use of repetition, has been felicitously
described by one critic as 'leaping and lingering'.

The poem continues as follows:

It fell about the Martinmass,
   When nights are lang and mirk [long and dark],
The carlin wife's three sons came hame,
   And their hats were o' the birk [birch].   20

It neither grew in syke [stream] nor ditch,
   Nor yet in ony sheugh [furrow, trench];
But at the gates o' Paradise,
   That birk grew fair eneugh [enough].

'Blow up the fire, my maidens,   25
   Bring water from the well;
For a' [all] my house shall feast this night,
   Since my three sons are well.'

And she has made to them a bed,
   She's made it large and wide,   30
And she's taen [taken] her mantle her about,
   Sat down at the bed-side.

The story leaps on again, to Martinmass (the feast of St
Martin, 11 November), when the three sons come home.
Clearly, it is their mother's curse in Stanza 4 which has
brought them back, the magical power of the spoken word.
The word *carlin(e)*, used of the Wife in lines 7 and 11, meant
'old woman', but could also mean 'witch', so perhaps we are
to understand that the Wife has more than ordinary powers.
The sons return, but they are dead, as we know from the
birch (birch-bark?) of which their hats are made: the birch
was a sacred tree associated with the dead. The sons are dead,
but they are 'In earthly flesh and blood', as the Wife had
wished in her curse: in the ballads, the dead do not usually
return as ghosts or spectres, but in bodily form. Hence the
Wife does not realise that they are dead, but believes that
her 'three sons are well' (28); but this has a terrible irony,
for there was a proverbial phrase, 'The dead are well'.
   The ballad ends as follows:

Up then crew the red, red cock,
   And up and crew the gray;
The eldest to the youngest said,   35
   'Tis time we were away.

The cock he hadna crawd but once,
   And clapp'd his wings at a',
When the youngest to the eldest said,
   Brother, we must awa.   40

'The cock doth craw, the day doth daw [dawn],
  The channerin [gnawing] worm doth chide;
Gin [if] we be mist out o' our place,
  A sair [grievous] pain we maun bide [must suffer].

'Fare ye weel, my mother dear!   45
  Fareweel to barn and byre!
And fare ye weel, the bonny lass
  That kindles my mother's fire!'

The crowing of the cock signals the dawn, when the dead are
obliged to return to their 'place'. The final two stanzas are
most moving: the horror of death is conveyed by the 'channerin worm' (42), and an emotional lift is given at the climax
of the poem by the internal rhyme in line 41 (*craw, draw*).
The final stanza evokes intensely the pathos of the longing of
the dead for the things of life — the mother, the farmstead,
and above all the 'bonny lass'.

   There is usually no authorial comment in a ballad, and this
may cause problems of interpretation. It could well be argued
that the Wife *does* know that her sons are dead, because of
the birch; and this would make the poem rather different.
Nor is there any authorial explanation about the status of the
dead sons, or where they have come from: the sixth stanza
suggests that they have come from Paradise (Heaven),
whereas the 'sair pain' of the eleventh rather indicates Purga-
tory; the 'channerin worm' instead suggests that they will
return to the grave; while the opening stanzas of the poem
give the impression (though they do not say so) that the sons
were lost in a storm at sea, and so might have no grave. This
kind of inconsistency, in which pagan ideas have a veneer of
Christianity, is common in the ballads.

'The Cruel Mother'

Not all ballads use 'ballad metre', and some have refrains, as
in the following short ballad:

She sat down below a thorn,
  Fine flowers in the valley
And there she has her sweet babe born
  And the green leaves they grow rarely.

'Smile na [not] sae [so] sweet, my bonnie babe,
And [if] ye smile sae sweet, ye'll smile me dead.'

She's taen [taken] out her little pen-knife,
And twinn'd [deprived] the sweet babe o [of] its life.

She's howket [dug] a grave by the light o the moon,
And there she's buried her sweet babe in.

As she was going to the church,
She saw a sweet babe in the porch.

'O sweet babe, and [if] thou were mine,
I wad cleed [would clothe] thee in the silk so fine.'

'O mother dear, when I was thine,
You did na prove to me sae kind.'

Again, there is no explanation of the background to the
story, and no comment, but we assume that the child is illegitimate and the mother unmarried. The poem has a wonderfully compressed, laconic quality, especially in the economy
of its final two lines. The absence of comment leaves it open
to the reader to interpret the ending as an example of the
supernatural, or as a hallucination produced by conscience
and post-natal trauma.

In performance, the refrains are repeated with each stanza.
It may be thought that the refrain is a meaningless one,
unrelated to the content of the poem. It could be argued,
however, that it introduces a contrast between human
society and nature: the mother is subject to the moral
censure of society, and this leads to her terrible act, whereas
the flowers and trees simply grow and reproduce, untouched
by moral codes.

Ballad diction

Oral literature tends to use a diction in which there are many
stock phrases or formulae. This is especially true of literature
which is composed orally, but is also a feature of much orally

performed literature, including the ballads. Many of the phrases in 'The Wife of Usher's Well' can be found in other ballads, either in identical form or in a very similar one: 'They hadna been a week from her' (5), 'It fell about the Martinmass' (17), 'Up then crew the red, red cock' (33). The ballads are fond of bright simple colours and of bright metals. In 'Sir Patrick Spens', the king is drinking 'the blude-red wine'. In 'Earl Brand', Lady Margaret rides on a milk-white steed; she thinks she sees the earl's blood in the water, but he says it is merely the reflection of his scarlet cloak. In 'The Twa Sisters', the younger sister has cherry cheeks and yellow hair. The dead knight in 'The Twa Corbies' has bonny blue eyes and golden hair. The false mermaid in 'Clerk Colvill' has a milk-white hand and a grass-green sleeve. In 'Fair Annie', the masts of the bride's ship shine like silver in one stanza, and like gold in the next. In 'Child Waters', the hero has a milk-white steed, while Ellen has a green gown and a girdle of gold. In 'The Demon Lover', the masts of the ship are of beaten gold. In 'Thomas Rhymer', the Queen of Elfland wears a skirt of grass-green silk, and rides a milk-white horse with fifty-nine silver bells on its mane. In 'Tam Lin', Janet has a green kirtle and yellow hair, as the poem frequently reminds us; when she rescues Tam Lin from the Queen of Fairies, she pulls him from his milk-white steed and covers him with her green mantle. Even in these few examples, some of the favourite ballad-phrases emerge clearly.

Other traditional ballads

The two ballads we have examined are both tragic, and this is true of many of the finest ballads. The commonest themes are violent death, sex (especially adultery), and the super-natural. 'Sir Patrick Spens' deals with death by drowning at sea, 'The Demon Lover' with the supernatural, 'The Unquiet Grave' with death and the supernatural. Many ballads tell a love-story which ends tragically with violent death: such are 'Earl Brand', 'Clerk Saunders', and 'Little Musgrave and Lady Barnard'. Some, like 'The Battle of Otterbourne', describe death in battle.

Not all ballads, however, are tragic. There are love-stories with a happy ending, like 'Young Beichan' and 'Fair Annie', and stories of the supernatural with a happy ending, like 'Tam Lin'. There are riddling ballads, in which a character successfully answers a series of riddles in order to escape from some dreadful fate: such are 'King John and the Abbot' and 'Riddles wisely expounded'.

Most ballads have the kind of narrative structure seen in 'The Wife of Usher's Well', with its characteristic leaping and lingering. But some ballads, like 'Lord Randal' and 'Edward', consist simply of dialogue between two characters; in the course of the dialogue the hearer learns of the events which have taken place, and at the end realises what the upshot is going to be. These are called 'situation ballads'. The best examples do not even contain introductory expressions like 'he said', but simply give the utterances of the two characters alternately. So in 'Edward', the mother and Edward speak in turn; she asks him why his sword is dripping with blood; after a number of false answers, which she rejects, he says that he has killed his father; we learn that he proposes to abandon his home and family and go into exile; the poem ends with Edward cursing his mother, and revealing that it was she who had instigated the murder. This, with its hypnotic repetitions and inexorable refrains, is one of the most powerful of all ballads. It is also a reminder of the international links of the ballads, for versions of what is essentially the same poem are to be found in Denmark, Sweden, Finland, and the United States.

Minstrel ballads and broadside ballads

The ballads we have been considering are folk-songs, sung by ordinary people just for the love of singing. But there were also professional ballads, sung and perhaps composed by minstrels. Minstrel-ballads are less impersonal than folk-ballads, and may include scene-setting and direct address to the audience. Examples are 'Chevy Chase', and the English ballads about Robin Hood from the fifteenth and sixteenth centuries. There was mutual influence between minstrel- and folk-ballads, and between both these and printed ballads.

In Shakespeare's *Winter's Tale* (IV.4), the pedlar Autolycus sells to his customers what they call ballads; they are poems to be sung to well-known tunes, mainly telling of marvellous and improbable events. These are plainly what we now call Broadside Ballads, poems printed on one side of a single sheet of paper, intended for singing. The broadside ballads include some versions of both minstrel- and folk-ballads, but also songs of many other kinds, including political polemic and accounts of topical happenings, like famous hangings. Many are by known authors, and they continued to be extremely popular right into the nineteenth century.

Touched-up ballads

When the literary world became interested in ballads and began making collections of them, there was a tendency for people to polish up and 'improve' the ballads they published. Sir Walter Scott admitted that, in his *Ministrelsy of the Scottish Border,* he had sometimes combined parts of different versions of the same poem, and polished up the originals. This had probably happened earlier, in the eighteenth century: just as Burns touched up folk-lyrics, so other Scots poets seem to have touched up ballads, and it is often these polished versions that have come down to us. 'Edward' is probably an example: it is undoubtedly a traditional ballad by origin, but the complexity of its metrical pattern and the neatness of its overall structure strongly suggest the hand of the improver. 'Sir Patrick Spens', first recorded in Percy's *Reliques* (1765), may be another example. Consider the stanza describing the Scots noblemen when the ship sank:

O our Scots nobles were richt laith [extremely unwilling]
    To weet their cork-heild schoone [shoes] ;
But lang owre [long before] a' the play were playd,
    Thair hats they swam aboone [above].

This dry, ironic comment on the Scots dandies and their fate is very fine, but is not in accord with the usual impersonality of the traditional ballad, and sounds like the work of an improver. But it is immediately followed (in Percy's version) by three stanzas which have an absolutely authentic ring: the wonderful ending of the poem, with the ladies waiting at home for the men who will never return, while Sir Patrick Spens lies fifty fathoms down, 'Wi the Scots lords at his feit'.

Literary ballads

At one time the ballad was despised in literary circles, but from the middle of the eighteenth century, as interest grew in popular literature, it became admired, and was often imitated by 'official' or 'educated' poets. From the time of the Romantics, ballad influence is common: Wordsworth and Coleridge called their seminal volume *Lyrical Ballads* (1798); and later examples of 'literary ballads' include Scott's 'Lochinvar', Keats's 'La Belle Dame sans Merci', Tennyson's 'The Revenge', Browning's 'Hervé Riel', D. G. Rossetti's 'The Blessèd Damozel', the *Barrack Room Ballads* of Rudyard Kipling (1865–1936), Auden's 'Miss Gee', 'James Honeyman', and 'Victor', together with innumerable poems by lesser-known authors. None of these poems, indeed, could for an instant be taken to be a genuine traditional ballad, and they differ widely from one another, ranging from Scott's simple narrative to Rossetti's preciosity. All of them, however, show in one way or another the influence of the ballad on 'official' literature.

In the older Commonwealth countries, in the period before full independence, the ballad was often cultivated as a means of expressing local patriotism and democratic feeling. Ballads about local folk-heroes, especially rebels or outcasts from established society, were felt to represent local attitudes, in contrast to metropolitan literature, which was seen as the property of an alien élite. The ballad movement was particularly strong in Australia. First, traditional folk-songs were adapted to local conditions. These 'Old Bush Songs' were usually against law and order, their heroes often being transported criminals ('Jim Jones at Botany Bay', 'The girl with the black velvet band'), or poachers ('Van Diemen's Land'), or bushrangers ('Bold Jack Donahoe', 'The wild colonial boy', 'Frank Gardiner', 'Brave Ben Hall'). Then, in the 1890s, urban poets began to write 'bush ballads' in imitation of these popular songs, as part of a nationalist and radical movement. Leading figures were A. B. ('Banjo') Paterson (1864—1941), who made a collection of Old Bush Songs, and whose own ballads include 'Clancy of the Overflow', 'The Man from Ironbark', and (perhaps) 'Waltzing Matilda'; and Henry Lawson (1867—1922), who produced such ballads as 'Talbragar', 'Ballad of the Drover', and 'The Lights of Cobb and Co.'. The ballads laid great stress on pioneering independence of spirit and on male comradeship. The Bush Ballad movement flourished from the 1890s to the 1930s. A journal is often central to a movement of this kind, and in this case the role was performed by the Sydney periodical *The Bulletin*, founded in 1880.

'The Ancient Mariner'

Of all English poems showing strong ballad-influence, the greatest is *The Rime of the Ancient Mariner,* one of Coleridge's few contributions to *Lyrical Ballads* (1798). It is about the supernatural, but also about a good deal more, for it deals with profound moral and spiritual problems and experiences, even if these cannot be reduced to a simple schema. Its story deals with evil-doing, retribution, spiritual suffering, regeneration, and final expiation.

The poem, which is in seven parts, opens in splendid ballad style, plunging into the action and then leaping into speech:

> It is an ancient Mariner,
> And he stoppeth one of three.
> 'By thy long grey beard and glittering eye,
> Now wherefore stopp'st thou me?
>
> The Bridegroom's doors are opened wide,   5
> For I am next of kin;
> The guests are met, the feast is set:
> May'st hear the merry din.'

But the Wedding Guest's protests are to no avail: he is spellbound by the Mariner's eye, and has to sit and listen to his story, which is the substance of the poem. The wedding, with its suggestion of love, sociability, and celebration, is in contrast to the life of the Mariner, who is an outcast and a wanderer. The wedding, with its 'merry din', also represents ordinary everyday life, in contrast to the extraordinary supernatural and spiritual world of the Mariner's voyage. We are periodically reminded of the Wedding-Guest framework throughout the poem, and the contrasts that it implies are kept fresh in our minds.

The Mariner relates how the fateful voyage had begun in a light-hearted mood, and the ship had sailed southwards in fair weather, until it had crossed the equator. Then it was driven southwards by a storm, until it reached the Antarctic:

> And now there came both mist and snow,
> And it grew wondrous cold:
> And ice, mast-high, came floating by,
> As green as emerald.
>
> And through the drifts the snowy clifts   55
> Did send a dismal sheen:
> Nor shapes of men nor beasts we ken —
> The ice was all between.

This is a thrilling piece of natural description, but the second stanza also conveys a sense of menace. It is now that the Albatross appears, and is welcomed by the mariners and fed by them; the ice splits, the helmsman steers the ship through the gap, and they sail northwards with a good wind behind. The Albatross accompanies them, coming every day 'for food or play', for nine days. Then comes the momentous deed on which the whole poem turns:

> 'God save thee, ancient Mariner!
> From the fiends, that plague thee thus! —   80
> Why look'st thou so?' — With my cross-bow
> I shot the Albatross.

The killing of the Albatross is an act of wanton destruction; no motive is given for it, no excuse ever offered. From it stem the disasters that befall the crew at the hands of super-

natural agents. At the simplest level, the killing of the Albatross can be seen as a sin against Nature, for which Nature
exacts retribution: the 'daemon' who punishes them is
clearly a nature-spirit. But there are suggestions that the
Albatross represents more than this: when it first appears,
the mariners welcome it 'As if it had been a Christian soul'
(65); later, when they are suffering from drought, the Albatross is hung round the Ancient Mariner's neck 'Instead of
the cross' (141–2); and one of the spirit-voices declares that
the Albatross had *loved* the Ancient Mariner (404). These
are only hints, but they make the reader feel that the Ancient
Mariner has committed some terrible sacrilegious act.

For a time, however, things seem to go well; in Part 2, the
ship sails on northward, and there is even a sense of adven-
ture and exhilaration:

> The fair breeze blew, the white foam flew,
> The furrow followed free;
> We were the first that ever burst   105
> Into that silent sea.

This suggests the excitement of the Discoveries of the sixteenth
and seventeenth centuries, about which Coleridge was an
avid reader, but also hints at spiritual exploration, the ventur-
ing into unknown realms of experience. But when the ship
reaches the equator it is becalmed; they run out of water, and
suffer agonies of thirst:

> Day after day, day after day,   115
> We stuck, nor breath nor motion;
> As idle as a painted ship
> Upon a painted ocean.

> Water, water, every where
> And all the boards did shrink;   120
> Water, water, every where,
> Nor any drop to drink.

> The very deep did rot: O Christ!
> That ever this should be!
> Yea, slimy things did crawl with legs   125
> Upon the slimy sea.

Nature, formerly so beautiful, has become grotesque and horri-
fying; and the external world mirrors the inner world, the
spiritual horror of the Mariner. Some of the crew learn in
dreams about the Spirit that is plaguing them; he has
followed them 'From the land of the mist and the snow'
(134). None of them can speak, for lack of water, but the
Mariner has evil looks from the rest of the crew, who know
that he is responsible for their sufferings.

In Part 3, a supernatural ship appears, containing two
spectral figures, Death and Life-in-Death. They dice for the
crew, and Life-in-Death wins the Ancient Mariner. The rest of
the crew drop dead in turn, each cursing the Ancient Mariner
with his eye.

In Part 4, the Ancient Mariner's spiritual agony continues,
and he wishes to die, but cannot. He cannot pray; his heart is
dry as dust; and the dead men still look at him as when they
died. But in this section too comes the Mariner's release from
his agony. It is anticipated in a striking change in the mood
and movement of the verse:

> The moving Moon went up the sky,
> And no where did abide:
> Softly she was going up,   265
> And a star or two beside —
>
> Her beams bemocked the sultry main,
> Like April hoar-frost spread;
> But where the ship's huge shadow lay,
> The charmèd water burnt alway   270
> A still and awful red.

This has a wonderful serenity, and the movement of the
moon and stars suggests a beneficent cosmic order. It has
often been pointed out that, in *The Ancient Mariner,* the sun
tends to be a destructive force, while the moon represents
spiritual illumination (as in 'Frost at Midnight'): it is the
'bloody Sun, at noon' (112) that torments the mariners
when they are becalmed, and now it is by moonlight that
spiritual healing comes to the Mariner. He watches the water-
snakes moving in the shadow of the ship, and admires their

beauty, their rich colours, their golden tracks; and the
moment of release comes when he blesses them:

> O happy living things! no tongue
> Their beauty might declare:
> A spring of love gushed from my heart,
> And I blessed them unaware: 285
> Sure my kind saint took pity on me,
> And I blessed them unaware.

The power to love has returned to the Mariner, and the
natural world is again beautiful; he finds that he can pray,
and the Albatross falls off his neck and sinks into the sea. It
has often been pointed out that the Mariner is a passive
character: things happen to him. Even the killing of the
Albatross, unmotivated as it is, seems like something that
befalls him. And now his release too just happens: he blesses
them *unaware.*

In Part 5, the Mariner sleeps, and when he wakes he finds
that it has rained, and everything is wet. Here again the
physical world mirrors the spiritual: the Mariner's spiritual
aridity has ended. But, although his redemption has begun,
he still has a long process of penance to undergo. A band of
angelic spirits animate the bodies of the dead crew, and they
sail the ship:

> The body of my brother's son   341
> Stood by me, knee to knee:
> The body and I pulled at one rope,
> But he said nought to me.

This gruesome episode underlines the Mariner's responsibility
towards the rest of the crew; he can now join in social labour
only with a body, not with his nephew. At dawn, the angelic
spirits leave the bodies of the crew, to sounds which prefigure
the Mariner's ultimate return home, for the associations are
English: the sky-lark (359), the hidden brook in the leafy
month of June (369–70).

In Part 6, the Mariner in a trance hears two nature-spirits
discussing what has happened to him. When he awakes, the

ship is sailing gently by moonlight, and the curse in the dead men's eyes is finally expiated. With sudden joy, the Mariner realises that the ship is sailing into his home harbour, from which she had set out; they had set out gaily by daylight, but he returns by moonlight: the everyday world has been replaced by one of strange spiritual knowledge. A boat approaches the ship, carrying the Hermit; the Mariner hopes for absolution from him: he will 'wash away/The Albatross's blood' (511–12).

In Part 7, as the Hermit's boat approaches, the ship suddenly splits with a loud and dreadful sound, and sinks like lead. On shore, the Mariner asks the Hermit to shrive him; at once, he is torn with the agony which forces him to recount his whole story. And periodically, he tells the Wedding Guest, this happens to him again. He wanders from land to land, and has strange power of speech; when he sees the person to whom he must retell his story, he is compelled to do so, and his auditor is compelled to listen.

The Mariner makes explicit the way in which the physical events of the story have been analogues of spiritual ones:

> O Wedding-Guest! this soul hath been
> Alone on a wide wide sea:
> So lonely 'twas, that God himself
> Scarce seemèd there to be.   600

He tags on a little moral to his story ('He prayeth well, who loveth well . . .') (612–17), which may seem a little too pat, too much like an attempt to summarise the rich suggestiveness of the poem into a Sunday-school aphorism; but it is, after all, a dramatic utterance: it is the Mariner speaking, not the poet.

The whole poem is one of great power and of haunting beauty. The natural descriptions are superb, but they are also the expression of inner experiences of extraordinary intensity.

4 *Themes and Topics*

There are no intrinsically 'poetic' subjects: poetry can be
written about anything whatever, and English poets have
ranged widely through the universe, through human affairs,
through human knowledge. It is true, however, that certain
subjects have been particularly popular, including sexual love,
nature, religion, public affairs, and death; and something will
now be said about the ways in which these major topics have
been treated.

Love Poetry

The theme of love is often handled in narrative poems, an
outstanding example being Chaucer's large-scale work *Troilus
and Criseyde*. More typically, however, it is a subject for lyric
poetry. Many love-lyrics are of a fairly obvious kind which
can occur in different periods. In the delightful fourteenth-
century lyric 'Alysoun', the poet rejoices in the coming of
Spring and in his love for Alysoun, expresses his longing for
her, and praises her beauty. In addition, a poet may assert his
undying loyalty, as Burns does in 'My love is like a red red
rose', or express his yearning for the beloved when they are
separated, as in the anonymous 'Western wind, when wilt
thou blow?' (*c.* 1500). Such themes are perennial, but there
are other ways of treating love which are more stylised.

Sixteenth-century conventions

In many sixteenth-century love-poems, and especially in the
sonnet sequences, there are conventions both of attitude and

of style. These go back partly to the courtly poetry of the Middle Ages, and partly to Petrarch and his Italian and French imitators. The lady addressed by the poet is usually unresponsive, even cruel: she is cold and chaste. The poet places her on a pedestal, worships her, hardly dares to approach her; he treasures the slightest favour she does him, and is terrified by her frown: her eye has power to kill. Her beauty is often described in terms of lilies, roses, precious stones, ivory, gold, and so on. There are common images to describe the poet's feelings; two of them, derived from Petrarch himself, are seen in the opening lines of a Wyatt sonnet:

> I find no peace, and all my war is done,
> I fear and hope, I burn and freeze like ice.

The conceit of the lover simultaneously burning and freezing is developed into a whole poem, the anonymous 'Thule, the period of cosmography', set to music by Thomas Weelkes (*c.* 1575—1623). An example of the conventional description of the lady's beauty is provided by Sonnet 15 in Spenser's *Amoretti* (1595), which compares various parts of her body to sapphires, rubies, pearls, ivory, gold, and silver.

Poetry of experience

In contrast to such stylised poetry is poetry concerned with the experience of love. The poet does not describe the lady, or praise her, but shows what loving her is like. A poet may write poems of both kinds: Wyatt writes Petrarchan poems, but also 'They flee from me'. In the first stanza of this, with its partially submerged comparison of the women to shy birds or animals, the poet remembers the past, when many women had loved him. In the second stanza, he recalls with intense nostalgia a particular episode of love-making. In the third, he considers his present abandoned plight, and the lady's 'strange fashion of forsaking'. It is the second stanza especially which creates vividly the experience of loving.

In Sonnet 130 ('My mistress' eyes are nothing like the sun'), Shakespeare laughs at the conventional description of the beloved. His mistress's lips are not as red as coral, her breasts are not like snow, there are no roses in her cheeks, her voice is not as pleasing as music. And yet this derision of convention is twisted round in the final couplet to give a conventional conclusion:

> And yet by heaven I think my love as rare,
> As any she [woman] belied with false compare
> [comparison].

Shakespeare's sonnets, which were published in 1609 but probably written in the 1590s, are pre-eminently explorations of the poet's experience of loving, in the tangled three-cornered relationship between the poet, the beautiful young man, and the faithless dark woman. In the best of them there is an honesty, a profundity of insight, an intensity of feeling, and a realisation of experience in language, which set them apart from all other Elizabethan sonnet sequences.

Donne, too, is pre-eminently a poet of experience. In the *Songs and Sonets*, he ranges widely over different kinds of experience and attitude: cynical promiscuity ('The Indifferent'), wondering experience of new love ('The Good Morrow'), joy in a continuing love ('The Anniversary'), despair of fulfilment ('Twicknam Garden'), grief at parting ('A Valediction: of Weeping'), complete desolation of loss ('A nocturnal upon St Lucy's day'), vindictive hostility to somebody formerly loved ('The Apparition'), exploration of the relationship between body and soul in love ('The Ecstasy'), and much more. This is one of the greatest collections of love-poems in the language.

Married love

Some of Donne's finest love-poems were almost certainly addressed to his wife, but this fact is not mentioned in them, and is indeed irrelevant. Some sixteenth-century love-poems on the contrary are clearly addressed to a married woman who is not the poet's wife: the Stella of Sidney's *Astrophel and Stella* was Lady Rich. There are also poems which celebrate married love, and these are especially likely to be written by poets with strongly Protestant sympathies, such as

Spenser in the sixteenth century and Milton in the seventeenth.
  Spenser's two finest shorter poems are both wedding-
celebrations. 'Prothalamion' (1596) celebrates the marriage
in London of two young noblewomen, who are figured in the
poem as swans swimming along the Thames. The poem is in
long stanzas, each of them ending with a famous refrain
which runs (with small variations):

> Against the Bridal day, which is not long:
> Sweet Thames run softly, till I end my song.

'Epithalamion' (1595) celebrates Spenser's own wedding. It,
too, is in long stanzas with a refrain. Its structure is chronological, tracing out the events of the wedding-day, with
mythological amplifications. It begins before dawn, with an
invocation to the sun to wake the poet's beloved, and to
nymphs to help to deck her. She awakes to happy bird-song,
and is prepared for the wedding. The minstrels play merry
music, and she comes out 'with portly pace'; the poet praises
her beauty, and the beauty of her mind. The temple gates are
opened wide for her, and she stands before the altar for the
wedding-ceremony. She is brought home with joy and jollity,
and the young men of the town ring the bells. Night comes,
and the bride is taken to the bridal bowers and put to bed.
The poet exorcises evil spirits and creatures of ill omen. The
moon peeps in at the window, and the poet asks for her
favour. He prays to Juno (goddess of wedlock and of child-
birth), and to the high heavens, asking for blessing on their
union, and for a large posterity which will have long and
lasting happiness on earth and then join the blessed saints in
Heaven. The whole poem is wonderfully joyful and festive,
combining gaiety with ritual, a rich sensuousness with a
seemly decorum.

Persuasions to love

One common type of love-lyric is the poem of persuasion,
like Marlowe's 'Come live with me and be my love'. Such
poems were common up to the eighteenth century, and
were often combined with the theme of transitoriness, as

in Herrick's 'Gather ye rosebuds': time passes swiftly, youth and beauty will fade, so love now before it is too late. There are innumerable poems in this tradition, but the masterpiece is Marvell's 'To his Coy Mistress'.

'To his Coy Mistress'. The poem displays great variation in tone and in pace. It falls into three sections. In the first, lines 1—20, the poet says that, if he and his beloved had illimitable time and space, it would be proper for her to be so modest and to repel his advances. She could find rubies beside the Ganges while he lamented by the Humber:

> I would
> Love you ten years before the Flood:
> And you should if you please refuse
> Till the Conversion of the Jews.   10

Their courtship could extend in time from before Noah's Flood until shortly before the Day of Judgment (when it was believed that the Jews would be converted to Christianity). And the lady, he says, deserves such protracted wooing.

This first section moves slowly and deliberately, and the tone is judicious and detached. The writing is witty, as in the striking *vegetable Love* (11), which refers to the traditional belief that the distinctive characteristic of the vegetable kingdom (as opposed to the animal kingdom or minerals) is the power of growth; the word does not suggest the kitchen (a later development in its meaning), but rather the slow growth of something like an oak-tree.

In the second section, lines 21—32, there is a sudden increase in pace, and the mood becomes restless:

> But at my back I always hear   21
> Time's wingèd chariot hurrying near:
> And yonder all before us lie
> Deserts of vast Eternity.

The pace slows down again for the solemn contemplation of the marble vault where the lady will lie in death, and then modulates into a sardonic reflection on death and love, concluding:

> The Grave's a fine and private place,   31
> But none I think do there embrace.

The final section, lines 33—46, is an ardent invitation to love, with energy of movement, rapid pace, and intensity of feeling. The invitation to love is also an invitation to live, and to live energetically, to 'tear our Pleasures with rough strife,/ Thorough the Iron gates of life', and to devour Time rather than be devoured by Time's 'slow-chapt power'. So, if we cannot make time stop, we will at least use it to the full:

> Thus, though we cannot make our Sun   45
> Stand still, yet we will make him run.

The structure of the whole poem is one of logical argument: (1) *If* it were so . . . (2) *But* it is not so . . . (3) *Therefore* let us love. Within this framework Marvell gives us a poem of enormous wit, clarity, poise, and emotional range; a poem, moreover, whose rhythmic energy and physical immediacy of experience are firmly rooted in idiomatic English. The strengths of the poem are brought out if one compares it with Herrick's 'Gather ye rosebuds', which is a charming poem but lightweight beside Marvell's. Compare Herrick's conventional poetic counters (sun, rosebuds, Old Time) with the original use of language in 'my vegetable love' and 'Deserts of vast Eternity'. Herrick's 'Old Time' is a trite personification, whereas Marvell's 'slow-chapt power' gives us the physical experience of people being inexorably ground down in Time's jaws.

Later love-poetry

After the seventeenth century, the more stylised forms of love-poetry, as found in the sonnet sequences and in persuasion-poems, gradually disappear. From the time of the Romantics, love-lyrics tend above all to express the emotions of the lover. Poets may praise their beloved, but this is usually subordinate to the expression of their passion, as in Byron's 'There be none of Beauty's daughters' and Shelley's 'To Constantia, singing' and Tennyson's 'Come into the garden, Maud'. Or the poet may express his grief at the loss of the beloved, either by death or by the ending of love. Some of the finest poems of Thomas Hardy (1840–1928) are of this kind, an example being 'Neutral Tones'. The poet recalls an episode in the past:

> We stood by a pond that winter day,
> And the sun was white, as though chidden of God,
> And a few leaves lay on the starving sod,
> — They had fallen from an ash, and were gray.

The woman standing by the pond with the poet no longer loves him: her eyes look at him as if at 'tedious riddles solved years ago'; words play between them on which has lost the more by their love; the smile on her mouth is 'the deadest thing/Alive enough to have strength to die'. Since that time, experience of the deceptions of love has recalled to the poet

> Your face, and the God-curst sun, and a tree,
> And a pond edged with grayish leaves.

It is the setting in which the poem is framed — the white sun, the pond, the gray leaves lying on the 'starving sod' — which creates the mood of the poem, the sense of emotional deadness, of a life from which colour has gone.

In the last fifty years, poems about love have often been about other things too. The poet may be concerned about his own integrity: he is watching for self-deceptions or for secret guilt, as in Auden's 'Dear, though the night be gone'. Or love may be one strand in a poem which handles other topics, for example social and political ones, as in Auden's 'The chimneys are smoking' and 'Easily, my dear, you move, easily your head'. These Auden poems date from the 1930s, when poetry often handled the relationship between private life and public affairs, between love and politics. Other examples are found in the work of Louis MacNeice (1907–63), like 'The Sunlight on the Garden', a technically brilliant poem making strict use of internal rhyme, and also a most moving one. It was written in 1938, when the Second World

War was clearly imminent, and deals with love and commitment; it regrets the ending of our 'freedom as free lances', but accepts the necessity for this, as the sun disappears from the European landscape and the light hardens and grows cold in the most private of gardens.

Pastoral Poetry and Nature Poetry

Our view of nature is coloured by the Romantic poets: to many people, Wordsworth's mountains seem the very stuff of poetry, and his 'Daffodils' the archetypal poem. In earlier ages, however, wild nature was often viewed with fear and abhorrence. In the Old English epic *Beowulf*, the 'misty moors' are the home of terrible beings which attack human civilisation. In the fourteenth-century poem *Sir Gawain and the Green Knight*, the mountains of northwestern England, through which Sir Gawain rides on his quest, are places of peril and pain and hardships: the cold streams dashing from the mountain-top are a source of discomfort, not of scenic beauty. This dislike of wild nature, and especially of mountains, was common until the later eighteenth century. Not that people were unresponsive to nature: poets through the centuries have rejoiced in bird-song and flowers and the burgeoning of plants in the Spring. But on the whole, people preferred nature to be tamed and domesticated: a fine field of wheat or a rich pasture cropped by cattle was preferable to a heath or moor or mountain.

Gardens

The domestication of nature is especially evident in gardens, and most strikingly in the gardens of great houses, with their size and (often) artistic pretensions; and it is not surprising that, in an age of patronage, poets celebrate them. A fine example is Ben Jonson's 'To Penshurst' (1616), a poem in praise of Penshurst Place in Kent, the home of the Sidney family and the birthplace of Sir Philip Sidney. The first half of the poem describes the grounds of the house, its walks, its trees, its copses. The poet delights in the beauty of the things he describes, but they are also useful things, contributing to the wellbeing of the house and neighbourhood: the lower land by the river has cattle, the middle ground has horses, every bank has rabbits, the higher ground provides pheasants, the River Medway and the fishponds offer carp and pike and eels, while the orchard produces a plenitude of fruit. Jonson describes these things with loving care, delighting simultaneously in the appearance of 'The purpled pheasant, with the speckled side', and the fact that it will crown the 'open table' of the house. Beauty and utility go hand in hand. In the second half of the poem Jonson praises the inhabitants of the house — their hospitality, generosity, justice and benevolence to their tenants, piety and virtue — and the good-neighbourly relations of the house with all around.

Another influence on garden-poetry was the traditional belief in a Golden Age of innocence and perfection in the remote past, sometimes associated with a garden. In Renaissance Europe, the classical Golden Age was sometimes linked to the Garden of the Hesperides. And in Christian belief, the original state of man's innocence was located in Paradise, the Garden of Eden. In these primordial states, there are no seasons, man does not have to labour (since the earth spontaneously produces all he needs), there is no conflict, and there is no decay or death. Such Paradisial traditions sometimes colour poems about gardens.

The Christian account of the Garden of Eden is amplified by Milton in *Paradise Lost*, notably in his description of the Garden in Book IV. A poem about a great-house garden which is coloured by such traditions is Marvell's 'The Garden': the poet contrasts the peace and innocence of the garden with the ambition and passion in the world outside, describes the spiritual state that can be achieved in it, and explicitly compares it to the Garden of Eden (but before the creation of Eve).

The eighteenth century was a great age of English landscape gardening, and the Augustan poets liked their Nature to be subject to the civilising hand of man. Formal gardens play a large part in the fourth of Pope's *Moral Essays* (1731–35), 'Of the use of riches'. The poem is about taste, and especially about the bad taste of ostentatious expense on grandiose buildings and gardens, such as those of 'Timon' (identified by some contemporaries with the Duke of Chandos). Pope gives advice on the laying out of a garden: you must follow Good Sense, never forget Nature, base your plans on 'the Genius of the place', and remember that the monumental buildings of Rome 'once were things of Use'; one of his illustrations of folly is the man who, in order to get a beautiful view from his house, cut down the trees which sheltered it, and left it exposed to the wind. After a satirical description of a visit to Timon's villa, he looks forward to a future age when Timon's ridiculously large parterre will be ploughed up and made productive again with 'Deep Harvests'; and he praises the kind of landowner

> Whose ample Lawns are not asham'd to feed
> The milky heifer and deserving steed;
> Whose rising Forests, not for pride or show,
> But future Buildings, future Navies grow.

As in Jonson, what is beautiful is also useful, and nature is made to serve the wellbeing of mankind.

Pastoral poetry

The myth of a Golden Age also plays a part in pastoral literature, which is about shepherds. They are not real shepherds, however, but idealised figures living in a world of imagined innocence and simplicity, remote from the troubles of the real world. The shepherds are also poets, composing songs and holding singing competitions with each other. They address love-songs to hard-hearted shepherdesses, lament the death of fellow-shepherds, sing the praises of great men. Pastoral literature sometimes has an allegorical meaning, or topical references below the surface. In any case, it is a projection of urban sophistication into an idealised rural setting, and the characters are really courtiers or scholars dressed up in shepherds' clothes. There is no attempt to give a realistic picture of rustic life.

The European pastoral tradition goes back to Greek poets

of Sicily in the third century BC, notably Theocritus, but more influential were the *Eclogues* (pastoral poems) of Virgil. These are set in an imaginary landscape, introduce supernatural characters, and evoke a Golden Age. They nevertheless have topical references — praising great men, and handling current problems like the eviction of farmers from their land during the civil wars.

There was little pastoral literature in the Middle Ages, but the tradition was revived in the Renaissance, and it became one of the most popular literary modes in Western Europe. In England, the revival began in the sixteenth century, and by the end of the century there was a flood of pastoral writing, much influenced by continental models; besides poems, there were long prose romances and pastoral dramas.

One poem modelled on Virgil's *Eclogues* is Spenser's *Shepherd's Calendar* (1579), a series of twelve dialogues between shepherds, one for each month. It includes many traditional features: singing contests, praise of great people, topical and political references, bewailing of unsuccessful love, a death followed by apotheosis (transformation into a God, exaltation to Heaven). The calendar-structure allows Spenser to combine multiplicity with unity, to put a great variety of things within a simple framework — different themes, attitudes, levels of seriousness. Some of the characters are thinly disguised real people, such as Queen Elizabeth I ('Eliza'), Archbishop Grindal ('Algrind'), Gabriel Harvey ('Hobbinol'), and Spenser himself ('Colin Clout'). There is a religious-political debate between Protestant and Catholic (or perhaps, more cunningly, between Puritan and non-Puritan Anglican). Other themes include poetry, love, the natural life and the civilised life, the humble life versus ambition, youth and age. The calendar framework gives the cycle of nature in contrast to life in cities, but also suggests man's own cycle of youth, maturity, old age, death: this is enacted in the poem by Colin Clout, who at the end of the December eclogue bids farewell to youth and love, and awaits death. The poem uses two main styles: a smooth style, making extensive use of the newly popular figures of rhetoric; and a rough style, used for humbler rustic characters, with irregular rhythms and many rusticisms or pseudo-rusticisms. Throughout, the reader is conscious of the combination of the literary with the rustic.

It was not only in set eclogues that pastoral influence appeared: Milton's 'Lycidas' (1638) is a pastoral elegy; and a multitude of lyrics, from the sixteenth century to the end of the eighteenth, present lovers under the guise of swains and shepherdesses. The word *swain*, which in the Middle Ages had been an everyday word for a country labourer or a servant, developed by about 1600 into a purely literary and pastoral word meaning 'country lover', '(poetic) shepherd'.

Pastoral was not without its critics. Samuel Johnson, in his *Life of Milton* (1779), referred to 'the common but childish imitation of pastoral life', and said of 'Lycidas' that 'Its form is that of a pastoral, easy, vulgar, and therefore disgusting'. What effectively ended the pastoral tradition, however, was the emergence of a new attitude to nature, especially in the poetry of Wordsworth.

Wordsworth and nature

A shift in attitudes to nature can be seen going on in the second half of the eighteenth century. Mountains cease to be terrifying or boring, and may be seen as picturesque, or as part of an exciting background to a 'Gothic' story, as in Gray's ode 'The Bard' (1757). In Blake's poetry there is a more fundamental change: a sense of the holiness and unity of all life, together with an insistence on its antitheses and contradictions, as in 'The Tiger' (did God make both the tiger and the lamb?).

The decisive voice, however, is that of Wordsworth. In the new urban environment of the Industrial Revolution, Nature becomes a healing and consoling force, and a moral educator, as in *The Prelude*. Not, indeed, Nature alone: traditional rural society and its values are equally important, as in 'Resolution and Independence' and 'Michael'; but the natural setting is seen as having a decisive influence on these rural characters and their moral qualities. Wordsworth goes further, and describes his experiences in moments of mystic vision of a unifying spirit running through Nature, as in 'The Simplon Pass'. These various aspects of Nature appear together in

'Lines composed a few miles above Tintern Abbey' (1798), in which the scenes and experiences are recorded with extraordinary concreteness and intensity; in its 159 lines 'Tintern Abbey' offers in concentrated form a great deal of what Wordsworth has to teach us and make us feel about Nature.

The influence of Wordsworth

In 1850, when Wordsworth died, Matthew Arnold (1822—88) wrote a set of Memorial Verses, in which the emphasis is on Wordsworth's consolatory and healing power in an 'iron time/Of doubts, disputes, distractions, fears'; and many other readers have testified to this power. Since Wordsworth's time, too, people have tended to take it for granted that wild nature is beautiful, and an eminently suitable subject for poetry. Poets may not indeed see nature as a healer and moral educator, and they may not have mystical experiences: a poet may simply use scenery as a beautiful backdrop to a story, as in Tennyson's 'Oenone', or merely rejoice in the English landscape for its own sake, as in some of the charming poems of John Clare (1793—1864). But in any case there has been a change in our sensibilities, and in the way we see natural objects, since the eighteenth century. To attribute such a change to Wordsworth alone would be absurd: large-scale changes of this kind are not produced by individuals, however eminent. But a great individual like Wordsworth can crystallise feelings which are suspended in a culture waiting to be precipitated; he can define and focus new feelings and attitudes, and so give them greater force and direction.

Nature in the twentieth century

In our own age, nature has continued to be one of the pre-occupations of poetry, though attitudes to it are often more complex than Wordsworth's. Even in Victorian times, there was the disturbing effect of the theories of Malthus and Darwin, and we have already seen how Tennyson was perturbed by 'Nature red in tooth and claw'. In this century, people have not been slow to point out that the English landscape which Wordsworth knew was one which had been deeply affected by the hand of man, even in the Lake District; and that the wilder landscapes that he admired, as in the Alps, are quite a different matter from a malaria-ridden jungle inhabited by deadly predators, where nature has a rather different aspect. Poets, moreover, are not likely to write simply about nature, but tend rather to consider it in relation to other topics.

Lawrence's 'Snake'

A poet with a strong feeling for nature was D. H. Lawrence (1885–1930), and some of his most attractive poems are the ones about birds, beasts, and flowers. We have already looked at the opening of one of these, 'Snake'. The broad structure of this poem is (a) Contemplation, (b) Conflict, (c) Action, (d) Reaction. In lines 1–21, the poet contemplates a new situation, the snake drinking at his water-trough. These lines give us superbly the heat of the day, the exotic setting, and the movements of the snake. The snake is identified with the dark depths of the earth: it has come out of a fissure in the earth-wall, and it is 'earth-brown, earth-golden from the burning bowels of the earth' (20). The heat, the water, and the depths of the earth function in the poem like natural principles, conflicting yet complementary (like the medieval 'elements', earth, air, fire, water). And the reference to 'Etna smoking' (21) reminds us of the fiery powers beneath the earth.

In the second section, lines 22–54, there is a conflict of feelings within the poet. The voices of his education tell him that he must kill the snake, because in Sicily the golden snakes are venomous. But he likes the snake, and feels honoured that it has come as his guest, even though he is also afraid. So he struggles with himself. Is he a coward? Is he perverse, to want to talk to the snake?

Then a change occurs in the situation: the snake finishes drinking, and begins to re-enter the hole in the earth-wall. If the poet is to act, it must be now, and in lines 55 to 62 he does act. But because of his conflict of feelings, his action is brief, half-hearted, and ineffective. He picks up a log and throws it, but with no serious intention of hitting the snake:

he throws it 'at the *water-trough*'. The snake writhes like lightning and disappears into the hole, and the situation has returned to normal — the man, the earth-wall, the heat. In the final section of the poem we have reaction:

> And immediately I regretted it.
> I thought how paltry, how vulgar, what a mean act!
> I despised myself and the voices of my accursed
>   human education.   65
>
> And I thought of the albatross,
> And I wished he would come back, my snake.
>
> For he seemed to me again like a king,
> Like a king in exile, uncrowned in the underworld,
> Now due to be crowned again.   70
> And so, I missed my chance with one of the lords
> Of life.
> And I have something to expiate;
> A pettiness.

The poet recognises, belatedly, that the voices of his human education were 'accursed' (65): they represent the man-made inhibitions that strangle the natural and instinctive life. He thinks of *The Ancient Mariner* and the killing of the albatross: his own attack on the snake (he implies) is a similar act. This widens the application of the poem: his act becomes symbolical, representing a betrayal of life. In his reaction, the poet apotheosises the snake, making it 'a king in exile'; the reference to the underworld brings in mythological associations (the classical god Dis), and also suggests the dark instinctive life of man below the level of consciousness, which is 'due to be crowned again'. And this king of the underworld is a lord, not of death, but of life.

Ted Hughes

Some of the finest poems of Ted Hughes (1930–) deal with birds or animals. He is intensely aware of the violence of the animal kingdom, but also of the role of the animal as victim.

He is equally aware of man's place in the evolutionary process, and of the differences between man and the other animals. He has an outstanding gift for capturing the appearance and movements of the creatures he deals with.

In 'Pike' (1960), the appearance of the small pike, 'green tigering the gold', and their movements, and the pond they swim in, are marvellously realised. The pike are 'killers from the egg', but they are also victims of evolution: their life is determined by their killers' jaws, 'not to be changed at this date'. In the course of the poem, the pike being considered become larger and larger, until at the end the poet, fishing a pond fifty yards across, is terrified by his imagination of pike so immense and old that, after nightfall, he is afraid to cast his line, but just stands with it motionless in the water, watching for what might move in the pond.

In 'Thrushes' (1960), there is a comparison between the birds and mankind. Once again, the appearance, and especially the movements, of the thrushes are superbly conveyed. What fascinates the poet is their 'bullet and automatic purpose': they listen on the lawn, strike, drag out 'some writhing thing'. There is no hesitation or doubt or procrastination. But 'With a man it is otherwise'. Men also kill, but 'Heroisms on horseback' are quite differently motivated from the thrush's automatic killing for food: the concept of heroism brings in socially determined criteria for killing. Men plan the future (the desk-diary), and they do things for their own sake, like making a work of art ('a tiny ivory ornament'). And men pray, and suffer moral conflict, and undergo intense religious experiences. At the end of the poem, the contrast is implicitly between man and the whole of the rest of the animal kingdom.

Religious Poetry

Some poems on religious themes are simple lyrics of praise or rejoicing, and before the Reformation these are often about the Virgin Mary, like the splendid early-fifteenth-century songs 'I sing of a maiden' and 'Adam lay ibounden'. Other poems are for devotional purposes; in the sixteenth century, the Psalms were especially popular for this, and there are numerous paraphrases of them, including verse ones by Wyatt and by Sidney. Yet other religious poems deal with religious experience, including doubt and struggle, and many of Donne's are of this kind.

John Donne

Donne's religious poems mostly date from the later part of his career, but they bear striking resemblances to the love-poetry of his earlier years, with the same passionate argumentativeness, restlessness, and metaphysical imagery; they may even use erotic images, as in the sonnet 'Batter my heart'.

One of his finest poems is 'Hymn to God my God, in my sickness', probably written a few days before he died in 1631. In the first stanza he recognises that he is near death:

> Since I am coming to that Holy room,
>   Where, with thy Choir of Saints for evermore,
> I shall be made thy Music; As I come
>   I tune the Instrument here at the door,
>   And what I must do then, think here before.   5

The 'Holy room' is Heaven, where the poet will become God's music. Now at the door of Heaven, he tunes the instrument (himself, his soul), in other words he puts himself in the right mental and spiritual state for death.

Having established the stanzaic pattern for the reader, the poet over-runs the end of Stanza 2:

> Whilst my Physicians by their love are grown
>   Cosmographers, and I their Map, who lie
> Flat on this bed, that by them may be shown
>   That this is my South-west discovery
>   *Per fretum febris,* by these straits to die,   10
>
> I joy, that in these straits I see my West;
>   For, though their currents yield return to none,
> What shall my West hurt me? As West and East
>   In all flat Maps (and I am one) are one,
>   So death doth touch the Resurrection.   15

The first four lines of Stanza 2 are all over-run, throwing emphasis on the opening words of the following lines. This is especially striking in lines 6—7: we reach *are grown*, and then, after the line-pause, are given the astonishing and quite unexpected word *Cosmographers* ('geographers, map-makers'), isolated at the beginning of the line. In line 8, *Flat* receives similar emphasis; this is to prepare the way for the crucial role of the word at the culmination of the image in the next stanza. The doctors, leaning lovingly over the dying poet on his bed, are like geographers studying a map. They will show that this is his *discovery* ('voyage of exploration') to the southwest (through the Straits of Magellan). The direction is westward because that is where the sun sets, and so symbolises death. *Per fretum febris* has two meanings: 'through the strait of fever' and 'through the raging heat of fever'. *Straits* (10) means both 'narrow seaway, channel', and 'difficulties, pains'. The adjective *strait* meant 'narrow, difficult, rigorous', as in the Biblical 'Strait is the gate, and narrow is the way, which leadeth unto life' (Matthew 7.14), which the original reader of the poem would have been reminded of.

We get to the end of Stanza 2 without having reached the main subject and verb of the sentence, *I joy*: Donne holds these back to the beginning of Stanza 3, so giving them enormous emphasis. The poet rejoices in his westward voyage, even though there is no return from death, because East and West are *one* ('identical'). A flat map of the earth is a projection of a globe, and a point on its western edge is identical with one on its eastern. So if a ship sails off the western edge of the map, it reappears on the eastern edge; similarly, Death adjoins the Resurrection. Moreover, as Donne had pointed out in one of his sermons, Christ is in one place in the Vulgate (the Latin version of the Bible) called *Oriens* ('rising, the East'). Christ is the East, the rising sun, but can be reached by sailing westward through death. So the apparently strange comparison of a dying man to a map is brought to a brilliant conclusion, which draws together the threads of all the references in the two stanzas. This remarkable poetic image *proves* nothing about Death and Resurrection, but it does convey triumphantly the poet's own complete conviction.

In Stanza 4, the poet points out that to get to the Pacific, or to the riches of the East, or to Jerusalem, you have to sail through straits (Behring, Magellan, Gibraltar). In Stanza 5 he refers to the traditional belief that Paradise and Calvary were at the same place, that Christ's cross stood on the same spot as Adam's apple-tree. He identifies the sweat on his own face (from the fever) with the sweat on Adam's face (from labour), which was part of his punishment for the Fall (Genesis 3.19): sickness, and death, and labour are all consequences of the Fall. He asks that the blood of the second Adam (Christ) may save his soul. In the final stanza, he identifies Christ's redeeming blood with his purple mantle of kingship; wrapped in this mantle, he asks God to receive him, and to give him the heavenly crown won for mankind by Christ's crown of thorns. In the past, as a priest, he has preached God's word to other souls; now he gives the text for his sermon for his own soul, 'Therefore that he may raise the Lord throws down'.

George Herbert

All the poems of George Herbert (1593–1633) are on religious subjects. Herbert came from a noble family, distinguished himself academically at Cambridge, and could well have had a career at court. Instead, he studied divinity, took holy orders, and was a parish-priest for a few years until his early death. His poetry is influenced by Donne's, but is simpler and more homely. The images often draw on everyday things: in 'Affliction (I)', he describes his early joy in God's service as a delight in God's 'furniture so fine' and 'glorious household-stuff' (as if he were a servant in a great household); 'Redemption' is an expanded metaphor, with the poet as tenant and God as the 'rich Lord' he holds from; and everyday menial work can become a glorification of God:

> A servant with this clause
> Makes drudgery divine:
> Who sweeps a room, as for thy laws,
> Makes that and th'action fine.
>
> ('The Elixir')

The room is made 'fine' by the sweeping, the action is made fine by the spirit in which it is done. In 'Jordan (I)', Herbert gives us his poetic credo: not for him is fiction, or pastoral, or love-poetry, or obscurity; he believes in truth and plainness. In 'Jordan (II)', he says that, when he began to write religious poetry, he had used ingenious and elaborate language, decorating the sense as if it were to be put up for sale; but then a voice whispered to him that this 'long pretence' was wide of the mark: in love there is a sweetness 'ready penn'd', and he merely needs to copy it out.

The poetry tends to be an extension of Herbert's pastoral work, aiming at the edification of others rather than concentrating (like Donne's) on his own experience. Some of the poems give straightforward moral advice, like 'The Church Porch'; some praise God, or rejoice in his service; some deal with the ritual and the symbols of the Church of England. Herbert's Anglicanism comes out in his rationality, and in his strong sense of form and order: images of building and architecture are common in his poetry, and the poems are constructed with great care.

Nevertheless, the poems do record the poet's own spiritual experiences. Often these are purely joyful, but there are vicissitudes. 'The Flower' conveys wonderfully a sense of spiritual refreshment and renewal, given by imagery of vegetation (a favourite of Herbert's), but the renewal is needed because of a period of aridity, when the poet's heart was shrivelled. In 'Discipline', the poet prays to God to throw away his rod and take a 'gentle path' with him. In 'Affliction (I)', he tells how his first delight in God's service had been followed by sorrow and pain. He feels a conflict between his upbringing and his vocation as a priest:

> Whereas my birth and spirit rather took
>   The way that takes the town;
> Thou didst betray me to a ling'ring book,
>   And wrap me in a gown.   40

God alternately rewards and punishes him, and he cannot tell what will happen next. He reads, and sighs, and wishes he were a tree, for then he would have some clear and useful function. The poem ends with a sudden impulsive burst of rebelliousness, immediately followed by the wonderful paradoxical appeal to God in its last two lines:

> Well, I will change the service, and go seek
>   Some other master out.
> Ah my dear God! though I am clean forgot,   65
> Let me not love thee, if I love thee not.

In 'The Collar', the rebellion against God begins the poem, with the splendidly colloquial and dramatic lines:

> I struck the board, and cried, No more.
>   I will abroad.
> What? shall I ever sigh and pine?
> My lines and life are free; free as the road
>   Loose as the wind, as large as store.   5

The poet continues to bang his fist on the table (strike the board), but the defiant tone becomes more and more exaggerated, revealing an underlying uncertainty which prepares us for the turn-round in the final two lines of the poem, which have a typical simplicity of submission.

In the poems of conflict we seem to be directly following the movement of the mind and feelings of a man who is supremely honest about his doubts and motives. But perhaps spiritual assurance is a more characteristic mood of Herbert's, which finds particularly fine expression in the poise and calm of 'Vertue', one of his loveliest poems.

After Herbert

Following Donne and Herbert, there is a tradition of 'metaphysical' religious poetry for the rest of the seventeenth century, the most interesting poets being Crashaw and Vaughan. Richard Crashaw (*c.* 1612—49) was a High-Church Anglican who became a Catholic, and his poetry reminds one of the art of the Counter-Reformation in Europe: it is extravagant, ardent, rhapsodic, voluptuous; it uses far-fetched comparisons and extreme conceits; it is devoted to the saints, as in the poems on St Teresa and St Mary Magdalene (a favourite subject of Counter-Reformation art). Henry Vaughan (1621–95) was influenced by Herbert, but lacked Herbert's interest in church ritual and also his sense of poetic form; he records moments of mystical experience, which alternate with times of spiritual aridity; he responds strongly to nature, as in 'Regeneration'; and, like Wordsworth later, he sees childhood as the time when we are nearest to God, and later life as a decline ('The Retreat').

In the Restoration period, Milton was writing a quite different kind of religious poetry: after *Paradise Lost,* he produced *Paradise Regained* (1671), a poem in four books on the temptation of Christ in the wilderness, written in a flat and unrhetorical style; and then *Samson Agonistes* (1671), a poetic drama on the Greek pattern about the death of the Biblical hero Samson, which shows Milton (in a situation analogous to Samson's) coming to terms with life after the collapse of the Commonwealth and the restoration of the monarchy. Dryden, too, wrote two long poems on religious topics: *Religio Laici* (1682) is a reasoned defence of the Church of England against sceptics, deists, Catholics, and Puritans; while *The Hind and the Panther* (1687) is an allegorical poem with animal characters, in defence of the Roman Catholic church (the poet having changed his religion in the interim).

The eighteenth century was not notable for its religious poetry. The Church of England was in a state of torpor and degeneracy, and perhaps the best religious poetry of the age is found in the hymns written by Nonconformists. Formerly, metrical versions of the psalms had been used in worship, and hymns had played little part (and were indeed regarded with suspicion by Anglicans until the nineteenth century). In the later seventeenth century, hymn-writing became commoner, and the movement flowered in Isaac Watts (1674–1748), a Nonconformist pastor whose hymns were enormously popular and influential, many of them still being in common use ('O God, our help in ages past', 'When I survey the wondrous cross', 'Jesus shall reign where'er the sun'). Later in the century, the Methodist movement was launched, originally as an attempt to revivify the Church of

England, later as an independent church, and this too had its own hymns, notably those of Charles Wesley (1707—88); he wrote several thousand, including 'Jesu, Lover of my soul', 'Hark, the herald angels sing', and 'Love divine, all loves excelling'.

The Romantic poets did not produce much religious poetry of distinction, though an exception should perhaps be made for Blake, since it could be argued that everything he wrote was religious; his beliefs are, however, so idiosyncratic that many readers would not recognise them as a religion. In the Victorian Age, poets struggled with religious doubt (Tennyson's *In Memoriam*) or regretted the loss of faith (Matthew Arnold's 'Dover Beach'); but there is only one religious poet in the age who has anything like the inwardness and power of the great seventeenth-century poets, and that is Gerard Manley Hopkins (1844—89).

Hopkins

Hopkins was a Roman Catholic by conversion, and became a Jesuit priest. Because of his influence in the present century, we tend to think of him as a 'modern' poet, and need to remind ourselves that he was a Victorian. Like Ruskin and Morris, he reacted against Victorian industrialism, both aesthetically and politically ('God's Grandeur', 'The Sea and the Skylark', 'Tom's Garland'). His conversion to Catholicism was in accord with one strand of Victorian thought, the High-Church reaction against liberalism seen in the Oxford Movement. He had a great sensitivity to nature, especially trees, water, and clouds, and a feeling for it akin to Wordsworth's, though he always saw God as immanent in nature. He was deeply and conventionally patriotic, as can be seen in the opening two lines of 'The Soldier'; and, during his years in Dublin, he was much disturbed to find that many of his fellow-priests were sympathetic to the Irish nationalist cause. Even in his use of language, strikingly original as it is, we are reminded that he lived in an age of German influence and of interest in folk traditions: he uses archaisms and dialect-words, and is fond of coining new compounds from native roots; a line like 'Though worlds of wanwood leafmeal lie'

('Spring and Fall') could only be written by a man steeped in the earlier history of English.

But he was a very unusual Victorian. Indeed, individuality and singularity played a considerable part in his view of the universe. He was interested in the unique being of everything, its self, which is different from all other selves, and he coined the verb *to selve*, meaning 'to be oneself, unique and distinctive'; he uses it, for example, in 'As kingfishers catch fire', a poem which asserts that the inner self of everything bodies itself forth in the outer shape and actions. And the most highly distinctive thing of all is the human individual. This insistence on singularity is in accordance with the Romantic rejection of the general in favour of the particular, but the form it takes in Hopkins is influenced by medieval Catholic philosophy.

The desire to capture the uniqueness of things leads to a singularity in style. Hopkins is ready to sacrifice grammar, syntax, even accepted word-forms and meanings, to capture the exact self that he perceives. The qualities that he prizes in verse are concentration, terseness, vividness, dramatic quality, and the sheer physical impact of language; and for these he is willing to sacrifice literary decorum and easy intelligibility.

Most of his poems are short: 'The Wreck of the Deutschland' (1876), which runs to 280 lines, is exceptional. In some, the main constituent is Hopkins's delight in natural beauty, as in 'Binsey Poplars' and 'Pied Beauty'; but this delight is often an expression of religious ecstasy, especially in earlier poems like 'Hurrahing in Harvest' and 'The Starlight Night'. In the directly religious poems, there is a strong sense both of God's terror and of his grace, as in 'The Wreck of the Deutschland'; and this poem also illustrates another common theme, the necessity for sacrifice. The supreme example of sacrifice is Christ, and another theme is the necessity of identifying oneself with Christ, indeed of becoming Christ, as in 'As kingfishers catch fire'. Other poems arise from Hopkins's pastoral work as a priest: his sympathy and love for people, his desire for the good of their souls, as in 'Felix Randall'. This theme is found in the octave of the sonnet 'The Candle Indoors', but in the sestet the poet turns in on himself, realising that he has been guilty of spiritual pride. There is honesty and a power of self-analysis, and these qualities are prominent in the poems of inner conflict, which are among Hopkins's finest work. One of these conflicts is between Hopkins's two vocations, as priest and as poet. This is seen in 'Spelt from Sibyl's Leaves'; the poem is about the change from life to death (compared to the change from day to night), a change which will submerge the multicoloured pattern of life into a simple question of black and white, right and wrong. But there is also in the poem a feeling for two different ways of life, two different ways of seeing the universe (the multicoloured and the black-and-white), and a gnawing doubt about the right choice.

The final sonnets

Among these poems of inner strain are Hopkins's final sonnets, sometimes called the 'terrible' sonnets, which record moods of darkness and spiritual desolation. This is a common experience in the lives of deeply religious people, and similar periods of darkness are recorded in the poetry of Herbert and of Vaughan. But Hopkins also felt that he had in some way stifled his creative impulse, made himself poetically infertile: this is clear in 'Thou art indeed just, Lord', and in the sonnet to Robert Bridges, and in 'To seem the stranger lies my lot'. In view of these repeated and moving expressions of grief at his creative infertility, it seems likely that the poet—priest conflict is one of the elements in the poems of desolation (in which the cause of desolation is often not mentioned) such as 'Carrion Comfort', 'No worst, there is none', and 'I wake and feel the fell of dark'. In these poems the mind torments itself, and the poet feels in conflict with God, or cut off from God. As an example of these final sonnets, let us look at 'No worst':

No worst, there is none. Pitched past pitch of grief,
More pangs will, schooled at forepangs, wilder wring.
Comforter, where, where is your comforting?
Mary, mother of us, where is your relief?

My cries heave, herds-long; huddle in a main, a chief   5
Woe, world-sorrow; on an age-old anvil wince and sing —
Then lull, then leave off. Fury had shrieked 'No ling-
ering! Let me be fell: force I must be brief.'

O the mind, mind has mountains; cliffs of fall
Frightful, sheer, no-man-fathomed. Hold them cheap   10
May who ne'er hung there. Nor does long our small
Durance deal with that steep or deep. Here! creep,
Wretch, under a comfort serves in a whirlwind: all
Life death does end and each day dies with sleep.

The opening words of the poem contain a reference to
Shakespeare's *King Lear* (IV.1), where Edgar is forced to
realise that things can always get worse: we can never say
that they are at the worst. The word *pitched* means both
'thrown' and 'tensioned, screwed up': the poet is thrown,
and the pangs (sharp pains, attacks of mental anguish) are
screwed up higher and higher. *Forepangs* is Hopkins's own
coinage: the pains are taught (*schooled*) to torture him more
savagely (*wilder wring*) by the pains that have gone before
(*forepangs*). The internal rhyme (*More pangs . . . forepangs*)
reinforces the idea of a repetitive process. In his anguish, the
poet calls on God in his aspect of Comforter (the Holy
Ghost, the third person of the Trinity), and on the Virgin
Mary. *Herds-long* (5) is another coinage, on the analogy of
adverbs like *sidelong* and *headlong*: his utterances of pain
follow one another like waves (*heave*), or like the echoing of
cries from animal to animal in a herd (*herds-long*). This idea
is continued in *huddle* (5), which suggests both the cowering
together of the animals and the compressing of all grief into
this grief. The poet and his cries are like a horseshoe being
hammered by a smith on an anvil; but this hammering,
clearly, is creative, so the image implies an acceptance by the
poet of his sufferings, which is why they *lull* and *leave off*
(7). His afflictions were necessarily (*force*) brief, but were
correspondingly terrible (*fell*). The Fury that has caused the
afflictions comes from classical mythology, and suggests
retributive justice, and the possibility of madness as a punishment. The placing of the line-division inside the word *lingering*
(7—8) really does make it linger.

In the sestet, the mental agony is now at a remove, though still vividly present to memory, as we see in the mountain-image: the mountain is not a Wordsworthian one, but a terrifying place of danger and loneliness, where we hang in peril over a precipice deeper than man can measure. The mood, however, is now more collected and composed. *Durance* (12) is used in its archaic sense 'endurance' or 'continuance', but also suggests its modern meaning, 'imprisonment'. In the last three lines, the poet withdraws into the comfort of sleep, and the thought that 'all/Life death does end'; but this is ambiguous: which is the subject of the sentence, and which the object? We are left balanced between the escape into death and sleep, and the thought that 'all life' puts an end to death.

The poem has enormous energy and immediacy, bringing home to us the drama of the tormented mind. A remarkable compression is achieved, especially by coinages like *forepangs* (2), *herds-long* (5), and *no-man-fathomed* (10). The movement is that of impassioned speech, counterpointed against the metrical pattern, and using the line-break to achieve emphasis, as in *chief/Woe* (5–6). Nothing could be further from the languid dream-world of Hopkins's contemporaries.

T. S. Eliot

The outstanding religious poet of our century has been Eliot. His earlier poems are not religious, though they have a moral passion which makes his later development unsurprising. *The Waste Land* (1922) is a statement of the fragmentation and spiritual aridity of modern urban civilisation, and is charged with horror and disgust at the futility and boredom and purposelessness of modern life (and even of modern death), and at the exercise of sex divorced from love and personal relationships. 'The Hollow Men' (1925) is a sardonic account of the people who live in this civilisation, 'Headpiece stuffed with straw'; it develops the more negative aspects of the earlier poem, and, although it contains some liturgical phrases, is more completely despairing, for the world ends 'Not with a bang but a whimper'.

Eliot's development thereafter is a movement towards the

acceptance of Christian faith. The movement is tentative, scrupulous, self-questioning: the poet knows that in the modern world faith is difficult, and that he cannot simply move back into an earlier age and accept religion in the way that Dante and Chaucer had. So there are no rhetorical assertions of faith, but instead a receptiveness, a submission to spiritual discipline, an attempt to construct faith. This movement towards faith is seen in 'Journey of the Magi' (1927) and 'Marina' (1929).

'Journey of the Magi'. In 'Journey of the Magi', the poem is spoken by a 'character', as is the case in many of Eliot's earlier poems: it is part of his technique for obtaining detachment and impersonality. In 'Journey of the Magi', the method enables him to present a state of doubt, of inbetweenness, without committing himself to it in his own voice. The speaker is one of the three 'wise men' who, says the Gospel according to St Matthew (2.1—12), came from the East, following a star, and gave gifts to the infant Christ. The speaker recounts, with haunting and vivid details, the hardships and frustrations and beauties of the journey, and the doubts of the Magi (voices in their ears saying that this was all folly), and their final arrival,

not a moment too soon 30
Finding the place; it was (you may say) satisfactory.

All this was a long time ago, and the speaker ruminates on it. Were they led all that way for Birth or for Death? There was a birth, but it was like a death — their death. The Magi had returned to their kingdoms (they are traditionally represented as kings), but were no longer at ease there, 'in the old dispensation'. So the poem presents a state between faith and non-faith: the Magi have witnessed the birth of Christ, but they still belong to a former era, 'With an alien people clutching their gods'.

'Marina'. By contrast, 'Marina' is not spoken by a character, but is in the poet's own voice, as are the great religious poems to follow, *Ash Wednesday* (1927—30) and *Four Quartets*

(1936—42). This is a significant change. We must not, indeed, read poetry as if it were autobiography, but the abandonment of a 'persona' to speak the poem is a sign that the poet has committed himself to faith.

'Marina' bears this out, for it is full of a sense of new-found joy and wonder. The title refers to a character in Shakespeare's *Pericles,* who is lost, believed dead, and then found again by her father; her finding seems to Pericles like a resurrection, a return from the dead; and her discovery transforms him from a state of utter despair to one of unimaginable joy. In the poem, the 'daughter' is associated with a lovely landscape and seascape, with rocks, and islands, and pine-scent, and the woodthrush singing. The things which horrified the poet in the past have 'become unsubstantial', as a result of 'this grace'. There follows the image of the building of a boat, a boat full of defects and weaknesses, but the poet's own, made half-consciously 'Between one June and another September'. The boat, clearly, is the faith which the poet has now achieved, and which accounts for the sense of renewal and freshness. The poem ends with a return to the beautiful landscape and daughter of the opening.

'Four Quartets'. Four Quartets is the culmination of Eliot's poetic career, and surely the greatest poem in the English language this century. It is a sequence of four linked poems, which are religious meditations, and, as its title indicates, has a structure analogous to that of a piece of music. Each of the four constituent poems is divided into five sections, the broad pattern being the same in all four; and Eliot himself used the musical word 'movements' to describe these sections. The first movement of each poem states its themes, which it relates to a landscape at a particular place referred to in the poem's title. The second movement develops the ideas of the first, and is in two parts: a lyrical part, rhymed and in short lines, and a more colloquial part, which treats the subject less figuratively and more conceptually. In the third movement the poet turns inwards, withdrawing from the world in the manner of a mystic. The fourth movement is short and lyrical. The fifth movement arrives at some kind of resolution, in which a part is played by a consideration of the problems of

the poet's own art; like the second movement, it is in two parts, but in the reverse order, the more lyrical part coming second.

Within this framework, themes are presented, dropped, picked up again later from another point of view or with new insights; until at the end of the whole work they are drawn together in a final affirmation. The central theme of the whole sequence is Time: the relationship of the present to the past and the future; the relationship of time-bound humans to that which is outside time; the history of human societies; memory, and the possible significance of particular intense memories; and the Passion of Christ eternally operative in Time. One of the subsidiary themes is the two different kinds of Christian life, the life of the Christian in the world and the life of the saint or mystic (a theme which Eliot treated more explicitly in his play *The Cocktail Party*, first performed in 1949); and the poem draws on the words of Christian mystics — St John of the Cross, Dame Julian of Norwich, Walter Hilton.

The poem is exploratory and tentative, even its resolutions being achieved by 'hints and guesses,/Hints followed by guesses' ('The Dry Salvages'); and this is why another recurrent theme is the poet's own art, and the difficulty in capturing elusive intuitions and experiences in words.

Some of the most intense and poignant passages in the poem are memories of moments in the past (real or imagined), like the rose-garden at the beginning of 'Burnt Norton', and the dawn scene in London after an air-raid in 'Little Gidding', when the poet meets a stranger who becomes a master-poet from the past (Dante, perhaps). Not only the intense and poignant passages but also the more casual and colloquial ones are striking for the constant *rightness* of their language. The phrasing, the placing of emphasis on particular words by repetition or the use of the line-ending, the perfect control of the poet's tone of voice, the absence on the one hand of rhetorical gestures and on the other of banality, the subtlety with which the 'hints and guesses' are crystallised — everything is inescapably right. And this is all done without the style in any way calling attention to itself, so that we are always attending to what the poet is saying, not how he is saying it. And this rightness is sustained, with hardly a falter, throughout the sequence.

Non-Christian poetry

Until the present century, religious poetry in English has inevitably been Christian. Before the eighteenth century, it was dangerous even to express doubt in Christianity, and even in later times sceptics needed to be discreet: Shelley was sent down from Oxford for publishing a pamphlet called *The Necessity of Atheism* (1811). In the eighteenth century, Deism was fashionable, and Pope's *Essay on Man* (1733–4) is influenced by Deist ideas, even though Pope was a Catholic. In the nineteenth century poets can express openly anti-religious and atheistic views, as is done by Algernon Charles Swinburne (1837–1909), for example in 'Hymn to Proserpine' (1866) and 'The Garden of Proserpine' (1866). The religion which is opposed in such poetry is, of course, Christianity.

In our own time, things have changed. Many poets writing in English today come from communities which are not Christian, and in due course there will no doubt be major poetry in English which is written from a distinctively Muslim or Hindu or Sikh point of view. In New Commonwealth countries in Africa, English poetry is now being written in defence of traditional African religions. This is part of the efforts of such countries to escape from westernisation and the colonial past, and to rediscover their own history, their own culture, their own poetic voice.

An outstanding example of this movement is Wole Soyinka, who has written poetry celebrating the Yoruba deity Ogun (god of creativity, of iron, of metal-working, and of war; guardian of the road; explorer; hunter; custodian of the sacred oath). The long poem *Idanre* (1967) deals with the creation of the world and the history of Ogun, the inevitable link between creativity and destructiveness, and the eternally cyclical nature of history. Soyinka does not mention other religions, but another Nigerian poet, Christopher Okigbo, is explicitly critical of Christianity. Okigbo was brought up as a Catholic, but in *Heavensgate* (1962) he says that Christianity has nothing to offer his people, and he rejects it in favour of traditional religion, represented by the river-goddess 'mother Idoto'.

Another poet deeply influenced by traditional African religion is Edward Braithwaite (1930–). He is from Barbados, but for seven years he lived in Ghana, and was profoundly impressed by the traditional village way of life, including its religion. When he returned to the West Indies he tried to rediscover there the African roots of his own community, and to create or revive for it a mythology and rituals. The second part of his monumental poetic trilogy *The Arrivants* (1967–9), called 'Masks', is a celebration of the traditional life and rituals which he had experienced in Ghana.

The Public World

In some ages and places, poetry has had a more obviously public function than it has in England today: Yoruba praise-poems and Homeric epics are part of the life of their community. In the sixteenth and seventeenth centuries, the writing of poetry was one of the normal accomplishments of the English upper classes, and there was a great deal of 'amateur' poetry. The professional poet (unless he wrote for the public theatre) depended for his livelihood on patronage: a great man might offer him the hospitality of his manor-house, or give him gifts of money, or obtain an employment for him. The existence of patronage encouraged the writing of poetry of compliment, and the age is full of flattering dedications, poetic epistles, and celebrations of particular events (like weddings). Jonson's 'To Penshurst' (1616) is the celebration of a noble family as well as of its manor-house, and Milton's *Comus* was presented in celebration of the installation of the Earl of Bridgewater as Lord President of Wales in 1634. Patronage continued to be common in the eighteenth century, but authors were increasingly becoming independent men of letters writing for the public, like Johnson.

Poets also wrote directly political poems, commenting upon public affairs. The comment might be oblique or allegorical, as in Spenser's poems, but there was also a tradition of openly polemical political poetry, for example in anonymous broadside ballads. Named authors also wrote political polemic, and John Skelton (*c.* 1460–1529) was audacious enough to publish two poems attacking Cardinal Wolsey, when the latter was the most powerful man in the country.

The Civil Wars

In the seventeenth century, the struggle between King and Parliament culminated in the Civil Wars, which broke out in 1642 and led to the execution of King Charles I (1649) and the establishment of a republic (the Commonwealth). Inevitably, poets were among the partisans on both sides. The great poet on the Parliamentary side was Milton, but during the Commonwealth period itself he wrote little poetry, being deeply involved in political arguments conducted in prose. There are some political poems, especially sonnets (like 'Avenge O Lord thy slaughter'd Saints'); but it was not until after the Restoration of the monarchy in 1660 that the experiences of the Commonwealth years bore fruit in his poetry: the great debates in Pandemonium in Book II of *Paradise Lost* obviously look back to the heroic revolutionary days of the Short Parliament and the Long Parliament in the early 1640s; while *Paradise Regained* and *Samson Agonistes* can be seen as part of his effort to adjust himself to a world in which his political ideals had been defeated.

On the Royalist side were the Cavalier Poets, whose very poetic manner is that of the court — urbane, witty, elegant, dashing. It is in their style that these poets show their Royalist sympathies, but there is also some overt political comment, as in one of Richard Lovelace's best-known poems, 'To Althea from prison'. It was written in 1642, when Lovelace had been imprisoned by the Long Parliament, and its theme is 'liberty despite imprisonment'. When Althea whispers to him through the bars of his prison, and he is 'fettered to her eye', he is nevertheless made free by love. When he and his companions steep their grief in wine and drink healths to the King, they are freer than 'Fishes that tipple in the deep'. When he sings (somewhat shrilly) the praises of his King, his 'sweetness, mercy, majesty', he is freer than the winds. 'Stone walls do not a prison make', and if the poet has freedom in his love and is free in his soul, only angels have a comparable liberty. The carefree carousing in Stanza 2, with its witty reference to the tippling of the fishes, shows the daredevil roistering side of the Cavalier outlook, which was to degenerate into the libertinism of the Restoration rakes.

Marvell's 'Horatian Ode'

But the most remarkable political poem of the Commonwealth period is Marvell's 'Horatian Ode'. This is nominally a partisan work, being addressed to Cromwell when, in 1650, he returned from Ireland to take part in a Scottish campaign; but in fact it shows a remarkable detachment and objectivity, and appreciates the qualities of both sides in the Civil Wars. It has a three-part structure: (1) Cromwell, (2) Charles I, (3) Cromwell as the servant of England. In the first part, Cromwell is an impersonal natural force, the lightning that blasted the King. The poet recognises Cromwell's admirable personal qualities, but in a tone of impartial weighing-up ('Much to the man is due'). As far as the rights and wrongs of the struggle are concerned, the poet recognises the existence of 'ancient rights'; but these cannot be maintained without power. Justice pleads the cause of ancient rights (the Crown), but Fate (the impersonal force of history embodied in Cromwell) is unmoved.

The brief second section on the King emphasises his personal qualities, not his political ones, and describes the dignity with which he behaved at his execution:

> He nothing common did or mean
> Upon that memorable Scene:
>   But with his keener Eye
>   The Axe's edge did try: 60
> Nor call'd the Gods with vulgar spite
> To vindicate his helpless Right,
>   But bow'd his comely Head,
>   Down as upon a Bed.

Meanwhile, the 'armed bands' who were the spectators 'Did clap their bloody hands' — an action which the reader *does* see as common and mean.

The third section hails Cromwell as the servant of the Republic, and as the bringer of foreign victories. This is not ironical, but all the same there is something equivocal about the ending of the poem, where Cromwell is told that he must 'Still keep [his] sword erect'. The cross on the hilt of the sword, obviously, is a spiritual weapon, but the blade is a material one which is used to keep the power which was won by force:

> The same Arts that did gain
> A Pow'r must it maintain.   120

This is double-edged: it seems to be saying that might is right, but it also points to the fate of those who live by this philosophy, the way they are trapped in it.

The poem as a whole is a detached, slightly ironical contemplation of the political scene, to which it applies civilised standards of feeling and conduct, while still recognising the inevitability of power-conflicts. The consciousness of both sides of the argument, the ability to inhabit simultaneously two different world-views, is perhaps above all what produces the metaphysical style in poetry. After the Restoration Marvell became much more partisan, and wrote poems attacking the corrupt governments of Charles II; these poems are in a different, quite unmetaphysical, style.

John Dryden

Dryden was a conservative politically, with a strong sense of the need for order and established authority. His three main satirical poems are attacks on the Whigs. *The Medal* (1682) is a lampoon on the Earl of Shaftesbury, leader of the Whig opposition to the government of Charles II. *MacFlecknoe* (1682) is a mock-heroic poem ridiculing the Whig poet Thomas Shadwell. While *Absolom and Achitophel* (1681), of which Dryden wrote Part 1, is a short satiric epic.

In *Absolom and Achitophel,* Dryden uses a Biblical story to represent the intrigues of the Duke of Monmouth, an

illegitimate son of Charles II, against his father. The poem
has a splendid comic opening:

> In pious times, ere Priestcraft did begin,
> Before Polygamy was made a Sin;
> When Man on many multiplied his kind,
> Ere one to one was cursedly confin'd,
> When Nature prompted and no Law denied   5
> Promiscuous Use of Concubine and Bride;
> Then Israel's Monarch, after Heaven's own heart,
> His vigorous warmth did, variously, impart
> To Wives and Slaves: And, wide as his Command,
> Scatter'd his Maker's Image through the Land.   10

King David, 'Isreal's Monarch', represents Charles II, who was
notorious for his many mistresses and illegitimate children,
which are here amusingly justified by reference to Old Testa-
ment polygamy; there is a jovial and almost insolent flouting
of decorum in this reference to the King.

The poem deals with the attempts in 1679—81 of Shaftesbury to have Monmouth declared heir to the throne in place
of the Catholic Duke of York (later to be James II). It is
famous for its character-sketches, like those of Zimri (the
Duke of Buckingham) and of Achitophel (Shaftesbury). The
portrait of Achitophel begins as follows:

> Of these the false Achitophel was first,   150
> A Name to all succeeding Ages curs'd.
> For close Designs and crooked Counsels fit,
> Sagacious, Bold, and Turbulent of wit,
> Restless, unfix'd in Principles and Place,
> In Pow'r unpleas'd, impatient of Disgrace;   155
> A fiery Soul, which working out its way,
> Fretted the Pigmy Body to decay:
> And o'erinformed the Tenement of Clay.
> A daring Pilot in extremity;
> Pleas'd with the Danger, when the Waves went high   160
> He sought the Storms; but, for a Calm unfit,
> Would Steer too nigh the Sands to boast his Wit.

This is an attack, but it is also a tribute: Shaftesbury emerges as a heroic figure, rather as Satan does in *Paradise Lost*. Pope's satirical portraits tend to belittle and denigrate their subjects, while Dryden's are more magnanimous, and often magnify. Dryden's couplets are less neat than Pope's, the narrative driving forward with great energy and often overrunning the couplet-end. The writing is notable for its clarity and vigour, and works by statement rather than suggestion.

The Augustans

After the 'Glorious Revolution' of 1688, which finally established the constitutional monarchy of the Protestant William and Mary, there was a century of broadly consensus politics in England: the political squabbles tended to be about who had power and patronage, rather than about fundamental differences of political philosophy. Satire flourished, for it is an advantage to a satirist to have an audience with an agreed set of assumptions; but the satire tended to be on individuals, or fashions, or affectations, rather than on political parties or governments. Pope was a Tory, but his poetic energies were not devoted to party warfare. Johnson, too, was a staunch Tory, but his great poetic satires, *London* (1738) and *The Vanity of Human Wishes* (1749), are moral meditations on the lot of mankind, charged with a deep melancholy; in them, the Augustan poetic style, which in Pope seemed the perfectly natural way of expressing his attitudes, has become slightly literary: the social conditions that produced the style are passing away, and Johnson's style is an attempt to maintain attitudes which are becoming outdated.

The Romantics

All this is changed by the coming of the Industrial Revolution and the French Revolution. Once again there are disputes about basic matters of politics and social organisation; poets no longer live in a society with tacitly agreed assumptions, and inevitably participate in the ideological conflicts of the time. Blake reacted strongly against the materialism, rationalism, and mechanical science of the eighteenth century, and believed that the imagination needs to be liberated from the fetters of reason. In his early work he was a strong supporter of the radical political doctrines of Paine and Godwin, as in *The French Revolution* (1791) and *America* (1793). But the rationalism and materialism of the radical movement were uncongenial to him, and his later writings are predominantly mystical. Wordsworth was first excited and then disillusioned by the French Revolution; he wrote little directly political poetry, but the changed political and social situation obviously has a bearing on his doctrine of poetry as the 'real language of men', and his turning for material to humble and rustic life.

Byron

Of the younger generation of Romantic poets, Byron and Shelley were the most overtly political, and both radicals. Byron's political masterpiece is *The Vision of Judgment* (1822). It was written on the death of George III ('although no tyrant, one/Who shielded tyrants'), and has a sardonic account of the hypocritical pomp of his funeral. The main action takes place at the gate of Heaven, where George arrives to ask for admission, accompanied by a troop of angels. He is followed, however, by Satan, who makes a counterclaim to his soul, gives a long account of the havoc caused by his reign, and summons a host of witnesses. The main target of the poem, however, is not the king himself, but the poet Robert Southey (1774—1843), who had been a radical but had later become a conservative and been made Poet Laureate; he had written a fulsome memorial poem on the death of the king. Southey, the poet says,

> had written much blank verse, and blanker prose,
> And more of both than anybody knows.

He begins reading one of his poems to the assembled company at the gate of Heaven, whereupon both devils and angels run away screaming in horror. At the fifth line, St Peter raises his keys and knocks the poet down. In the subsequent confusion King George slips into Heaven,

> And when the tumult dwindled to a calm,
> I left him practising the hundredth psalm.

The poem is in the 'medley' style we have already met in *Don Juan,* ranging through the colloquial, the melodramatic, the reckless, the flippant, the serious. It is a splendid satire, with superb comic moments.

Shelley

Shelley's lyrical drama *Prometheus Unbound* (1820) is an expression of his political ideas: the wrongness of all violence; the perfectibility of man; the evil effects of all government; the dependence of government on opinion, so that the chains will fall off of themselves 'when the magic of opinion is dissolved'; and consequently the belief in a completely peaceful social revolution. In *Prometheus Unbound,* Jupiter symbolises all tyranny and oppression: despots, prisons, armies, and traditional moral codes and religions. The Titan Prometheus represents suffering mankind, who eventually overthrows Jupiter and is united with his bride Asia (Nature). Jupiter falls as soon as Prometheus withdraws his curse and forgives him: the change is brought about by the power of love. The actual mechanism by which Jupiter is made to fall is clumsy: he is dethroned by his own son Demogorgon, who perhaps represents the dissolving of the magic of opinion, though this is not clear. The final act of the drama is a lyrical rejoicing at the liberation of mankind, at the new era of light and happiness about to begin.

One striking thing about *Prometheus Unbound* is that it does not contain a single human being among its characters: we have a Titan, a God, Furies, spirits, but no men or women. And in general one of the deficiencies of Shelley's poetry is its weak grasp on external reality. A remarkable exception, however, is *The Mask of Anarchy,* a poem inspired by the so-called 'Peterloo Massacre' of 1819, when an unarmed crowd of peaceful demonstrators near Manchester was attacked by dragoons, and many killed. The poem is a vision, but one of frightening clarity and solidity. The poet sees a procession of the political leaders of England, like Viscount Castlereagh:

I met Murder on the way —   5
He had a mask like Castlereagh —
Very smooth he looked, yet grim;
Seven blood-hounds followed him.

This has a remarkable directness and power, and a concise
gnomic quality that reminds us of Blake. The poet's eye is
firmly on the object he is describing, not on himself. And the
poem continues on the same level, with its vision of Anarchy
on his white horse, of the maniac maid Hope, and of the
sufferings of the English people, who are exhorted in a final
magnificent invocation to overthrow tyranny. If Shelley had
often written like this, he would have been one of the great
political poets, but *The Mask of Anarchy* is not in the main-
stream of his work. In her notes on the poem, Mrs Shelley
says apologetically that 'The poem was written for the people,
and is therefore in a more popular tone than usual'. If Shelley
had written more often 'for the people' instead of for himself
and his friends, he would perhaps have been a more effective
poet.

The Victorians

In the Victorian age, the political turmoil died down, with
rising living-standards and the collapse in the 1840s of the
Chartist movement. There was less concern with fundamental
social change, and more concern with the righting of particular social evils and injustices; and the battle for these was
carried on in prose rather than in poetry, especially in the
novel. There was a widespread belief in Progress and in the
possibility of peaceful social change, though to many progres-
sives the path often seemed desperately slow and difficult, as
in 'Say not the struggle nought availeth' by Arthur Hugh
Clough (1819—61), who also gave us that satirical comment
on Victorian hypocrisy, 'The Latest Decalogue'.

The First World War

The war of 1914—18 was a great shock to Western civilisation,
the first major sign of the crisis that was upon it. It was also

the first war in which huge conscript armies confronted one another with modern weapons of mass-destruction. For the soldiers involved, especially in the trench-warfare of the Western Front, it was an appalling and quite unforeseen experience, and was made worse by the gap between the home front and the fighting front: the civilian population in England waved flags and made patriotic speeches, unaware of the reality of life in the front line. The front-line experiences of this war found expression in some remarkable writing, both prose and verse, notably by Robert Graves (1895–), Siegfried Sassoon (1886–1967), Isaac Rosenberg (1890– 1918), and Wilfred Owen (1893–1918).

Owen was an infantry-officer on the Western Front, and was killed in action just one week before the Armistice in 1918. The experiences his poetry describes are searing ones, but the poems are astonishingly poised, and full of human sympathy. There is no nursing of indignation, no sensationalism, no self-indulgence. We feel that he is not writing about his own sufferings, but those of the troops around him, with whom he feels a deep comradeship; and he wishes to make these sufferings known to the public at home, to strike at the conscience of England. In 'Insensibility' he reflects that the men are fortunate who become calloused before they die, who lose feeling and imagination; but in the final stanza he turns in denunciation on those at home in England who are callous, who *by choice* have made themselves immune to pity. In 'The Send-Off' he watches troops marching from camp to the train which will begin their journey to France and to the front, and thinks how few of them will creep back, uncelebrated, to their villages. In 'Exposure' he recreates with extraordinary intensity the misery of life in the trenches on a winter night, and in 'Dulce et Decorum Est' the horror of a gas-attack. In 'Futility', a poem where the syntax mirrors wonderfully the movement of the poet's thought, he contemplates a dead comrade and wonders what the point was of life arising on earth at all. In 'Miners' there is a moving comparison between the troops and coal-miners, and the poet, watching the coal in his hearth, thinks how he and his comrades will be forgotten, 'Lost in the ground', while future years warm their hands 'well-cheered/By our lives' ember'. These are just a few of the more striking among about fifty poems that Owen wrote about the War.

We have already looked at the opening of one of the finest of them, 'Strange Meeting', in which the poet dreams that he escapes from battle into a subterranean hall, which he realises is Hell. It is like a dugout in the trench-warfare above, with men lying sleeping and groaning, and one of them recognises him and springs up, lifting his hands as if in blessing. This stranger tells the poet of the similarity between the two of them, and of the loss caused by his death, for he was one who could have told of 'The pity of war, the pity war distilled'. At the end of the poem the stranger reveals his identity:

> I would have poured my spirit without stint
> But not through wounds; not on the cess of war.
> Foreheads of men have bled where no wounds were.
> I am the enemy you killed, my friend.   40
> I knew you in this dark; for so you frowned
> Yesterday through me as you jabbed and killed.
> I parried; but my hands were loath and cold.
> Let us sleep now . . .

The reference in line 39 is to the stigmata, the marks or wounds corresponding to the five wounds of Christ, which are said to appear on certain people, especially saints. Wounds, the poet is suggesting, can be produced from internal causes: the sensitive man bleeds simply from imagination. The forehead suggests Christ's crown of thorns, but also reminds us of Cain, the first murderer, who killed his own brother and had a mark placed on his brow by God (Genesis 4.1–15). The climactic line, line 40, gains its impact from the paradoxical collocation of *friend* and *enemy*. This makes us conscious of the double meanings of the words: (1) persons for whom one has feelings of affection or of hostility, (2) persons who are on the same side or on the opposite side in a war. The description of the killing which follows has a disturbing immediacy, and reminds us that Owen's compassion was not limited to the British troops, but also embraced the 'enemy'.

The 1930s

T. S. Eliot was conservative in outlook, Anglo-Catholic in religion and royalist in politics. But in the 1930s there was a group of poets with left-wing political sympathies, in reaction to the great economic depression of the period and the increasing threat of war from Hitler's Germany and Mussolini's Italy. This threat led to a movement in many European countries for an anti-fascist 'popular front', a broad alliance stretching from liberals to communists; and the crucial political event for many young people of that generation was the Spanish Civil War. The three most prominent 'leftist' poets of the period were W. H. Auden, Cecil Day-Lewis (1904–72), and Stephen Spender (1909–). They were not working-class poets, but Oxford-educated men from the professional classes whose political sympathies were engaged because of the social situation in that particular period. Hence they sometimes felt a conflict between the demands of politics and the desire to preserve their personal integrity; they felt caught between two different worlds, two different sets of moral imperatives. This is especially the case with Day-Lewis, as in 'The Conflict' and 'In me two worlds'.

They differed from Eliot in another way. He, though American by origin, was deeply European in feeling and sympathies: he felt Western European culture as a single tradition, and himself a part of it. The 1930s poets, by contrast, were intensely English, and none more so than Auden, the one really major poet in the group. In Auden's poetry of the 1930s there is a deep feeling both for the English landscape and for English history and tradition, as can be seen in poems like 'O love, the interest itself in thoughtless Heaven', 'Look, stranger', and 'Here on the cropped grass'. He is both fascinated and appalled by the derelict industrial landscape created in England by the Great Depression, as in the poem which begins:

> Get there if you can and see the land you once were
>   proud to own
> Though the roads have almost vanished and the
>   expresses never run:

Smokeless chimneys, damaged bridges, rotting wharves
and choked canals,
Tramlines buckled, smashed trucks lying on their side
across the rails.

His response to the situation often sounds straightforwardly
Marxist, as in 'Brothers, who when the sirens roar', but this is
only one strand in a complex web of beliefs and attitudes.
Another thread is his belief in 'healers' (which implies individual therapy rather than social action); he refers to
'Lawrence, Blake and Homer Lane, once healers in our
English land'; and Freud is prominent among the healers that
he admires. The poem 'Sir, no man's enemy' is an invocation
to such a healer. Auden has a strong sense of history, and a
considerable interest in technology, but he often suggests
that the driving-force in history is Love, as in 'O love, the
interest itself' and in 'Our hunting fathers', a poem which
contrasts the liberal and rational ideas of our ancestors with
the illicit underground activity necessary today.

This complex of ideas, and especially the linking of Freud
and Marx, is characteristic of the 1930s; but after Auden had
left England for America in 1939, the Marxist element fell
out, and the poet moved towards a religious view of the
world. In this he was not alone, for the views of many
writers of the 1930s changed considerably after the outbreak
of the Second World War.

Post-colonial poetry

Some of the most interesting writing in English in recent
decades has come from former British dominions and colonies
which achieved independence and full nationhood after the
Second World War. The most impressive works have perhaps
been novels, but there is also some fine poetry, which often
deals with the public world. Many poets have reacted against
modern industrial civilisation, and especially against suburban
and middle-class values and way of life; this reaction is seen,
for example, in some of the satirical poems of A. D. Hope,
such as 'Australia', 'Standardization', 'Crossing the frontier',
and 'The Brides'.

Another common theme has been the conflict between local and European values: as we have seen, the traditional way of life is upheld by Okot p'Bitek in East Africa, by Wole Soyinka in West Africa, by Edward Brathwaite in the West Indies. There are counter-currents, however: in Australia, Judith Wright sometimes dreams nostalgically of the pioneering past, but A. D. Hope rejects what he sees as the provinciality of much nationalist feeling, and regards Australian literature as part of a European tradition. And in the West Indies, the internalisation of cultural conflicts is seen in the poetry of Derek Walcott. Himself a mulatto, and brought up as a Methodist in the predominantly black and Catholic island of St Lucia, Walcott is deeply conscious of the divisions and tensions within the Caribbean community; he looks forward, however, to the fusion of its various elements into a homogeneous local culture.

In African writers, the black liberation movements in South Africa and Zimbabwe provide another obvious theme. Soyinka's *Ogun Abimañ* (1976) is a prophetic work, centred on the Ogun mythology and invoking the spirit of the Zulu warrior-king Shaka, which looks forward to the complete liberation of *Abimañ*, 'the Black Nation'.

Other Themes

The poetic topics we have considered are not mutually exclusive: a poem does not have to be concerned *only* with love, or Nature, or religion, or politics: it can contain many strands. And there are other topics quite commonly handled, which can be briefly mentioned.

Death

Death is a recurrent theme, and we have already seen it as a favourite topic in the Ballads. A poet may directly express his grief at the death of somebody loved, as in Tennyson's *In Memoriam*. He may express similar feelings more obliquely, or dramatically, as is often done by A. E. Housman (1859–1935), for example in 'Bredon Hill'. He may write about his own death, but this calls for exceptional purity of feeling, since the subject easily arouses self-pity or self-indulgence; successful examples include the moving 'Requiem' by Robert Louis Stevenson (1850—94), 'Remember me when I am gone away' by Christina Rossetti (1830—94), and the opening lines of Day-Lewis's 'Suppose that we, tomorrow or the next day'. Or he may use more formal modes of writing about death, such as epitaph and elegy.

An epitaph was originally an inscription on a tomb, and hence came to mean also a short poem suitable for this purpose. A real epitaph is seen in Ben Jonson's tender poem on the death of the boy-actor Pavy ('Weep with me, all you that read'), and a fictional one in the wonderful dirge for Fidele in Shakespeare's *Cymbeline.* An epitaph may also be comic or satirical, as with Rochester's epitaph on Charles II.

An elegy is a song of lamentation, especially a lament for the dead. It may be an expression of personal grief, like Matthew Arnold's 'Thyrsis', or it may be a formal and public poem like Tennyson's 'Ode on the Death of Wellington'. It may handle concerns to which the death in question is only incidental, and this is the case with one of the great formal elegies, Milton's 'Lycidas' (1638).

'Lycidas'

'Lycidas' is an elegy on the death of Edward King, 'a learned friend' drowned in the Irish Sea. It is largely about Milton's own fears and problems, for he is keenly aware of the parallels between King and himself, and this leads him to consider the possibility of his own early death, and to question the value of the poetic career to which he is dedicating himself. But it is also about many other things in which Milton was interested (such as the corrupt state of the Church), and the multiplicity of interests gives the poem a great richness.

In form it is a pastoral elegy, which has a long European history. It draws heavily on this tradition, and almost every episode in it has a parallel in ancient or Renaissance pastoral; even the introduction of St Peter has Renaissance precedent. Many of the features go back to the Greek pastoral poets or to Virgil. These include the broad pattern of lamentation followed by apotheosis (Lycidas is not dead after all, but in Heaven); the lament of Nature for the dead man; the series of questions ('Where were ye . . .?'); the procession of mourners, each of whom says something; and the heaping of flowers on the dead.

The poem combines, or moves between, pagan and Christian ideas, and Milton adapts pagan forms to Christian use with surprising ease, as when the traditional apotheosis becomes the Christian consolation of Heaven. In part, this may be because the Greek pastoral elegies were in origin lamentations for the god of fertility (Adonis, Thammuz), who dies and is lamented; and such mystery-religions influenced early Christian thought. The figure of Christ walking on the waters fits naturally into the symbolism of the poem, as does the story of Orpheus, another god of the mystery-cults. It is not to be thought, of course, that Milton was conscious of these affinities; but he has certainly seized on one of the key-concepts of the fertility-rites — water — and made it the central image of the poem. Water pervades 'Lycidas', from tears to the 'sounding seas', and is double-edged: it is the bringer of life but also of death, the stream that nourishes the Sicilian flowers but also the sea which drowned Lycidas.

Out of these traditional materials, Milton creates a great original poem. It is highly decorous, always saying the right thing, but is also highly charged emotionally. The passage about the corrupt clergy, for example, has enormous vigour and power, the pastoral imagery taking on a new meaning and also a new and striking reality. And when the poet turns from the poetic fancy of the flowers on Lycidas's hearse to the reality of his body washing about in the Irish Sea or beyond, a poignant personal note enters the poem, and at the same time Milton's imagination is fired (as often) by ideas of space and distance, the legendary and remote (the bottom of the monstrous world, with its Beowulf-like suggestions). Then, after the intense vision of Heaven, he puts a framework round the poem, and himself outside it, as the 'uncouth Swain' becomes the singer of the poem: the elegy for the dead has been celebrated; the problems it raised in the poet's mind have been wrestled with and resolved; and now it must be put behind us and life must go on — 'Tomorrow to fresh woods, and Pastures new'.

Moral meditation

Poems on death shade off into comments or meditations on death, as in the splendid lyric by Thomas Nashe (1567–1601), 'In time of pestilence', with its sombre refrain:

> I am sick, I must die,
> Lord, have mercy on us.

Its theme, the vanity and transitoriness of all earthly things, is a traditional one, handled by numerous poets. One of the finest poems of the kind is Gray's *Elegy written in a Country Churchyard* (1751), which is in a meditative and melancholy style, rising at times to a solemn high style resembling that of Johnson. The poem is a triumph of literary tact, handling its traditional materials with an Augustan decorousness and with a perfect control of tone.

Moral meditation may range over many subjects besides death. Pope's four *Moral Essays*, which are among his finest works, have the general titles 'Of the knowledge and characters of men', 'Of the characters of women', and 'Of the use of riches' (twice). Johnson, in *London* and *The Vanity of Human Wishes,* also ranges widely; the former poem is famous for its account of poverty in London, and the latter for its passages on the hard lot of the scholar and on Charles XII of Sweden, but they contain a great deal more of majestic and melancholy moralising.

Light verse

Many of the poems we have considered are extremely amusing — some of those of Chaucer, for example, and of Dryden, and Pope, and Byron. Yet these poems are also serious: we must not confuse seriousness with solemnity. Other poems are not uproariously comic, and yet delight us by their wit, as in many poems of Donne, Marvell, and Pope.

There are other poems, however, in which the humour, the

amusement, is the sole or the main aim. Some critics hesitate to recognise these as poetry, and such work is often referred to as Light Verse, or Comic Verse. Certainly the aims of such writing are extremely modest, and yet it seems to fall within our definition of poetry. There are many kinds of light verse, including epigrams, parodies, punning poems, nonsense-verses, and others.

An epigram is a short, concise, and witty poem, usually ending with some ingenious turn of thought. An example is Rochester's epitaph on King Charles II:

> Here lies our Sovereign Lord the King,
> Whose word no man relies on,
> Who never said a foolish thing,
> Nor ever did a wise one.

Parody is a work in the style or manner of a given author (or class of authors) which aims to make these appear ridiculous, by exaggerating them or by applying them to grotesquely inappropriate subjects. Many of the poems in the *Alice* books by Lewis Carroll (1832—98) are parodies of poems well-known in his time: 'How doth the little crocodile', for example, is a parody of Isaac Watts's 'How doth the little busy bee'. Carroll also wrote a parody of Swinburne, called 'The Manlet', but it is less telling than 'Octopus', by A. C. Hilton (1851—77), which is a hilarious send-up of Swinburne's 'Dolores'. There are many parodies of T. S. Eliot's poetry, the outstanding one being 'Chard Whitlow' by Henry Reed (1914—).

Slightly different is the following witty triolet by Hopkins:

> 'The child is father to the man.'
> How can he be? The words are wild.
> Suck any sense from that who can:
> 'The child is father to the man.'
> No; what the poet did write ran,
> 'The man is father to the child.'
> 'The child is father to the man!'
> How *can* he be? The words are wild.

Here Hopkins wilfully misunderstands a line from Wordsworth's poem 'My heart leaps up', by interpreting it literally.
(In fact Wordsworth wrote '*of* the man', so Hopkins is mis-
quoting him.)

Some set forms are used solely for comic purposes, notably
the limerick. The following is an example by Edward Lear
(1812—88):

> There was an Old Man with a beard,
> Who said, 'It is just as I feared! —
> Two Owls and a Hen,
> Four Larks and a Wren,
> Have all built their nests in my beard!'

A more recently invented comic form is the clerihew; this is a
four-line poem rhyming a a b b, with lines of any length; it is
normally about a well-known person, this person's name pro-
viding the first rhyme-word.

A poem may consist of a series of puns. Thomas Hood
(1799—1845) wrote many poems of this kind, such as 'Faithless Nellie Gray', which begins as follows:

> Ben Battle was a soldier bold,
> And used to war's alarms;
> But a cannon-ball took off his legs,
> So he laid down his arms.

And so it continues for another sixteen stanzas.

Other types of light verse include comic narrative poems in
which the farcical incidents are an end in themselves, such as
'John Gilpin', by William Cowper (1731—1800); delightful
comic fantasy, such as Edward Lear's 'The Jumblies' and
'The Dong with a Luminous Nose'; the comic treatment of
gruesome happenings, as in the *Cautionary Verses* of Hilaire
Belloc (1870—1953) and the *Ruthless Rhymes* of Harry
Graham (1874—1936); and the sustained narrative nonsense-
poem, of which the supreme and irresistible example is Lewis
Carroll's *The Hunting of the Snark* (1876).

These poems will not give us any profound experiences or
insights, but they can be very delightful, and they serve to

remind us of the enormous range of things that we call poetry: from the light-hearted send-up to the 'terrible sonnet', from the four-line epigram to the twelve-book epic, from the elegant love-poem to the churchyard elegy, from the flattering dedication to the merciless satire, from the popular ballad to the esoteric work for a literary élite. These can all be poetry, which covers a range of experience as wide as that of life itself.

Suggestions For Further Reading

Most major English poets are easily available, either complete or in substantial selections, in such series as the Oxford Standard Authors (Oxford University Press) and the Penguin English Poets (Penguin Books). The *Collected Poems* of W. B. Yeats are published by Macmillan, T. S. Eliot's *Collected Poems 1909–62* by Faber & Faber, and Wilfred Owen's *Poems* by Chatto & Windus. The poems of W. H. Auden that are mentioned come from the two volumes called *Poems* (Faber & Faber, 1930) and *Look, Stranger!* (Faber & Faber, 1936); those of Ted Hughes from *Lupercal* (Faber & Faber, 1960); those of William Empson from *Collected Poems* (Chatto & Windus, 1956); those of Cecil Day-Lewis from *A Time to Dance* (Hogarth Press, 1935); that of Louis Mac-Neice from *The Earth Compels* (Faber & Faber, 1938); and that of Philip Larkin from *The Less Deceived* (Marvell Press, 1955). Many minor poets (such as Nashe, Ralegh, Rochester, Clough) are most easily found in anthologies. For the ballads, there is a one-volume abridgement of F. J. Child's *English and Scottish Popular Ballads,* edited by H. C. Sargent and G. L. Kittredge (Harrap, 1922); and the complete five-volume version of the work is available in paperback (Dover Books, 1965); there are also numerous anthologies of ballads. A collection of Australian ballads is provided by Douglas Stewart and Nancy Keesing, *The Pacific Book of Bush Ballads* (Angus & Robertson, 1967).

The number of general books on English poetry is enormous, and it would be impossible to list them here. Some of them are straightforward chronological histories, like Douglas Bush, *English Poetry* (Methuen, 1952); some adopt a chronological order, but select particular authors and topics, like P. Hobsbaum, *Tradition and Experiment in English Poetry* (Macmillan, 1979); some deal with technical aspects, like Marjorie Boulton, *Anatomy of Poetry* (Routledge & Kegan Paul, 1953); many are practical-criticism books, reproducing a number of poems and analysing them, or giving exercises on them, like C. B. Cox and A. E. Dyson, *The Practical Criticism of Poetry* (Edward Arnold, 1975), Laurence Lerner, *An Introduction to English Poetry* (Edward Arnold, 1975), and the enormous *Understanding Poetry* by C. Brooks and R. P. Warren (Henry Holt, 1938); some are discursive books which arrange their material according to topics (the nature of poetry, its origins, metre, types of poetry, and so on), like James Reeves, *Understanding Poetry* (Pan Books, 1967), F. W. Bateson, *English Poetry* (Longmans, 1950), and Denys Thompson, *The Uses of Poetry* (Cambridge University Press, 1978).

On individual poets, types of poetry, and periods of poetry, the number of works is daunting. The elementary student who wishes to find critical works on a particular author or poem would be well advised to begin by looking at a general history of English literature, and following the recommendations made in its bibliography. One excellent history for this purpose, with useful bibliographies, is *The New Pelican Guide to English Literature*, edited by Boris Ford, published in eight paperback volumes by Pelican Books; another more recent history is *The Macmillan History of Literature* (in preparation) edited by A. Norman Jeffares, published in twelve volumes by Macmillan Press. On oral literature (worldwide, not just English) see Ruth Finnegan, *Oral Poetry* (Cambridge University Press, 1977). A good general introduction to the English and Scottish ballads is M. Hodgart, *The Ballads* (Hutchinson University Library, 1950). For an introduction to recent Commonwealth literature, see Bruce King, *The New English Literatures* (Macmillan, 1980).

Index